# A

# *Resilient*

# CROWN

# A
# *Resilient*
# CROWN

## CANADA'S MONARCHY AT THE PLATINUM JUBILEE

EDITED BY

D. MICHAEL JACKSON

CHRISTOPHER McCREERY

DUNDURN
PRESS

Publisher: Scott Fraser | Acquiring editor: Kathryn Lane | Editor: Laurie Miller
Cover and interior design: Karen Alexiou

**Library and Archives Canada Cataloguing in Publication**

Title: A resilient Crown : Canada's monarchy at the Platinum Jubilee / edited by D. Michael
  Jackson, Christopher McCreery.
Names: Jackson, D. Michael, editor. | McCreery, Christopher, editor.
Description: Includes index.
Identifiers: Canadiana (print) 20220212120 | Canadiana (ebook) 20220212279 | ISBN
  9781459749702 (softcover) | ISBN 9781459749719 (PDF) | ISBN 9781459749726 (EPUB)
Subjects: LCSH: Monarchy—Canada. | LCSH: Heads of state—Canada. | LCSH: Canada—
  Politics and government.
Classification: LCC JL15 .R47 2022 | DDC 320.471—dc23

We acknowledge the support of the Canada Council for the Arts and the Ontario Arts Council for our publishing program. We also acknowledge the financial support of the Government of Ontario, through the Ontario Book Publishing Tax Credit and Ontario Creates, and the Government of Canada.

Care has been taken to trace the ownership of copyright material used in this book. The authors and the publisher welcome any information enabling them to rectify any references or credits in subsequent editions.

The publisher is not responsible for websites or their content unless they are owned by the publisher.

Printed and bound in Canada.

Dundurn Press
1382 Queen Street East
Toronto, Ontario, Canada M4L 1C9
dundurn.com, @dundurnpress 𝕏 f ⊙

# Contents

## PERSPECTIVES ON THE CROWN IN CANADA

# Preface

*D. Michael Jackson and Christopher McCreery*

This work is the sixth publication overseen by the Institute for the Study of the Crown in Canada. Established in 2014, the Institute has grown from an informal network that gathered for the first time in 2005 at the University of Toronto's Massey College. The inaugural meeting convened a diverse array of people from a variety of backgrounds, each interested in promoting knowledge and understanding of Canada's constitutional monarchy. The head of the College at the time, John Fraser, was founding president of the Institute. It has expanded beyond the confines of a small graduate college to encompass writers, practitioners, and scholars across Canada and in Australia, New Zealand, and the United Kingdom.

With its mission to enhance understanding of Canada's federal and provincial constitutional arrangements, and in particular the role of the Crown in Canada, the Institute commissions studies, papers, and conferences that examine the constitutional, historical, and institutional reality of the Crown. It seeks alliances, associations, or liaison status with viceregal offices, appropriate public policy and governance institutes, Indigenous organizations, academic and general publishers, and parallel institutions in other countries with similar constitutional arrangements. The Institute is a resource for further studies in this area, as well as making available recognized scholars and other spokespersons in the field of constitutional monarchy.

The work contained herein is that of the authors alone and should not be interpreted as official policy or statements on behalf of the government departments, agencies, or other organizations that the authors are currently or previously have been in the employ of.

*A Resilient Crown: Canada's Monarchy at the Platinum Jubilee* draws on the expertise and experience of a number of scholars and practitioners in the domain of the Canadian Crown — constitutional, Indigenous, viceregal, historical, and personal. We express our appreciation to all of them for their stimulating contributions to and involvement in this publication. We are also grateful to a number of generous donors for their support of the Institute and for helping to make this project possible; notably, the Honourable Margaret McCain, CC, ONB, twenty-seventh lieutenant governor of New Brunswick, and the Honourable Henry N.R. Jackman, OC, OOnt, CD, twenty-fifth lieutenant governor of Ontario.

We also gratefully acknowledge the team at Dundurn Press for their understanding and support for a project involving multiple authors and demanding timelines. We particularly thank Scott Fraser, president and publisher; Kathryn Lane, associate publisher; Elena Radic, managing editor; Sara D'Agostino, contracts, rights, and administration manager; Laura Boyle, art director; and cover designer Karen Alexiou.

Dundurn Press are to be commended for their promotion of Canadian authors in many diverse fields, among them that of the Canadian Crown. Several of those involved in the Institute for the Study of the Crown in Canada have reason to be grateful to Dundurn for publishing their work. It is the editors' hope that *A Resilient Crown* will be a worthy addition to the literature on Canada's constitutional monarchy — and a fitting tribute to Her Majesty Queen Elizabeth II on the occasion of her Platinum Jubilee.

## PREVIOUS PUBLICATIONS OF THE INSTITUTE

Jackson, D. Michael, ed. *The Canadian Kingdom: 150 Years of Constitutional Monarchy.* Toronto: Dundurn, 2018.
Jackson, D. Michael, ed. *Royal Progress: Canada's Monarchy in the Age of Disruption.* Toronto: Dundurn, 2020.

Canada's emblem for the Platinum Jubilee of Her Majesty Queen Elizabeth II in 2022, designed by the Canadian Heraldic Authority, Office of the Secretary to the Governor General.

Jackson, D. Michael, and Philippe Lagassé, ed. *Canada and the Crown: Essays on Constitutional Monarchy*. Montreal and Kingston: McGill-Queen's University Press, 2013.

Smith, Jennifer, and D. Michael Jackson, ed. *The Evolving Canadian Crown*. Montreal and Kingston: McGill-Queen's University Press, 2012.

Tidridge, Nathan. *The Queen at the Council Fire: The Treaty of Niagara, Reconciliation, and the Dignified Crown in Canada*. Toronto: Dundurn, 2015.

## OTHER PUBLICATIONS BY DUNDURN AUTHORS

Harris, Carolyn. *Raising Royalty: 1000 Years of Royal Parenting*. Toronto: Dundurn, 2017.

Jackson, D. Michael. *The Crown and Canadian Federalism*. Toronto: Dundurn, 2013.

Johnson, David. *Battle Royal: Monarchists vs. Republicans and the Crown of Canada*. Toronto: Dundurn, 2018.

McCreery, Christopher. *The Canadian Honours System* (2nd edition). Toronto: Dundurn, 2015.

McCreery, Christopher. *Commemorative Medals of the Queen's Reign in Canada, 1952–2012*. Toronto: Dundurn, 2012.

McCreery, Christopher. *Fifty Years Honouring Canadians: The Order of Canada, 1967–2017*. Toronto: Dundurn, 2017.

McCreery, Christopher. *On Her Majesty's Service: Royal Honours and Recognition in Canada*. Toronto: Dundurn, 2008.

Tidridge, Nathan. *Canada's Constitutional Monarchy*. Toronto: Dundurn, 2011.

Tidridge, Nathan. *Prince Edward, Duke of Kent: Father of the Canadian Crown*. Toronto: Dundurn, 2013.

# Introduction

*D. Michael Jackson and Christopher McCreery*

The Platinum Jubilee of Queen Elizabeth II's accession to the throne as Queen of Canada and of a host of other realms is an opportune moment to reflect upon the Crown's presence in Canadian life, as well as the Queen's remarkable seventy years of service. Canada has grown and changed greatly over the course of the Queen's reign, yet her role, and that of the Crown in the broadest sense, have not faded into obscurity as many predicted in the 1970s and 1980s.

When the government of Prime Minister Pierre Trudeau introduced the contentious Bill C-60, *An Act to Amend the Constitution of Canada*, in 1978, proposing to royally demote the Queen by labelling the governor general as head of state and "the First Canadian," the library shelves had few useful resources to offer. Eugene Forsey's *The Royal Power of Dissolution in the British Commonwealth* (1944), John T. Saywell's *The Office of Lieutenant Governor* (1957), Frank MacKinnon's *The Crown in Canada* (1976), and Jacques Monet's *The Canadian Crown/La Monarchie au Canada* (1979) were the principal resources. There were also the standard academic studies of Canadian government, such as R. MacGregor Dawson's *The Government of Canada* (1945) and Alexander Brady's *Democracy in the Dominions* (1952), which contained robust examinations of the Crown's role. By the 1970s, less and less attention was being given to the Crown's legal and symbolic functions.

However, from the 1990s, and especially following the Queen's Golden Jubilee in 2002, there has been a proliferation of writing and commentary on the Canadian Crown, its past, present, and future. The diversity and breadth of the written discourse have grown immensely, considering the few resources that were available at the time of the constitutional debates of the late 1970s and 1980s. David E. Smith's *The Invisible Crown*, first published in 1995,[1] marked a significant turning point in academic attention to the Crown. It was followed by numerous books on monarchical topics, some, like the present volume, contributed by the newly formed Institute for the Study of the Crown in Canada. To this output we can add publications in the sister realms of Australia, New Zealand, and the United Kingdom. Evidently the constitutional monarchy exemplified by Queen Elizabeth II remains topical in the twenty-first century.

Elizabeth II is the only head of state 85 percent of Canadians have ever known. Over the same period we have seen twelve prime ministers and 128 premiers serve in office. The passing of the Queen's consort, the Duke of Edinburgh, in April 2021 brought into sharper focus the reality that an inevitable transition of the Crown is on the horizon. Naturally, this has sparked discussion and debate about the monarchy's purpose and future in what will be the post-Elizabethan era. The revitalization of Canada's vice-regal family over the last forty years through increasingly active and publicly engaged governors general and lieutenant governors has helped to afford the Crown a renewed and increased locally focused profile. Despite the challenges posed by the precipitous departure of Julie Payette from the post of governor general in 2021 and the associated fallout of the circumstances surrounding her three years in office, the continuity of the institution was ably demonstrated when Chief Justice Richard Wagner assumed for six months the role of administrator of the government of Canada.

The transition of Barbados from one of the Queen's realms into a parliamentary republic headed by a president in 2021 naturally fostered greater discussion of constitutional monarchy, if not among the public, then certainly within the media. Polling related to Canadians' support for the Queen has remained largely unchanged over the last decade, although there appears to be a slight shift in attitudes toward constitutional monarchy and its future. This may well be a byproduct of the controversy surrounding Payette's tenure and a civil society that is increasingly skeptical of all structures of authority, especially in the post-pandemic world; or it could signal a deeper change.

The long-term influence of the increased social media presence of Canada's governor general and lieutenant governors, combined with the strong online media presence of the Prince of Wales, who has taken on an increasingly prominent role, remains to be assessed. Aside from those aspects of the Crown's function that are very focused on the institution and key office holders, there is the less tangible but highly significant role that the Crown has to play as part of reconciliation between Canadians and Indigenous Peoples. The foundational nature of this relationship, woven into the constitutional and historical fabric of the country, has only recently entered the public sphere as something more than just a symbolic connection.

*A Resilient Crown: Canada's Monarchy at the Platinum Jubilee* is divided into four parts, each containing chapters that examine a specific aspect of Canada's monarchy.

In Part I, "A *Constitutional* Monarchy," legal and constitutional aspects of the Crown are discussed, opening with Warren J. Newman's "The Queen, the Crown, and the Structure of the Constitution." The Crown, says Newman, and more particularly, the Queen and her representatives, the governor general and the provincial lieutenant governors, are integral to the institutional and structural architecture of the Constitution of Canada. This chapter introduces the key elements and basic principles inherent in that constitutional framework.

The chapter by Jonathan Shanks, "The Crown's Contemporary Constitutional Legitimacy," examines the role and status of the Crown during the reign of Elizabeth II. The monarchical institution is continuously being reassessed by parliamentarians, professors, government officials, interest groups, the media, and the public. Shanks sees the modern Crown as resilient and multifaceted, successfully accommodating a monarchical past with a democratic future.

The monarchy in Canada is shielded from hasty abolition, let alone radical change, by its constitutionally protected status. Andrew Heard examines the intricacies of that status in "Canada's Entrenched Monarchy: The 'Offices' of the Queen and Her Representatives." Under the *Constitution Act, 1982*, the unanimous consent of Parliament and the provinces is needed to alter the "offices" of the Queen, governor general, and lieutenant governors. But the definition of those "offices" and extent of their constitutional protection are difficult to determine. Heard explores different ways to define these offices and offers some thoughts on which is preferable.

Part II, "The Canadian Crown and Indigenous Peoples," focuses on an integral, historic, and highly topical dimension of the Canadian Crown. Keith Thor Carlson addresses this dimension in "The Promise of the Crown in Indigenous-Settler Relations." Indigenous people suffered at the hands of the settler colonial majority, which worked to dislocate them from their ancestral lands and resources, deny them the ability to govern themselves according to their traditions, and assimilate them into the body politic. One of the few effective checks on settler society, asserts Carlson, has been the Crown.

But how do Indigenous people view that Crown? In Winnipeg on July 1, 2021, demonstrators overturned statues of Queen Victoria and Queen Elizabeth to protest the colonialism that suppressed the identity and culture of the First Nations, Inuit, and Métis peoples. Serge Joyal, in "Overturning Royal Monuments," considers whether it is now possible to acknowledge past wrongs, restore the honour of the Crown, and retain the value of these royal symbols and all they mean in our constitutional order.

In "Treaty Spaces: The Chapels Royal in Canada," John Fraser, Carolyn King, and Nathan Tidridge describe one of these symbols, Canada's third chapel royal, authorized by Queen Elizabeth II in 2017, and explain how it continues a tradition unique to this land that stretches back centuries. The Queen's newest chapel is rooted in this history, while also part of a reawakening in the twenty-first century by the Crown's representatives regarding their responsibilities and relationships with Indigenous Peoples across this land.

The contributors to Part III, "Representing the Sovereign," discuss the role and status of the viceregal representatives — the domestic manifestations and instruments of the Canadian Crown. Barbara J. Messamore begins her chapter, "The Enduring Crown in Canada: Reflections on the Office of Governor General at the Platinum Jubilee," by acknowledging that for both the Queen and the office of governor general 2021 was a challenging year: Governor General Julie Payette resigned and Buckingham Palace had to face damaging news stories. Nonetheless, the Crown is weathering the storms and remains a robust institution.

In "The Lieutenant Governors — Second Fiddles or Coordinate Viceregals?" D. Michael Jackson underlines the coordinate status of the provincial Crown and its representatives with their national counterpart. In addition to essential constitutional duties, lieutenant governors play a major role as symbols of the Crown and their provinces, notably in Indigenous relations and citizen recognition. The federal government, argues Jackson, should reform the currently flawed process of viceregal appointments. The Canadian Crown functions best as a partnership between its national and provincial viceregal representatives.

Christopher McCreery studies a little-known aspect of the Crown in "The Spare Fire Extinguisher: The Role and Function of the Administrator." This is a separate office discharged by the chief justice of the Supreme Court during periods when the governor general is unable to exercise his or her function on account of death, incapacity, removal, or absence. The chapter delves into the origins, role, and development of this supplementary, yet important, safeguard in our constitutional order, imbued with the same legal and constitutional powers as the governor general yet lacking the same moral and symbolic authority.

The final part of the book, titled "Perspectives on the Crown in Canada," offers four different views of how the monarchy is perceived by Canadians. Arthur Milnes reveals a unique and privileged perspective in "The Prime Ministers and the Queen." Through exclusive interviews with five former prime ministers, and by examining the memoirs of late prime ministers, Milnes takes us on a journey through our nation's political history with Her Majesty and her Canadian first ministers. It is a record of first-hand knowledge of Canadian prime ministers that will likely never be surpassed.

In "The Rise and Fall of French Canadian Loyalism," Damien-Claude Bélanger examines French Canadian loyalism to the Crown. Loyalism served the interests of various groups within French Canadian society and expressed a desire among its exponents for Quebec to find a place within the British Empire. The doctrine survived the tumultuous 1830s, but it could not survive the imperialist reaction of the late nineteenth and early twentieth centuries. French Canadian loyalism disappeared because it had become untenable, but also because it was no longer politically useful.

Carolyn Harris offers a contrasting view in "Royal Tours During the Reign of Queen Elizabeth II." Although the format of the tours has changed, she says, the themes have remained consistent, including a focus on Canada's environment, culture, and economy, royal patronage of Canadian philanthropic organizations and institutions, commemoration of historic anniversaries, and meetings with Canadians of all backgrounds. Subsequent monarchs will face the challenge of maintaining steady engagement with a smaller number of working members of the royal family.

Our work concludes with an emotive piece by Canada's twenty-eighth governor general, the Right Honourable David Johnston, "Queen Elizabeth II: A Personal Tribute." This essay provides vivid reflections on interactions with Queen Elizabeth from 2010 to 2017, reflecting on the more personal aspects of the Queen's reign — her personality and her devotion to peoples throughout the Commonwealth. It describes three of Elizabeth II's enduring and inspiring characteristics: graciousness, service, and faith; and illustrates these through her words and actions.

———————

The complex, adaptive, and constantly evolving nature of the monarchy headed by Queen Elizabeth II has been described in other realms in terms such as "chameleon" and "shapeshifting."[2] For our part, we give the final word to the author of this book's first chapter. Warren J. Newman aptly observes that "the Crown itself, while in certain respects an abstract and occasionally elusive concept ... remains subtly and profoundly embedded in Canada's constitutional structure .... It is, as the evocative title of this book suggests, a truly *resilient* Crown."

# *Part One*

---

# A *Constitutional* Monarchy

# 1

# The Crown, the Queen, and the Structure of the Constitution

*Warren J. Newman*[i]

## INTRODUCTION

The Constitution of Canada reserves a central place for the Queen, and more broadly, the Crown, in its preamble and substantive provisions. The latter embody a series of underlying fundamental principles which are, in turn, protected by a web of unwritten conventions, practices, and understandings that govern how regal powers ought to be exercised and constitutional machinery should operate. The prerogatives appertaining to the Crown recognized by the common law, as well as the provisions of certain statutes of a constitutional character, complete the portrait.

---

i   Senior General Counsel, Constitutional, Administrative and International Law Section, Department of Justice of Canada. The views expressed in this chapter are those of the author in his academic capacity and do not bind the Department of Justice or the Government of Canada.

The modest ambition of this chapter is to provide an overview of and introduction to the constitutional framework outlined above, particularly as it relates to the relevant features of the monarchy in Canada. It is only by gaining an accurate understanding of the basic constitutional structure that one can then begin to appreciate the subtle, complex, and dynamic interactions that take place in applying the formal laws and underlying principles of the Constitution in relation to the Crown in Canada.

Happily, one need not possess the vocation of a constitutional lawyer, historian, or political scientist to grasp these truths. All it takes is an overall sense of the constitutional design — the "constitutional architecture," as the Supreme Court of Canada has called it — to realize the extent to which the institutions and principles of monarchy form an integral, and indeed pivotal, part of our constitution.

## THE CONSTITUTION OF CANADA

The formal Constitution of Canada, as defined by the *Constitution Act, 1982*, begins with the *Constitution Act, 1867* — the original *British North America Act* — and includes more than thirty statutes, amendments, and other instruments. Naturally, as our constitution is the fruit of evolution, not revolution, a venerable constitutional tradition has also sustained its growth and interpretation. "Behind the written word is an historical lineage stretching back through the ages," the Supreme Court emphasized in the *Quebec Secession Reference*.[1] It is one that has been receptive to upholding principles such as legality, continuity, stability, and the rule of law, as well as the protection of minorities, and adhering to time-honoured conventions that have maintained the spirit as much as the letter of the Constitution.

The original provinces desired to be "federally united into One Dominion under the Crown of the United Kingdom," in the words of the preamble to the *Constitution Act, 1867*, with "a Constitution similar in Principle to that of the United Kingdom." Moreover, it was held to be expedient not only to provide for legislative authority in the new Dominion of Canada, "but also that the Nature of the Executive Government therein be declared."[2] The nature of that government was to be monarchical, but, as in the United Kingdom, it would be a limited, or constitutional, monarchy, not an absolute one. Executive power as well as legislative authority would be exercised within the context of cabinet government and a parliamentary democracy and institutions founded on the Westminster model.

## THE CROWN

Explicit references to the Crown in the text of the Constitution of Canada are few and far between, but they are significant. Mention has already been made of the preamble to the *Constitution Act, 1867* and its reference to provinces desirous of uniting federally into a single Dominion "under the Crown of the United Kingdom." How and when the concept of the indivisibility of the Crown was relaxed and ultimately abandoned is a subject for protracted discussion and further refinement, and just when it became both a legal phenomenon as well as a political one is still a neat question. However, political and legal sovereignty tended to go hand in hand in the gradual transformation of the British Empire into the Commonwealth, so that the Dominions became recognized, in the terms of the Report of the Imperial Conference of 1926, as being "autonomous Communities within the British Empire, equal in status, in no way subordinate one to another in any aspect of their domestic or external affairs, though united by a common allegiance to the Crown, and freely associated as members of the British Commonwealth of Nations."[3]

With the Imperial Conference of 1930 and the ensuing enactment by the British Parliament of the *Statute of Westminster, 1931*, this concept of autonomy, if not outright independence, was reflected in most of the substantive provisions of the statute, but also in the preamble. The second recital in particular underscored, as part of the new constitutional position of equality, that it was now appropriate to affirm that "inasmuch as the Crown is the symbol of the free association of the members of the British Commonwealth, and as they are united by a common allegiance to the Crown," changes to law touching the succession to the Throne or the royal style and titles would hereafter require, as a matter of constitutional convention, the assent not only of the United Kingdom Parliament but also of the Parliaments of the Dominions.[4]

In Canada, the basic federal structure of the country led early on to the recognition that the sovereign was at the head not only of the Dominion (or central) government but also of the provincial governments, so that one could speak of the Crown "in right of" Canada and the Crown "in right of" each province. The *Constitution Act, 1867* had deftly and pragmatically sidestepped the question of divisibility by simply speaking of Canada or the provinces, jointly or severally, in such provisions as were necessary to differentiate between those two orders of government,[5] or occasionally referring to the Government of Canada and the governments of the respective provinces.[6]

The relative paucity of specific references to the Crown in our constitutional texts is hardly surprising. The Crown is the symbol of monarchical government, but as Maitland noted, aside from the splendid, bejewelled headpieces reposing in the Tower of London, the Crown is essentially an abstract concept. This does not diminish its importance to our form of government; in fact, the Crown is omnipresent in the modern administrative state in both its federal and provincial manifestations, even if largely invisible to many in its daily workings and influence.[7] And the remarkable power of symbolism and the importance of ceremonial, decorative, and formal rites, customs, and practices in sustaining the dignity, status, and place of the Crown as the abiding image of Canadian sovereignty should not be underestimated.[8]

More to the present point, the Constitution gives substance to the Crown not only through its structuring of executive, legislative, and judicial power but also by its many references to the Queen and her viceregal representatives in Canada — the governor general and the provincial lieutenant governors.

## THE QUEEN

The provisions of the *Constitution Act, 1867* are replete with mentions of "the Queen," "Her Majesty," or "Her Majesty the Queen." Naturally, the Queen to whom the constitutional text referred was Victoria, the reigning monarch at the time. It is this Queen who, in the thirtieth year of her reign, lawfully declared by proclamation the date of the union of the provinces of Canada, Nova Scotia, and New Brunswick into "One Dominion under the Name of Canada,"[9] and in whose name the various constitutional powers set out in the Act were initially exercised. It was also to "Her Majesty Queen Victoria" that allegiance was sworn by a prescribed oath.[10]

That the provisions of the *Constitution Act, 1867* referring to "Her Majesty the Queen" extended as well "to the Heirs and Successors of Her Majesty, Kings and Queens of the United Kingdom" was never in doubt, but was made explicit,[11] and this rule of recognition (or of identification or symmetry) continues to underlie our basic constitutional structure.[12] While we may properly speak of Queen Elizabeth II as the Queen of Canada, Her Majesty is the Queen of Canada because she is the Queen of the United Kingdom. That will also be the case for Her Majesty's successor as heir to the Throne, Prince Charles, when he becomes king.[13]

## EXECUTIVE POWER

Plenary executive power is affirmed, by the terms of the *Constitution Act, 1867*, to continue to repose in Her Majesty; indeed, "the Executive Government and Authority of and over Canada" is declared by section 9 to continue to be vested in "the Queen."[14] The exercise of executive powers is generally carried out in the Queen's name by the governor general, whose office is established not by the act itself, but by a royal instrument, the letters patent, and whose role is recognized throughout the relevant provisions of the act. Significantly, the act does establish the Queen's Privy Council for Canada, "to aid and advise in the Government of Canada," composed of privy councillors chosen and summoned by the governor general.[15] Since the effective part of the Privy Council is made up of ministers of the Crown who have the confidence of the House of Commons to which they have been elected as members, the Privy Council provides an essential part of the legal footing for the principle of cabinet government, as well as the array of constitutional conventions that protect the related principles of responsible and representative government, by channelling the exercise of sovereign executive power in democratically-acceptable ways. It is also for this reason that the oft-used term *governor in council* is short-hand for "the Governor General acting by and with the Advice of the Queen's Privy Council for Canada."

The Queen also enjoys and occasionally exercises, on the advice of the ministers of the Crown, ancient prerogative powers, and it was once stated authoritatively that "the prerogative of the Queen, when it has not been expressly limited by local law or statute, is as extensive in Her Majesty's colonial possessions as in Great Britain."[16] Canada is no longer a colony, of course, and there are some notable differences in the functioning of Crown prerogatives in Canada and in the United Kingdom,[17] but the role of the prerogative as a limited but significant source of executive legal power continues to this day.[18]

Each province is headed by a lieutenant governor, appointed by the governor in council, who holds office during the pleasure of the governor general, but is not removable (except for cause) within five years from his or her appointment.[19] The appointment of the lieutenant governor by the governor in council (and the payment of a salary fixed and provided by the Parliament of Canada[20]) does not place the lieutenant governor in a position of hierarchical subordination to the governor general, or make that officer any less a representative of the Queen. Lord Watson, writing on behalf of the Judicial Committee of the Privy Council (JCPC), observed:

> There is no constitutional anomaly in an executive officer of the Crown receiving his appointment at the hands of a governing body who have no powers and no functions except as representatives of

the Crown. The act of the Governor-General and his Council in making the appointment is, within the meaning of the statute, the act of the Crown; and a Lieutenant-Governor, when appointed, is as much the representative of Her Majesty for all purposes of provincial government as the Governor-General himself is for all purposes of Dominion government.[21]

Each lieutenant governor appoints officers to an executive council composed effectively of the province's ministers of the Crown (themselves chosen on the basis of the principle of responsible government). Thus, the executive power of the Crown in right of the province is exercised by the lieutenant governor in council; that is, the lieutenant governor acting by and with the advice of the executive council.[22]

## LEGISLATIVE POWER

Federal legislative power too is, in formal terms, exercised by the Queen, but on the advice and consent of the two Houses of Parliament. The opening words of section 91 of the *Constitution Act, 1867* state that "it shall be lawful for the Queen, by and with the Advice and Consent of the Senate and House of Commons, to make Laws for the Peace, Order, and good Government of Canada." Indeed, as is the case with the United Kingdom Parliament, the Parliament of Canada — the central legislature — is by law composed of the Queen and both Houses.[23] It is the Queen-in-Parliament who exercises legislative authority and parliamentary sovereignty. No legislative bill can be enacted without passage by both Houses and the granting of royal assent; that is, "the Queen's Assent" declared by the governor general "in the Queen's Name."[24]

Provincial legislative power is exercised by legislatures composed of the lieutenant governor of the province and a legislative assembly. Like the House of Commons, the legislative assembly is the deliberative and elected part of the legislature but cannot enact legislation without the participation of the lieutenant governor and the granting of royal assent to legislative bills duly passed by the assembly. Noted Viscount Haldane, in another significant judgment of the JCPC, "when the Lieutenant-Governor gives to or withholds his assent from a Bill :.. it is in contemplation of law the Sovereign that so gives or withholds assent. Moreover, in accordance with the analogy of the British Constitution which the Act of 1867 adopts, the Lieutenant-Governor who represents the Sovereign is part of the Legislature."[25]

The power of the governor general to reserve a bill for the "Signification of the Queen's Pleasure" and for the Queen-in-council to disallow an Act of the Canadian Parliament effectively lapsed with the recognition that Canada is on an equal footing in its relations with the United Kingdom and, as the Balfour Report's famous declaration stated, "in no way subordinate one to another in any aspect of their domestic or external affairs."[26] The powers of reservation and disallowance, insofar as they extend to the bills and acts of provincial legislatures, have fallen into disuse, with the understanding that in a federation like ours, it is the courts of law that normally provide the most appropriate mechanism for the constitutional review of the validity of laws. Like the power to withhold royal assent to bills, the powers of reservation and disallowance have been severely curtailed and limited by the federal principle and constitutional convention. It is only where the effect of provincial laws "cuts directly across the operation of federal law or creates serious disorder particularly beyond the boundaries of the province enacting them" that the power of disallowance might still be considered.[27]

## JUDICIAL POWER

The notion of the Crown as the fount of justice survived in the nomenclature of some provincial superior courts as the *Court of Queen's Bench,* and in the prerogative writs that still form part of the inherent jurisdiction of those courts. The powers of appointment are still in the hands of those who represent the Crown, even as courts have asserted and sustained, as fundamental constitutional principles, the separation of powers and judicial independence. Section 96 of the *Constitution Act, 1867* is, on its face, a bald power of appointment by the governor general of the judges of the superior courts of the provinces, but it has been generously construed, in light of the principle of the rule of law, as a bulwark protecting the independence of the judiciary and access to open courts.[28]

So has section 99, which protects the tenure of office of judges during good behaviour and makes them removable only by the governor general on address of the Senate and the House of Commons.[29] The judicial inquiry powers of the Canadian Judicial Council established pursuant to the *Judges Act* are in keeping with sections 96 to 100 of the *Constitution Act, 1867,* which not only embody the principle of judicial independence inherited from the *Act of Settlement* of 1701, but also place the appointment, the tenure, and the remuneration of superior court judges within the competence of the governor general, the Houses of Parliament, and Parliament itself, respectively.

The Supreme Court of Canada, the Federal Court, the Federal Court of Appeal, and the Tax Court of Canada are all courts established by Parliament for the better administration of the laws of Canada within the meaning of section 101 of the *Constitution Act, 1867.* The Supreme Court is also the "General Court of Appeal for Canada." The judges of these courts are appointed by the governor in council. The Supreme Court has determined that its composition — including the eligibility requirements for appointment — as well as its independence as a judicial institution are constitutionally protected.[30]

## CONSTITUTIONAL PROTECTION AND ENTRENCHMENT

The office of the Queen and those of the governor general and the lieutenant governors of the provinces are entrenched as part of the basic structure of the Constitution. As such, these institutions are protected from changes to their fundamental roles and essential characteristics except by resort to the most stringent of the procedures for constitutional amendment, the unanimous consent procedure. Section 41(*a*) of the *Constitution Act, 1982* provides that an amendment to the Constitution of Canada in relation to "the office of the Queen, the Governor General and the Lieutenant Governor of a province" may be made by a proclamation issued by the governor general only where authorized by resolutions of the Senate and House of Commons and of the legislative assembly of each of the ten provinces.

The scope of the office of the Queen, and the offices of her viceregal representatives in Canada, includes the constitutional status, dignity, and powers flowing from or conferred upon those offices by the Constitution. This does not mean that these offices are immutable and immune from change, both formal and informal. As we have noted, unwritten constitutional principles and conventions control and channel the exercise of executive powers, and the constitutional structure has built within it the advisory roles of the Queen's Privy Council for Canada and the executive councils of the provinces. Beyond that, statutes that implement constitutional principles and conventions, without rising to the level of formal constitutional amendments themselves, have assisted in modernizing aspects of these institutions without altering their fundamental features.

The office of the lieutenant governor has been expressly protected from amendments by the legislature to the constitution of the province since 1867. The first of the classes of subjects in relation to which matters the legislature was empowered by section 92 of the *Constitution Act, 1867* to make laws, was "the Amendment from Time to Time, notwithstanding anything in this Act, of the Constitution of the Province, except as regards the Office of the Lieutenant Governor." That section was repealed and replaced by section 45 of the *Constitution Act, 1982*, which subordinated the legislature's power to amend the provincial constitution to section 41, and thus maintained the protection afforded to the lieutenant governor's office.

The office includes the constitutionally-recognized powers of the office. In *Re Initiative and Referendum Act*, Viscount Haldane affirmed: "The analogy of the British Constitution is that on which the entire scheme is founded, and that analogy points to the impropriety, in the absence of clear and unmistakable language, of construing s. 92 as permitting the abrogation of any power which the Crown possesses through a person who directly represents it."[31] This included, in that instance, the power to signify royal assent to legislative bills, a power which, although conferred on the governor general to assent (in the Queen's name) to bills passed by the federal houses, extended to the lieutenant governor.[32] As well, in reasons for judgment rendered in the *OPSEU* case, Justice Beetz of the Supreme Court of Canada wrote that it was "uncertain, to say the least, that a province could touch upon the power of the Lieutenant Governor to dissolve the legislature, or his power to dismiss ministers, without unconstitutionally touching his office itself. It may very well be that the principle of responsible government could, to the extent it depends on those important royal powers, be entrenched to a substantial extent."[33] Nor could the power to amend the constitution of the province be utilized "to bring about a profound constitutional upheaval by the introduction of political institutions foreign to and incompatible with the Canadian system."[34]

The Parliament of Canada possesses a limited power to make laws amending the Constitution of Canada in relation to the executive government of Canada or the Senate and House of Commons. This power, which is now set out in section 44 of the *Constitution Act, 1982*, is also subject to section 41 and thus to the unanimous consent procedure as concerns the offices of the Queen and the governor general. In the *Senate Reform Reference*, the Supreme Court stated that while "neither level of government acting alone can alter the fundamental nature and role of the institutions provided for in the Constitution," nonetheless, "those institutions can be maintained and even changed to some extent under ss. 44 and 45, provided that their fundamental nature and role remain intact."[35]

Recent examples of statutes at the federal level that have contributed to updating aspects of the monarchical system, without altering the fundamental characteristics of the institutions involved, include the *Royal Assent Act*, which sets out a procedure for signifying the royal assent in writing;[36] amendments to the *Governor General's Act*, which in tandem with an increase in salary commensurate with the dignity and importance of the office subjected that salary to income tax;[37] and the *Succession to the Throne Act, 2013*, which signified the Parliament of Canada's assent to a modernization in the law respecting royal succession, in accordance with the constitutional convention recorded in the second recital of the preamble to the *Statute of Westminster, 1931*. None of these changes required a constitutional amendment made pursuant to the unanimous consent procedure of section 41 of the *Constitution Act, 1982*.[38]

## CANADIAN SOVEREIGNTY

The Crown in Canada has proved remarkably resilient in adapting to the evolution of the country, first from a colony to an autonomous Dominion within the Empire and the Commonwealth, and thence to a fully independent state. The basic structure of the Constitution of Canada did not change much in that regard: executive power remains vested in the Queen, laws continue to be enacted by the Queen-in-Parliament (or by the lieutenant governors with the legislative assemblies), and the judiciary is appointed by the representatives of the Crown. Nonetheless, the *Canada Act, 1982* completed the work begun by the *Statute of Westminster, 1931* in formalizing Canada's independence: it provided that upon the coming into force (by proclamation of the Queen) of the *Constitution Act, 1982*, no act of the United Kingdom Parliament enacted henceforth would extend to Canada as part of its law.[39]

The Queen of Canada is now the head of a sovereign state, but one which preserves, in a modern setting, an ancient fealty to the Crown, the symbol, as the *Statute of Westminster* put it, of "the free association" of those members of the Commonwealth that remain "united by a common allegiance" to the Crown. Canada, Australia, and New Zealand, as well as the other realms that continue to recognize Her Majesty as head of state, each cherish and express their independence in ways appropriate to their individual history, peoples, and political culture, but have also found the legal and conventional means to maintain the essential forms, institutions, and traditions of monarchical and parliamentary government without compromising this independence.

Legal continuity and stability have been important values in Canada[40] and are reflected in our country's gradual accretion of independence. Thus, for example, the *Royal Style and Titles Act* of 1953, in signifying the Parliament of Canada's assent to the issuance of a royal proclamation establishing Her Majesty's style and titles for Canada, perfectly embodied the delicately-balanced desire of the Commonwealth countries "that it would be in accord with the established constitutional position that each member country should use for its own purposes a form suitable to its own particular circumstances but retaining a substantial element common to all." Each country was "to secure the appropriate constitutional approval" for the changes envisaged, which meant, in Canada's case — and in accordance with the constitutional convention recorded in the second recital in the preamble to the *Statute of Westminster, 1931*, which Canada had continuously respected — the statutory assent of Parliament.[41]

So, too, the *Succession to the Throne Act, 2013* simply and elegantly signified the Parliament of Canada's assent to alterations in the law respecting the succession to the Throne that were presented in a legislative bill laid before the United Kingdom Parliament, so as to make royal succession not depend on gender and to end the disqualification arising from marrying a Roman Catholic. The enactment of the *Succession to the Throne Act, 2013* was as much the tangible expression of a sovereign Parliament and an independent Canadian state as it was of adherence to a long-established constitutional convention that has placed the Canadian Parliament, and the Parliaments of the other Commonwealth realms that recognize the Queen as head of state, on a footing of equality with the Parliament of the United Kingdom.[42]

That the Crown in right of Canada and the provinces, respectively, has succeeded to any powers and prerogatives of the Crown in right of the United Kingdom in relation to lands and territories now forming part of Canada has also been made clear, both in case law[43] and in instruments such as the Royal Proclamation issued on behalf of Queen Elizabeth II designating July 28th of every year as a day of commemoration of the Acadian people:

> Whereas Canada is no longer a British colony but a sovereign
> state, by and under the Constitution of Canada;

Whereas when Canada became a sovereign state, with regard to Canada, the Crown in right of Canada and of the provinces succeeded to the powers and prerogatives of the Crown in right of the United Kingdom;

Whereas We, in Our role as Queen of Canada, exercise the executive power by and under the Constitution of Canada;[44]

The Proclamation, issued by and with the advice of the Queen's Privy Council for Canada, noted that on July 28, 1755, "the Crown, in the course of administering the affairs of the British colony of Nova Scotia, made the decision to deport the Acadian people," which continued until 1763 and led to tragic consequences. The Queen acknowledged these historical facts "and the trials and suffering experienced by the Acadian people during the Great Upheaval" that was the deportation, and also underscored the "remarkable contribution to Canadian society the Acadian people have made for almost 400 years."[45]

## RECONCILIATION AND THE HONOUR OF THE CROWN

Canada's sovereignty as an independent state and the place of the Crown within the Canadian constitutional framework have given rise to a burgeoning jurisprudence on the legal development and application of the principle of the honour of the Crown in relation to the national project of reconciliation with the Indigenous Peoples of Canada, whose "aboriginal and treaty rights" are "recognized and affirmed" by section 35 of the *Constitution Act, 1982.*

The Royal Proclamation issued by King George III on October 7, 1763, had sought to organize the governments of lands and territories in America acquired and "secured to our Crown" through the Treaty of Paris concluded on February 10 of that year. With respect to the Indigenous Peoples, the King declared with some candour that "whereas it is just and reasonable, and essential to our Interest, and the Security of our Colonies, that the several Nations or Tribes of Indians with whom we are connected, and who live under our Protection, should not be molested or disturbed in the Possession of such Parts of our Dominions and Territories as, not having been ceded to or purchased by Us, are reserved to them, or any of them, as their Hunting Grounds." His Majesty, "with the Advice of our Privy Council," declared it to be his royal will and pleasure that certain lands "which, not having been ceded to or purchased by Us as aforesaid, are reserved to the said Indians," and "to reserve under our Sovereignty, Protection, and Dominion, for the use of the said Indians, all the Lands and Territories not included within the Limits of our said Three new Governments," or within the territory granted to the Hudson's Bay Company, or lands and territories lying westward "of the Sources of the Rivers which fill into the Sea from the West and North West as aforesaid."

The proclamation thus defined certain lands as "Lands reserved for the Indians" (a term that was later to make its way into subsection 91(24) of the *Constitution Act, 1867* as a head of federal legislative authority) and enjoined the governors of the colonies and settlers and other subjects alike from granting warrants to survey, issuing patents, or purchasing or taking possession of reserved lands. Recognizing that "great Frauds and Abuses" had been committed "in purchasing Lands of the Indians, to the great Prejudice of our Interests, and to the great Dissatisfaction of the said Indians," and in order "to prevent such Irregularities for the future, and to the end that the Indians may be convinced of our Justice and determined Resolution to remove all reasonable Cause of Discontent," the King's proclamation also enjoined private persons from presuming to make any purchases of lands reserved to the Indians "within those parts of our Colonies where, We have thought proper to allow Settlement," but that if any Indians should be inclined to dispose of the said lands "the same shall be purchased only for Us, in our Name, at some public Meeting or Assembly of the said Indians, to be held for that purpose by the Governor or Commander in Chief of our Colony."

That, beyond its assertion of Crown sovereignty, the proclamation reads today in the eyes of many as Eurocentric, paternalistic, prolix, and generally archaic in tone, if not arcane in meaning, cannot be easily denied. That it

27

was, even in its time, the product of expediency and pragmatic self-interest as much as principle is evident even on its face. That it has proved to be, however, the reflection of a higher interest, of reason, justice, and a promise of honourable fair dealing explains why, for example, as early as 1886 in the *St. Catherine's Milling* case, it was described by one judge as "the Indian Bill of Rights,"[46] and why the dissenting judges in *Calder* called the proclamation evidence of "a remarkably enlightened attitude" at a time "when other exploring nations were showing a ruthless disregard of native rights."[47] In another early decision in 1909, *Province of Ontario v. Dominion of Canada*, Justice Idington of the Supreme Court described the policy underlying the proclamation in a manner that began to forge the links between treaties, fair dealing, and "the honour of the Crown":

> A line of policy begotten of prudence, humanity and justice adopted by the British Crown to be observed in all future dealings with the Indians in respect of such rights as they might suppose themselves to possess was outlined in the Royal Proclamation of 1763 erecting, after the Treaty of Paris in that year, amongst others, a separate government for Quebec, ceded by that treaty to the British Crown.
>
> That policy adhered to thenceforward, by those responsible for the honour of the Crown led to many treaties whereby Indians agreed to surrender such rights as they were supposed to have in areas respectively specified in such treaties.[48]

In a more recent series of cases, notably marked by a watershed trilogy of decisions in 2004, including *Haida Nation v. British Columbia*, the Supreme Court of Canada has elaborated the scope and content of the "honour of the Crown" as a constitutional principle, which derives "from the Crown's assertion of sovereignty in the face of prior Aboriginal occupation"[49] and is "not a mere incantation, but rather a core precept that finds its application in concrete practices"[50] and "cannot be interpreted narrowly or technically."[51] Thus, the Crown "must act honourably in accordance with its historical and future relationship with the Aboriginal peoples." The honour of the Crown also overlays specific constitutional obligations "made for the overarching purpose of reconciling Aboriginal interests with the Crown's sovereignty," as was the case with section 31 of the *Manitoba Act, 1870,*[52] and informs a generous interpretation of section 35 of the *Constitution Act, 1982,* such that Parliament's legislative power under section 91(24) of the *Constitution Act, 1867* in relation to "Indians, and Lands reserved for the Indians"[53] must be read together with section 35: "in other words, federal power must be reconciled with federal duty," in keeping with "holding the Crown to a high standard of honorable dealing with respect to the aboriginal peoples of Canada."[54]

The duty to consult that flows from the constitutional principle of the honour of the Crown does not apply to the legislative process, as the duty is concerned with executive action, whereas other constitutional principles, including the separation of powers, parliamentary sovereignty, and parliamentary privilege, come into play in the development, introduction, and enactment of legislation.[55] Whether the honour of the Crown, taken as a constitutional principle, is itself "capable of grounding the constitutional invalidation of legislation" has not been decided by the Supreme Court, "but if it is, it is unique in this regard," given that unwritten constitutional principles are not a substitute for written constitutional provisions and "cannot serve as bases for invalidating legislation."[56]

The installation of Mary Simon as the thirtieth governor general since Confederation, and Canada's first Indigenous governor general, marks an important turning point on the road to reconciliation.

## CONCLUSION

The Queen and her Canadian representatives, the governor general and the lieutenant governors, are present throughout the provisions of the Constitution of Canada, and their offices, including their constitutional status and powers, are protected from facile abolition or alteration by the

Constitution's amending procedures. At the same time, our monarchical institutions, informed by fundamental principles such as responsible government and controlled in the exercise of their formal powers by a web of conventional understandings as well as the rule of law, have continued to evolve and to be responsive to modern democratic values. Venerable concepts such as the honour of the Crown have been refreshed and applied by the courts in a manner that furthers, or ought to further, reconciliation with Indigenous Peoples in Canada, and statutes have also contributed to modernizing aspects of the monarchical system without requiring complex constitutional amendments to date. As for the Crown itself, while in certain respects an abstract and occasionally elusive concept, it remains subtly and profoundly embedded in Canada's constitutional structure, the formal institutional architecture being only the most obvious manifestation. It is, as the evocative title of this book suggests, a truly resilient Crown.

# 2

# The Crown's Contemporary Constitutional Legitimacy

*Jonathan Shanks*

The Crown, like many Canadian institutions of government, is continuously being examined and reassessed. The modern Crown is resilient and multifaceted and presents several avenues for consideration by academics, judges, parliamentarians, government officials, journalists, interest groups, and the public. The reign of Queen Elizabeth II has been remarkable in its longevity, the longest of any British monarch. She is the only sovereign that most of her subjects have known, and the demise of the Crown is not familiar to Canadians today in the way that it was in the first half of the twentieth century, which saw four sovereigns on the throne between the death of Queen Victoria in 1901 and the accession of Elizabeth II in 1952. Perhaps this explains why the Queen herself is sometimes perceived as more popular than the institution that she represents. In November 2021, the Angus Reid Institute published public opinion research showing that 55 percent of Canadians support the monarchy under Elizabeth II, while only 34 percent say they would support it when Prince Charles becomes king. The Queen's Platinum Jubilee provides an opportunity to reflect on Her

Majesty's extraordinary contribution to public life. It is likewise an opportunity to explore how Canada has accommodated a monarchical past with a democratic future and to examine the Canadian Crown's contemporary constitutional legitimacy.

When the emperor of Japan abdicated in favour of his son in 2019, *The Economist* observed as follows: "If monarchy did not exist, nobody would invent it today. Its legitimacy stems from ancient ritual and childish stories, not from a system based on reason and intended to achieve good governance."[1] This has long been acknowledged by those who study monarchical forms of government. In his 1947 presidential address to the Canadian Political Science Association, Robert MacGregor Dawson observed that the Westminster system of government "was the product of a series of historical accidents, experiments, and temporary expedients, so haphazard in its origin and development that no one could have planned it in advance, or, even if this had been possible, would have been so rash as to suggest that it could ever have been made to work."[2] The identification by *The Economist* of the origins of monarchy in ritual and stories also resonated with Dawson, who wrote in the first edition of his influential book, *The Government of Canada*:

> Once upon a time, runs the fairy tale, there was a King who was very important and who did very big and very important things. He owned a nice shiny crown, which he would wear on especially grand occasions; but most of the time he kept it on a red velvet cushion. Then somebody made a Magic. The crown was carefully stored in the Tower; the King moved over to the cushion and was transformed into a special kind of Crown with a capital letter; and this new Crown became in the process something else, no one knows exactly what, for it is one thing today, another thing tomorrow, and two or three things the day after that. The name given to the Magic is Constitutional Development.[3]

There is no question that both the British and Canadian systems of government have developed incrementally in response to events rather than by grand design. Dawson noted that the "personal King of history has thus been in large measure displaced by or transformed into the modern Crown."[4] This contrasted with Europe's continental monarchs, many of whom were deposed. At the beginning of the First World War in 1914, every country in Europe aside from France, Portugal, and Switzerland had a hereditary monarch as its head of state. By 1950, only seven of twenty-five monarchies survived: Britain, Belgium, Denmark, Greece, the Netherlands, Norway, and Sweden.[5] The British retained familiar monarchical forms, but power had gradually shifted from the sovereign to chief ministers, Parliament, and the courts. The survival of kings and queens and the institutional survival of the Crown were ensured by the accommodation of parliamentary sovereignty, representative and responsible government, and the rule of law. Most of this occurred prior to and during the reign of the Queen's great-great-grandmother, Queen Victoria, when the modern form of constitutional monarchy took shape in the United Kingdom and was replicated in Canada, with accommodation for a variety of local conditions.

The Platinum Jubilee is therefore an opportune juncture to reflect on the Queen's constitutional position when she acceded to the throne in 1952 and to examine how it has evolved over the seventy years of her reign. As Warren Newman has explained in chapter 1, the structural constitutional fundamentals have not changed. The Queen is, alongside the Senate and the House of Commons, a part of the Parliament of Canada and laws are formally enacted in her name.[6] The Constitution also vests executive authority in the Queen.[7] Parliament and the provincial legislatures routinely assign powers, duties, and functions to the Queen's representatives, the governor general and the lieutenant governors, acting in conjunction with their respective councils. In some areas not covered by statutes, the royal prerogative continues to disperse power throughout Canada's system of government by allowing for the exercise of the non-statutory powers that are inherent in the Crown. Formally, the Crown has steadfastly remained at the centre of Canada's system of government.

When Elizabeth II became Queen on February 6, 1952, the Canadian accession proclamation referred to her as "Elizabeth the Second by the Grace of God, of Great Britain, Ireland and the British Dominions beyond the Seas QUEEN, Defender of the Faith, Supreme Liege Lady in and over Canada."[8]

This was in keeping with the royal style and titles of her father, George VI, but by 1952 these were out of step with the constitutional practice and development that had taken place in the early twentieth century. The reference to Ireland did not take into account the partition of the Republic of Ireland. There was also no mention of the Queen's role in relation to the Commonwealth. Although initially the successor to the British Empire, it had evolved from the "British Commonwealth" to a "Commonwealth of Nations," including republics that did not recognize the Queen as head of state. Furthermore, the expression "British Dominions" implied subordination by then outdated for countries such as Canada.

In addition, the royal style and titles harkened back to the theory of an indivisible Crown, which had been contradicted by events and overtaken by both political commitments and legal developments about the nature of the Crown and the exercise of its powers. Commenting contemporaneously, Stanley de Smith noted that "the time was ripe for changes to be made in the royal titles that would bring them into accord with the widespread view that the concept of the indivisibility of the Crown had become an anachronism."[9] The question about whether the Crown could act differently in relation to different jurisdictions had been settled in Canada as it related to the federal government and the provinces by the Judicial Committee of the Privy Council in 1892.[10] In *Liquidators of the Maritime Bank of Canada v. Receiver General of New Brunswick*, without any grappling with the divisibility of the Crown under that label, Lord Watson confirmed that Confederation had not severed the Crown's relationship with the provinces and that the Crown in right of each of the provinces enjoyed, within their constitutional sphere, the same relationship with the Crown as the Crown in right of Canada.

This was, in some senses, incremental judicial innovation of the type long known to the common law. However, it was also an interpretation harmonious with the structure of the *Constitution Act, 1867*, which expressly acknowledged that the governor general was to carry on "the Government of Canada on behalf and in the Name of the Queen" and in doing so was to be advised by "the Queen's Privy Council for Canada."[11] The lieutenant governors were to carry on "the Government of the Province" with the advice of the executive council of the province.[12] Furthermore, public property and revenues were vested separately in the Crown in right of Canada and the Crown in right of each province respectively.[13] Delivering the Hamlyn Lectures in 1969, Bora Laskin commented that it required a sophistry to maintain the concept of the indivisibility of the Crown following this decision.[14]

In advance of the coronation in 1953, Commonwealth representatives agreed to modernize the royal style and titles so that each country could adopt its own royal style and titles suited to its own circumstances, while incorporating a substantial element common to all that would recognize the sovereign as Queen of her other realms and territories and Head of the Commonwealth.[15] In December 1952, Prime Minister Louis St. Laurent informed the House of Commons that the Canadian royal style and titles would be "Elizabeth the Second, by the Grace of God of the United Kingdom, Canada and Her other Realms and Territories Queen, Head of the Commonwealth, Defender of the Faith."[16] In accordance with the second recital of the *Statute of Westminster*, these titles and royal style were assented to by the Parliament of Canada and subsequently proclaimed by the Queen on May 29, 1953, shortly before the coronation.[17]

The modernized royal style and titles proclaimed that Elizabeth II was the Queen of Canada. What did that entail in the 1950s? To a large extent, the updates to the royal style and titles were in response to the developments that had already taken place to reflect the Crown's actual position. By 1952, the fundamental understandings and structures had been put in place to allow the Queen to act as Queen of Canada and for a Canadian Crown to later develop and flourish as an institution of government. In 1947, on the advice of Prime Minister Mackenzie King, George VI had issued the updated *Letters Patent Constituting the Office of Governor General of Canada*, which authorized the governor general to "exercise all powers and authorities" of the sovereign respecting Canada.[18] Elizabeth II became Queen of Canada in an era when Canada already had equality of status with the United Kingdom and when the understanding that she would only act in Canadian matters on Canadian advice was well-established both in law and in practice. It was therefore appropriate for the new Great Seal of Canada to substitute for the traditional Latin an inscription in English and French: Queen of Canada — Reine du Canada.[19]

From the beginning of her reign, Elizabeth II was Queen of Canada both in law and in fact. Over the last seventy years, the Crown has been further Canadianized. The Queen remains the central figure, is still personally involved in some matters relating to Canada, and has been present for many significant moments in Canadian history. Over her reign, she has been represented by the first Canadian-born governor general, two governors general who were naturalized citizens, having immigrated to Canada, as well as the first Indigenous governor general, and more than 125 individuals from many different backgrounds have served as lieutenant governors in the provinces.

Since 1952, the governor general has gradually taken on a number of the Queen's responsibilities, namely in relation to the Table of Titles and certain diplomatic appointments and communications.[20] Despite the governor general's assumption of many responsibilities, the Queen remains personally involved in matters directly affecting the sovereign. These include the appointment and removal of the governor general, amendments to the *Letters Patent Constituting the Office of the Governor General* and the issuance of supplementary letters patent, approving the proposal of any alterations to the royal style and titles, the granting of honours — including the creation of new honours or the modification of existing honours, granting of royal patronage, appointing colonels-in-chief of Canadian regiments, appointing the Canadian secretary to the Queen, approving designs for Canadian coinage, granting permission for the inclusion of the crown in Canadian grants of arms and badges, and the use of royal seals.[21] The Queen has also shown an interest in Canadian affairs and remained involved in Canadian matters, for example by reading the speech from the throne in 1957 and 1977, approving the exceptional appointment of additional senators in 1990, proclaiming the *Constitution Act, 1982*, honouring Canadians, extending royal patronage to a variety of Canadian organizations, and visiting Canada many times.

In addition to the responsibilities that the governor general has assumed from the Queen, the governor general and lieutenant governors (the "viceregals") perform other functions as the Queen's representatives in Canada. They have a fundamental role in the continuity of democratic government by ensuring that Canada always has a prime minister and each province a premier. This choice is nearly always made obvious by the outcome of an election or the leadership selection process of a political party, but it must nevertheless be formalized through an invitation from the governor general or lieutenant governor to become first minister and form a government. The representatives of the Crown act in accordance with the constitutional conventions and practices that have developed in Canada, for example furthering the democratic principle by having the power to dismiss a government that attempts to cling to office in the face of another political party securing a majority of seats in an election.[22] Or, more recently and less hypothetically, by refusing a request for a dissolution, in 2017, by a premier who had lost the confidence of the legislative assembly fifty-two days after an election.[23]

The viceregals also grant royal assent to legislation and approve several thousands of legal instruments in various forms, formalizing the decisions taken by ministers and the Cabinet, including regulations, appointments, proclamations, and various other executive instruments. In appropriate circumstances, they can exercise the so-called reserve powers by delaying or refusing to act on the advice of ministers.

Nearly all these roles illustrate what Dawson characterized as the "superficial absurdity of the dual nature of the executive power."[24] What he meant was that decisions made in the name of the Queen or her representatives have effectively been made by the prime minister or ministers. The absurdity is quite superficial because it reveals the core of the constitutional principle of responsible government and the associated conventions that protect that principle. In short, it accommodates the democratic element that has allowed the monarchy to survive. The formal levers of powers with all their associated pomp, symbols, and seals are exercised on the advice of ministers who are responsible to the House of Commons and the provincial legislative assemblies and through them the people of Canada.

In addition to approving the issuance of legal instruments, the viceregals carry out a range of ceremonial, diplomatic, and social responsibilities. The development of national and provincial honours systems has given the Crown a central non-partisan role in recognizing excellence, long service, bravery, volunteerism, and other types of service to Canada both nationally and locally.

Another development during the reign of Elizabeth II was the Canadianizing of the symbols associated with the Crown in Canada. Although based on elements borrowed from France, the United Kingdom, and Indigenous sources, Canada has augmented these symbols to give expression to its independence.[25] The Queen issued letters patent in 1988 authorizing the governor general to grant armorial bearings, which led to the establishment of the Canadian Heraldic Authority to design flags, badges, coats of arms, and other symbols for Canadian individuals and organizations.

The rules governing the succession to the throne have garnered little attention since 1701, when the British Parliament provided that William III and Mary II would assume the Crown jointly and that the Protestant line of succession would be assured by settling it on James I's granddaughter, Sophia of Hanover, and her Protestant heirs. In 2011, the then sixteen countries who then recognized the Queen as head of state agreed to two changes to the law of the succession to the throne at a Commonwealth Heads of Government meeting.[26] The first ended the system of male preference, where a younger son could displace an elder daughter in the line of succession. The second removed the requirement that marrying a Roman Catholic resulted in ineligibility to succeed to the Crown. The Parliament of Canada enacted the *Succession to the Throne Act, 2013*, assenting to the alteration of the law touching the succession to the throne in accordance with the constitutional convention recorded in the second recital of the *Statute of Westminster, 1931*. The United Kingdom statute implementing these changes came into force in March 2015.[27]

Appearing before the Standing Senate Committee on Legal and Constitutional Affairs, the then minister of justice, Rob Nicholson, explained that the provisions and structure of the Constitution of Canada provide that "whoever, at any given period is the Queen or King of the United Kingdom is, at the same time, the Queen or King of Canada."[28] This was also the view of Canadian legal scholars Peter Hogg and Mark Walters.[29] Others, notably Australian constitutional scholar Anne Twomey, canvassed how other jurisdictions dealt with the law concerning royal succession. Twomey suggested that the law touching the succession to the throne operates seamlessly in the United Kingdom, but that difficulties may arise "in relation to the Realms as they are no longer subject to British political or legal sovereignty."[30] In particular, Twomey was critical of the Canadian approach, premised on a rule of recognition, taking the view that Canada should have enacted substantive Canadian law to give effect to the changes made in the United Kingdom. Although Twomey characterized the Canadian approach as "a stark case of short-term political pragmatism taking priority over fundamental constitutional principle," its proponents contend that it was supported "not only by sound legal principle but also by Canadian practice and tradition."[31]

The Canadian *Succession to the Throne Act, 2013* survived challenges in the Quebec Superior Court and Court of Appeal, and the Supreme Court of Canada refused leave to appeal.[32] The legal position, as accepted by the Canadian courts, is that the United Kingdom Parliament was not legislating for Canada when it modernized the law of the succession to the throne. It amended the United Kingdom laws that determine who is the sovereign of the United Kingdom. The Canadian rule — that Canada takes the queen or king as we find them, as determined by the United Kingdom Parliament — was not changed. To alter this basic rule of symmetry would require resort to the unanimous consent amending procedure in section 41 of the *Constitution Act, 1982*. To maintain it does not require any Canadian action beyond the conventional requirement of assenting to the change as was done in the *Succession to the Throne Act, 2013*.

It is not unusual in the heat of litigation for there to be strongly held views advanced by way of zealous advocacy, sometimes involving creative or even exaggerated arguments. However, one observer has continued to advance unusual arguments concerning the outcome of the litigation regarding the alteration to the law of the succession to the throne and a couple of cases rejecting challenges to the oath of allegiance to the Queen. Philippe Lagassé argues that these court cases have "hollowed" the Canadian Crown, variously asserting that Canada now has a "Potemkin monarchy," that "Elizabeth II may be the first and last genuine Queen of Canada," and that the Canadian monarchy "remains intrinsically British and colonial."[33] These assertions would appear to be based on Lagassé's consistent preoccupation with an obscure legal fiction: the Crown's ostensible status as a corporation sole.[34] Overemphasizing this legal fiction, disparaged as it was by Maitland[35] and contextualized as it has been by many others,[36] is reminiscent of that villain of Greek mythology, Procrustes, who accosted travellers and forced them to fit in his iron bed by either stretching them or cutting off their limbs. Lagassé's views are provocative, but do not align with the Canadian Crown's constitutional development and current position. It is notable that the concept of the Crown as a corporation sole was not mentioned in the reasons for judgment in any of the cases dealing with the succession to the throne or the oath of allegiance. While it is not surprising that this concept was irrelevant to both the legal reasoning and the outcomes in those cases, political philosophers might also take inspiration from American philosopher Nelson Goodman, who wrote that "you may decry some of these scruples and protest that there are more things on heaven and earth than are dreamt of in my philosophy. I am concerned, rather, that there should not be more things dreamt of in my philosophy than there are in heaven or earth."[37]

Others have long recognized the promise and limits of theorizing about the nature of the Crown. Some have occasionally also been alarmist about particular constitutional developments, such as when Arthur Berriedale Keith in 1928 colourfully denounced "the suggestion that the King can act directly on the advice of Dominion ministers" as a "constitutional monstrosity, which would be fatal to the security of the position of the Crown."[38] When Stanley de Smith was writing about the 1953 changes to the royal style and titles, he noted that

> analysis of the juridical character of the Commonwealth and of the fundamental rules of the legal order that it embodies has for long been an unrewarding pursuit for the constitutional lawyer. What has been asserted to be legally impossible has in fact occurred with a disconcerting frequency. The books have had to be re-written, the statements of principle expressed more tentatively and with a diminishing confidence that they will not soon be whittled down by exceptions until the exceptions become

recognised as the true rule. The doctrine of the indivisibility of the Crown has perhaps been the chief victim of the reluctance of political facts to conform to the requirements of the legal purist.[39]

On the subject of whether the oath of allegiance was "owed merely to 'the King,' and not to 'the King of Canada,'" de Smith noted that the "controversy had been stripped of all but a vestige of practical significance."[40] Similarly, W.P.M. Kennedy concluded that the changes to the royal style and titles were directed "neither by theory nor by doctrine," forming "material for legal arguments ... fruitless and barren and with little meaning in the lurid light of recent history."[41]

In the *Oxford Handbook of the Canadian Constitution*, Timothy Endicott and Peter Oliver examined the role of theory in Canadian constitutional law and observed that Canada's "constitutional heritage did involve a long and complex history of theorizing about constitutional law and constitutional morality; however, the theorizing was always very incomplete and controversial, and the practical impact of theory was often rather unclear, because of the English knack (restored with the restoration of the monarchy after the Civil War) for pragmatic muddling through."[42]

This modest examination of the Crown during the reign of Elizabeth II reveals a mature Canadian Crown. The Crown's formal legitimacy flows from the Constitution of Canada and the protection afforded to the offices of the Queen, the governor general, and the lieutenant governors in the constitutional amending procedures. The Crown also has a deeper legitimacy in Canada forged not merely as a British export, but through Canadian experience. The Crown's incremental development has allowed Canada to have one of the oldest written constitutions in the world, but also a viable and vibrant form of government that has adapted to keep pace with contemporary democratic values. Canada's trajectory from colony to nation involved neither revolution nor citizen assemblies to design a different form of government. Rather, Canada's independence was secured through the incremental development of shared understandings about how the representatives of the Crown would behave and how the Crown's powers would be exercised. This allowed Canada's system of government to mature within the stability, predictability, and continuity of a constitutional framework that once promoted the colonial interests of the British Empire, but that has evolved and adapted to sustain Canada as a modern democratic and independent country.

# 3

# Canada's Entrenched Monarchy: The "Offices" of the Queen and Her Representatives

*Andrew Heard*

As Canada celebrates the Platinum Jubilee of our sovereign, Queen Elizabeth II, it is useful to explore the constitutional status and protection of the monarchy in our country. At the time of Confederation, the new Dominion of Canada was declared to be united "under the Crown of the United Kingdom and Ireland" and executive authority of and over Canada was "to continue and be vested in the Queen."[1] This statement was, in a sense, a legal redundancy as Canada was at that time, and remained for many years, an integral part of the British Empire.

While the Queen was explicitly integrated into the fabric of Canada's national government by the *Constitution Act, 1867*, the Queen was not originally viewed by many as being a part of provincial government — just as she is not a part of municipal or territorial governments even today. However, a great deal has changed in the years since.

There has been an effective localization of the Queen into Canada's political culture and government.[2] Canadian ministers, not British, now advise the Queen on Canadian affairs. The Queen acquired a local title in 1953, recognizing her as the Queen of Canada. New letters patent in 1947 delegated most of the Queen's powers "in respect of Canada" to the governor general. And a succession of judicial decisions established that the Queen is an inherent element of provincial governments and legislatures. The lieutenant governors are held to be direct representatives of the monarch rather than of the federal government that appoints them, and lieutenant governors possess all the prerogative powers of the Crown relevant to provincial governance.[3]

Constitutional monarchy remains a framing principle of Canada's constitution. Most important aspects of federal and provincial government are conducted in the Queen's name and, when needed, signed by one of the Queen's local representatives, from the passage of legislation to the conduct of government.

An important question therefore arises: how can one make changes to the legal framework of the monarchy? This question arises not just in the grand context of how Canadians might one day abolish their ties to the monarchy or elect their governors, but in such practical questions as whether one can have an effective fixed-date election law, provide for administrators to act in the case of a lieutenant governor's death, require a governor to be bilingual, or even just to change the title given to the governor general or lieutenant governors.

Canada finally acquired the power to amend its Constitution with the passage of the *Constitution Act, 1982*. The framers of this law consciously chose the highest level of protection for our monarchic offices: section 41(a) requires unanimous federal and provincial consent to any changes to the Constitution involving "the office of the Queen, the Governor General, and Lieutenant Governor of a province." The federal minister of justice at the time, Jean Chrétien, told the joint parliamentary committee considering the draft *Constitution Act* in 1981 that the federal government had deliberately chosen the exact wording formerly agreed to by all the provincial negotiators for the Victoria Charter in 1971.[4] In contrast, the Fulton-Favreau formula proposed in 1964 would have seen amendments to the basic monarchic elements subject only to agreement from seven provinces with 50 percent of the population; furthermore, the national Parliament would have been able to legislate unilaterally on "the functions of the Queen and the Governor General in relation to the Parliament or Government of Canada."[5] One motivation in 1981 for the provincial premiers to support the unanimous protections of section 41(a) was reportedly the very fresh memory of the Trudeau government's controversial proposal to redefine unilaterally the roles of the governor general and the Queen in Bill C-60.[6] As well, the election of a separatist government in Quebec in 1976 may have raised the prospect of incremental republicanism.

It is clear, therefore, that Canada's basic monarchic structure was intended to be altered only with the unanimous consent of Parliament and all provincial legislatures. But unfortunately it is not clear which particular laws relating to the monarchy require unanimity, which may be changed by another joint federal-provincial process not requiring unanimity, or which can still be altered by ordinary legislation.

This chapter explores the surprisingly complex set of issues raised by the two critical elements of section 41(a). Unanimity applies to changes that would involve both 1) an alteration to "the Constitution of Canada," rather than some other element of law or convention, and 2) a substantive aspect of a monarchic office. Problems arise in determining just what is part of the formal Constitution of Canada, given the complex web of constitutional, statute, and common law relating to these offices. That legal framework is in turn fundamentally altered by constitutional conventions that ultimately determine the powers in reality. Secondly, there are competing conceptions of what is meant by an "office"; four models will be discussed later in this chapter. One must also be mindful that there are issues specific to each of the three sets of offices; the legal and constitutional positions of the Queen, the governor general, and the lieutenant governors are in many ways each unique, despite all being linked by common threads.

The difficulty lies in finding a balance between the obvious intent to put foundational aspects of the monarchy out of reach of unilateral changes, on the one hand, and the need of each government in Canada to change the structure and powers of their institutions and public officials, on the other. Part of this delicate balance must be a recognition and protection of a fundamental rule of the British constitution that Canada was explicitly modelled on, that the common-law powers of the Crown are subject to the legislative power of Parliament.[7] This principle lies at the heart of our modern constitutional monarchy and parliamentary democracy. It was the result of hard-fought battles in England between parliamentary and royalist forces over the centuries, involving civil war as well as the execution and exile of kings, culminating in the Glorious Revolution of 1688 and the passage of the *Crown and Parliament Act*, as well as the *Bill of Rights*. But ultimately, the challenge stems from the way in which the Crown is woven into the fibre of all three branches of government.

This discussion begins with a review of the constitutional framework of these problems, both the variety of laws shaping the monarchy in Canada and the possible processes for amending relevant constitutional provisions, and then moves on to an analysis of competing conceptions of an "office." What exactly is the scope of the offices referred to in section 41(a) and to which aspects of the Constitution does unanimity apply? The unfolding discussion on these questions may help identify some answers.

## THE MONARCHY'S CONSTITUTIONAL FOUNDATIONS

The powers of the Queen, governor general, and lieutenant governors are found in a wide range of legal settings and those laws are in turn fundamentally altered by constitutional convention. There are, in the first instance, explicit references in the documents of Canada's formal Constitution. A host of federal and provincial statutes reference the governor general or lieutenant governors, touching on specific powers, such as the unique power of the lieutenant governor to return a bill to the legislative assembly for suggested revision, found in British Columbia's *Constitution Act*, salaries and pensions for the viceregal officers, or the wide range of statutes radically transforming or eliminating specific common-law powers and immunities of the Crown.

As well, important matters are found in the common law, particularly the prerogative powers of the Crown. There are a variety of prerogative powers, relating to the legislature, conduct of foreign affairs, national defence, issuance of passports, acquisition and administration of foreign territories, structure of the executive, appointments, granting honours, creation of reserves for Indigenous communities, immunities and privileges, and the prerogative to deal with emergencies.[8] While many aspects of the prerogative have been displaced by statute, not all legislative measures have extinguished the related prerogatives. Some documents issued under those prerogative powers are pivotal, such as the *Letters Patent, 1947,* detailing the appointment and general powers of the governor general. Certain United Kingdom statutes not included within Canada's formal Constitution also possibly apply to our sovereign as well, such as the 1688 *Bill of Rights,* the *Act of Settlement,* the *Regency Act, 1937,* and the *Succession to the Crown Act, 2013.*[9] Key judicial decisions are also at the heart of these offices, particularly the decisions of the Judicial Committee of the Privy Council extending the royal presence and prerogative powers into provincial government.

The pervasive reach of these laws provides a theoretical framing of our system of government in Canada that places the monarchic officers in central positions of power. However, that framework is transformed into a constitutional monarchy, with true power determined through the constitutional conventions and principles firmly establishing parliamentary government as the defining character of modern Canadian governance.

Just how changes may be made to these laws is governed by the amending formulas set out in the *Constitution Act, 1982.* The highest level of protection is given in section 41(a), which stipulates that amendments to the Constitution of Canada relating to "the office of the Queen, the Governor General and the Lieutenant Governor of a province" can be done only with the unanimous consent of all provincial legislative assemblies and both Houses of Parliament. But this does not mean all matters relating to the Crown in Canada. Some other changes may be made through the "7 & 50" formula of section 38, with amendments authorized by Parliament and the assemblies of at least seven provinces that together have 50 percent of the national population. For example, the governor general's power to appoint senators is clearly central to "the method of selecting senators" that falls within section 38.

One should also allow for potential amendments to be made under section 43 as well; amendments applying "to one or more but not all provinces" may be made when authorized by Parliament and the legislative assemblies of the provinces involved. In addition, both the national parliament and provincial legislatures are empowered to make certain constitutional changes on their own.

There is also the potential of some minor matters relating to the Queen, governor general, or lieutenant governors that could be achieved through ordinary legislation by either Parliament or a provincial legislature acting alone — provided the changes do not impact their offices.[10] If the subject matter is not required to be dealt with through either section 41 or section 38, then according to section 44 Parliament may pass ordinary legislation "amending the Constitution of Canada in relation to executive government of Canada or the Senate and House of Commons." Provincial legislatures are also authorized to make certain changes through section 45: "Subject to section 41, the legislature of each province may exclusively make laws amending the constitution of the province." In a larger sense, this complex set of amending rules embodies the inherent tension in any federal country between the autonomy of each government and the need for collective agreement to alter common bonds.

A number of puzzles quickly arise when one tries to sort out which amending procedure should be used for any particular change. With respect to the requirement of unanimity, one needs to determine whether a proposed change involves the "office." As we will see in the discussions to follow, this is not an easy question to answer. The governor general's power to appoint senators under section 24 of the *Constitution Act, 1867* and the joint process of appointing extra senators involving both the Queen and governor general under section 26 clearly fall under the 7 & 50 formula, thanks to section 42(1)(b) of the *Constitution Act, 1982*. But it is not immediately clear how one would make changes to the governor general's power to appoint and remove judges of provincially constituted superior courts under sections 96 and 99(1) of the *Constitution Act, 1867.* Is this power integral to the "office" of the governor general or is it a matter that might be amended through section 38? It is definitely not an issue simply relating to the executive or Parliament that would allow changes by ordinary statute under section 44. While the power to appoint judges is part of a historic status of the sovereign as the "font of justice," it is not a functional aspect of the monarch's role in the modern era.

Another set of issues relate to the provincial legislatures' ability to unilaterally amend "the constitution of the province." The first dilemma is whether a proposed change does in fact impinge on the office of the lieutenant governor or is peripheral to the matters protected by unanimous consent. For example, if New Brunswick wished to pass a law requiring the lieutenant governor to be able to speak both French and English, would this be a matter of the provincial constitution to be legislated on unilaterally, or would it alter the office of the lieutenant governor? Furthermore, while provincial legislatures are barred from making changes to the "office" of lieutenant governor, it is not clear whether they can make changes to anything else considered to be part of "the Constitution of Canada." Would they have to follow a joint amendment with Parliament under section 43? If provincial legislation could not amend the Constitution of Canada with respect to "the constitution of the province" it would seem unnecessary to stipulate that the province's powers under section 45 are subject to section 41. And yet, to accept that provincial legislation under section 45 can amend the Constitution would seem to run counter the wording of section 43, which states that amendments to the Constitution relating to one or more provinces, but not all, may be made "*only where so authorized* by resolutions of the Senate and House of Commons and of the legislative assembly of each province to which the amendment applies" (emphasis added).[11]

Further complications relate to distinguishing powers granted to the Queen or governor personally from those entrusted to the Queen or governor in council (cabinet).[12] A further question arises as to whether those personal powers relate to the monarchic character of the empowered actors, or serve some other governance objective. For example, when presented with a bill for royal assent, the governor general and lieutenant governors are given the personal power to reserve the bill for consideration by the next level of government's cabinet.[13] The fate of bills reserved by a lieutenant governor is determined by the governor general in council, while bills reserved by a governor general are settled by the Queen in council in London. The power of reservation is clearly a statutory invention, unrelated to the historic prerogatives of the British monarch. It was put in place not to reinforce the monarchic element of government, but to ensure the policy priorities of a superior level of government would prevail over a subordinate legislature. The British government's imperial polices were enforced over Canada's national legislation, while the Dominion cabinet's national priorities were given precedence over provincial policies through the reservation and disallowance of provincial legislation.

Important consequences flow from determining what comprises "the Constitution of Canada," because ordinary legislation would suffice if a proposed change does not involve the formal constitution. In some sense the bar should be set quite high to cross this threshold, as section 52(1) of the *Constitution Act, 1982* declares: "The Constitution of Canada is the supreme law of Canada, and any law that is inconsistent with the provisions of the Constitution is, to the extent of the inconsistency, of no force or effect." There once was some hope that a definitive answer could be given to this issue, as section 52(2) goes on to state that "the Constitution of Canada" includes the *Canada Act, 1982*, the *Constitution Act, 1982*, a specific list of documents found in the appendix of this act, and any amendments made to all those documents.

However, the Supreme Court of Canada has stepped well beyond this list in two ways. First, the court has underlined that section 52(2) says the Constitution *includes*, indicating the list of documents is not exhaustive. In a 2014 case, the court held that three sections of the *Supreme Court Act* relating to the composition of the court must be considered part of the Constitution.[14] And the court has made clear that the content of the Constitution of Canada must extend to the basic "constitutional architecture" of institutions at the heart of our system of government.[15] A pressing question to emerge from this expansive view is whether the letters patent are part of the formal constitution.

A second important expansion of the Constitution's content flows from the Supreme Court's decisions to recognize unwritten principles as part of our constitutional law. In *New Brunswick Broadcasting*, the court established that the preamble to the *Constitution Act, 1867* was the source for fundamental constitutional matters not explicitly referred to elsewhere.[16] In another case, Chief Justice Lamer described the Preamble as "the grand entrance hall" to the constitution.[17] Of particular interest is the preamble's reference to Canada's being "federally united into One Dominion under the Crown of the United Kingdom of Great Britain and Ireland, with a Constitution similar in Principle to that of the United Kingdom." Over the years, the Supreme Court has found that Canada's constitution includes a number of unwritten principles: judicial independence,[18] the rule of law,[19] parliamentary privilege,[20] federalism,[21] and democracy.[22] But, as the Supreme Court made clear in 2021, these unwritten principles are just interpretive guides to understanding the Constitution and cannot to be used to strike down legislation.[23]

## THE "OFFICE"

Although it is an everyday term, there is much debate over just what is entailed in the "office" referred to in section 41(a). The most authoritative pronouncement on this matter so far comes from the Quebec Court of Appeal's decision in the *Motard* case. In response to a challenge that changes to the rules of succession to the throne should have been made in Canada through section 41(a) and not through United Kingdom legislation, the court held that

> simply put, s. 41(a) of the *Constitution Act, 1982* protects the institution of the monarchy, not the procedural rules by which a person accedes to the throne. The amendments made by the British Parliament to the rules of royal succession did not have any impact on the "office of the Queen" in Canada. The 2013

Canadian Assent Act did not alter the powers, status or constitutional role devolved upon the Queen. Thus, it did not pertain to the "office of the Queen."[24]

While the court ruled that the office of the Queen relates to its "powers, status or constitutional role," each of those three terms involves a certain degree of ambiguity, especially in regard to what powers the judges may have had in mind.

Following that decision, Warren Newman took quite a sweeping view of the matter when he wrote about the protection afforded through section 41(a): "That constitutional protection extends to the constitutional status and dignity of the Queen's (or, depending on the incumbent, the King's) office as head of the Canadian state, the executive and legislative roles constitutionally conferred upon the Queen and her representatives, and the related constitutional powers and prerogatives of the regal officer and viceregal representatives."[25] Without further nuancing, this approach could potentially include a wide swath of statutory and common-law powers of the Queen and governors.

Philippe Lagassé and Patrick Baud drew from a range of judicial decisions to argue that the defining question that distinguishes whether a matter is part of the "office" is if the governor or Queen has any personal discretion in exercising the powers.[26] While there is sound logic to this approach, it is not without significant problems. Ultimately, it relies on constitutional conventions to determine whether a matter is to be protected by unanimous consent or not, as convention — not law — determines what the Queen and governors may or may not do personally. The problem with that is two-fold. First, conventions can and do change and evolve over time, even if there is a small core of fundamental conventions whose terms are clear, widely accepted, and whose breach would result in some constitutional harm. For example, lieutenant governors quite actively used the powers of reservation and refusal of assent in the early decades after Confederation, but those powers have since been effectively nullified by convention.

Secondly, the discretion to refuse advice is very broad, touching on a wide array of powers that in no other circumstance would involve personal discretion for the Queen or governors. The governors may, in exceptional circumstances, refuse to act on unconstitutional advice involving almost any of the legal documents that require their formal signature.[27] For example, a governor may refuse to appoint a wide range of officials when advised by a first minister who has clearly lost an election to an opposition party with a majority of seats; these appointments could include positions that would never normally be an area where the governor could exercise personal discretion, such as the appointment of ambassadors, judges, or senators. Other examples of refused advice over the years include financial and contractual matters, along with the dismissal of individual ministers; none of these are normally matters over which a governor has personal discretion. So, would one say that the reserve power to refuse advice on a broad range of matters is part of the offices of the Queen and her governors, because they may exercise personal discretion in this regard? Or, are all the matters that might be subject to a viceregal refusal part of the governor's office?

However, one argument that could be made in favour of Lagassé and Baud's proposal is the Supreme Court position that unwritten principles can be used to interpret provisions of the Constitution.[28] So in theory the principles of constitutional monarchy and parliamentary democracy could be employed to define section 41(a)'s reach as they suggest. But in doing so, a court would be essentially crystalizing constitutional convention into law that could be changed only with unanimous federal-provincial consent. To the extent that judges include within the "office" powers that the cabinet or first minister almost always determine the use of, rather than their governor, the courts would entrench everyday cabinet power behind the almost impenetrable requirement of unanimity.

## DIFFERENT CONCEPTIONS OF THE "OFFICE"

At this juncture, it is useful to reflect on common analytical approaches that might define the offices mentioned in section 41(a). Four basic alternative models can be identified for the three sets of offices that can be amended only through unanimous federal-provincial agreement, although none is free from either conceptual or practical concerns. These models may be summed up as comprising minimalist, formalist, personal power, and all-inclusive approaches to the offices. The discussions that follow are by necessity abbreviated and the models themselves could be further refined. They are also illustrations of alternative views, rather than an exhaustive classification of options.

## The Minimalist Office

In the most restrictive conception of the "offices" of the Queen and governors, only the basic existence and character of those offices would require section 41(a), to preserve the monarchic framework of Canada's system of government. In this view, matters requiring unanimous consent would extend to the office's existence and position in Canada's system of government. This first model would reflect the fundamental character and role of the offices, given the Supreme Court's insistence on respecting a constitutional architecture. This would protect the office of the Queen as a constitutional, hereditary monarchy whose powers are exercised by the current monarch of the United Kingdom. As well, the roles of the governor general and lieutenant governors as limited-term, appointed representatives of the sovereign would be protected. In theory, one could adopt this approach while distinguishing the existence and character of the office from the powers to be exercised by the office holder.

There is much to recommend such a limited notion of the monarchic offices. As the unanimous consent of all ten provincial legislatures and of Parliament is a very elusive achievement, one might argue this requirement should be left to the most fundamental transformations of our system of government or national character.[29] In this sense, to sever ties with the Queen or to empower an elected governor general to wield effective political power would radically transform our system of government in ways that, for example, eliminating the governor general's power to appoint the speaker of the Senate could not. This model would not leave the powers of the Queen and governors to the mercy of unilateral legislation, as they could still be subject to joint federal-provincial agreement through section 38.

## The Formalist Office

This model would build on the first by including almost all explicit references in the formal constitution to the existence of the office and personally assigned powers. This approach is consistent with the Quebec Court of Appeal's view in *Motard* that the office of the Queen extends to "the powers, status or constitutional role devolved upon the Queen."[30] But an exception to this rule of thumb would be the appointment of senators, because section 42(1)(c) of the *Constitution Act, 1982* stipulates that the method of selecting senators is a matter to be pursued through section 38, the 7 & 50 formula. This option would accommodate the ruling of the Judicial Committee of the Privy Council in the *Re Initiative & Referendum Act*, which held that a province may not create a new law-making power by referendum that excludes the lieutenant governor as a constituent element of the legislature.[31]

However, the diverse legal foundations for the lieutenant governors across the ten provinces pose a difficulty here. For example, Doug Stoltz underlines that the powers of the lieutenant governors with respect to their legislatures are on a different constitutional footing in the four Atlantic provinces and British Columbia from the rest of Canada. Those five provinces have their lieutenant governors' powers expressly based on those of pre-Confederation governors, and in his view are not part of the formal Constitution of Canada.[32]

Another broader issue is the extent to which the courts might interpret the ambit of the preamble in the *Constitution Act, 1867*. The courts would have to determine whether the reference to "a constitution similar in principle to that of the United Kingdom" brings into section 41(a)'s orbit all the specific powers of the monarch that are founded on common law or constitutional convention. This could be problematic on a number of levels, given the reliance on conventions as well as Parliament's power to legislate on common-law prerogative powers.

As a result, it might be analytically prudent to distinguish this model as restricting itself to only those direct textual references to the Queen, governor general, and lieutenant governors found in the formal documents of the Constitution. However, such a literalist approach would not be consistent with the Supreme Court's vision of the Constitution as something much more than a textual entity, involving a whole "architecture." This model may have to be flexible enough to protect some other aspects of the monarchic offices that are necessary implications of the monarchic and parliamentary principles of government, the basic role and function of key institutions, or the institutional interests shared by federal and provincial governments.

## The Personal Powers Office

The personal powers model includes all matters that may be assigned to or exercised by the Queen, governor general, and lieutenant governors individually. This model may be the closest to the Lagassé and Baud proposal, mentioned earlier, for interpreting section 41(a). This model would have to encompass changes to certain statutory and common-law prerogative powers, in order to cover the actual powers that may be exercised by either the Queen or governors. It might also prevent legislative changes from nullifying personal discretion currently permitted by convention. This focus on the personal powers of the Queen and governors would exclude powers granted explicitly to the governor in council. However, one practical problem is the variety of statutory provisions, particularly at the provincial level; in some jurisdictions, matters that were once the legal powers of the lieutenant governor individually have been made governor-in-council powers. One can also find legislation that has increased the personal powers of a governor. For example, British Columbia's lieutenant governor is unique in Canada in having been granted the option to return legislation to the legislature for further consideration, instead of the usual three options of granting or refusing royal assent and reserving the bill for the federal cabinet's review. The result is something of a patchwork quilt across the country. Would the Supreme Court allow such variation or enforce uniformity? It is unclear if this model would include powers assigned to a governor but in truth never exercised personally by them. An example is the requirement for the royal recommendation, required by sections 54 and 90 of the *Constitution Act, 1867,* for important financial legislation to proceed through the legislature.

However, this recommendation is exercised entirely by ministers, usually without their governors being consulted or informed.

Most problematically, the inclusion of the wide range of legal sources for the personal powers covered by this model could undermine a key precept of the United Kingdom's constitution, that the common-law prerogatives of the Crown are subject to legislative revision or extinction by ordinary legislation. Significant transformations of the prerogative powers of the Crown have already been achieved through legislation at both federal and provincial levels over the years. Crown immunities and privileges have been refined multiple times. The prerogative power of pardon and mercy has been transformed into a statutory framework.[33] The power to structure and redefine the existence and responsibilities of government departments as well as the terms of employment of servants of the Crown are matters of royal prerogative now entrusted with the governors in council in most jurisdictions and could be included in this approach. Even the traditional power to appoint individuals to be ministers of specific portfolios has been changed by statute in some but not all provinces from a personal power of the lieutenant governor to one held by the governor in council.[34] These are just a few examples of how Canadian legislation has transformed common-law powers of the Crown into governor-in-council powers. It is essential that legislatures retain this ability to adapt and evolve the powers of the Crown in an organic and continuing way. In effect, this principle is so important it should be recognized as part of the constitutional architecture the Supreme Court of Canada has referred to. If all common-law prerogative powers were subject to the rigours of section 41(a), Canada's constitutional framework would be tied into a suffocating straitjacket. For example, unanimous provincial consent would be needed for any further attempt to legislate on the royal prerogatives relating to foreign relations and national defence.

## The All-Inclusive Office

This model encompasses the many ways in which the operations of government hinge on the presence or participation of the Queen, governor general, or lieutenant governors and their advisers. All actions by governors in council would be included in this view of the office, since it is an inherent part of their position for governors to sign orders in council and other documents. The governors' engagement, however formal and nondiscretionary, is required for government actions to be authorized, published, and acted upon. Most of these powers are defined in the Constitution or legislation as belonging to the governor in council rather than the governor personally. For example, the powers to disallow or to grant assent to reserved provincial legislation and to hear appeals from provincial denominational education rights issues belong to the governor general in council. Lieutenant governors and provincial administrators are appointed by the governor general in council, as well. An almost incalculably vast set of powers are given to the governors in council at both levels of government through legislation; some imply acknowledgement of the Crown's symbolic framing role in our system of government, and others because the common-law prerogative powers once belonging personally to the monarch have been legislated to belong to the governor in council. For example, Canadian law vests control over public lands in the governor in council; this is no small matter, considering that 90 percent of the territory of Canada was estimated to be Crown land in 2010.[35]

The almost limitless potential of this model's reach should make it an impractical candidate for determining the nature of the office protected by unanimous consent. The intent of section 41(a) must be to protect the offices of the Queen, governor general, and lieutenant governors without implicating so much of the work of national and provincial governments.

## CONUNDRUMS FOR THE COURTS

It should be evident after these discussions that the courts will have to make some difficult and nuanced choices in determining which matters are both part of the formal constitution and integral to the offices of the Queen or her representatives. Two very practical questions will at some point have to be answered when courts come to interpret what matters are or are not part of the Constitution to which section 41(a) applies. The first is whether the whole panoply of common-law prerogative powers are part of the formal constitution requiring joint federal-provincial consent to changes. As discussed earlier in this chapter, the inclusion of the common-law prerogative powers of the Crown would eliminate an essential principle of the British parliamentary democracy upon which Canada is modelled, that Parliament may alter or dispense with the Crown's common-law prerogatives. The healthy evolution across Canada's eleven provincial and federal governments that this principle has afforded would be stifled if unanimity were required for future changes to the remaining prerogative powers. The second question is whether the *Letters Patent, 1947* are part of the Constitution and subject to section 41(a). This is a more complex issue to deal with, as this document authorizes the appointment of not just the governor general, but the administrator to act in the governor general's absence, incapacity, or death. As well, several specific powers of the sovereign are explicitly delegated to the governor general, including the command of Canada's military forces, along with the general delegation of the monarch's powers "in respect of Canada." With the importance of its contents, it is not surprising that Monahan et al. argue that the *Letters Patent* should indeed be considered part of the Constitution, "at least to the extent that it creates the office of the governor general and defines the powers of office."[36]

However, the courts could exclude the *Letters Patent* from the Constitution through the same logic by which the Quebec Court of Appeal excluded the laws of succession to the throne. The *Constitution Act, 1867* only details some powers of the Queen with respect to Canada, not how someone becomes the Queen. Similarly, the *Constitution Act, 1867* details some powers of the governor general without specifying all of these powers or how someone becomes governor general. It was a firm presumption in 1867 that the governor general would be appointed by letters patent through the prerogative powers of the Crown and that the monarch might delegate varying powers over time to the governor general; such has been the case ever since. Much is made of the delegation of most of the Queen's powers to the governor general in the 1947 *Letters Patent*, even though much of that delegation is in fact redundant. The courts had already ruled that the Canadian governors possessed all the prerogative powers relevant to their level of government. In effect, all the Queen's powers with respect to the provinces were delegated to the lieutenant governors without the need for letters patent. It was only a matter of convention and political practice that the governor general was initially prevented from exercising some of the powers relating to the conduct of foreign relations until the 1970s, in that the Queen personally signed certain treaties and issued letters of credence for Canadian ambassadors and high commissioners.

When it comes time to define the monarchic offices in more detail than *Motard* provided, the courts will have to select among competing visions of those offices, as illustrated by the four models discussed in this chapter. Judges might be tempted to embrace a "broad and purposive" interpretation of the Constitution, as the Supreme Court is wont to expound on occasion. Such an approach to protecting the monarchy would likely lead to an expansive notion of the "office" protected by section 41(a). If so, one should pause to consider another subject protected from change by the requirement for a unanimous consent. Section 41(c) lists, "subject to section 43, the use of the English or the French language." Here, it only makes sense to follow a narrow interpretation of the ambit of both the Constitution and "the use of" English or French.[37] Otherwise, one would have to resort to formal amendments under either section 41(a) for national matters or joint federal-provincial consent for changes to individual provinces' approaches to bilingualism. If one accepts that bilingualism is now a defining principle of Canada's polity, one might argue quite forcefully, based on the Supreme Court's logic in the *Supreme Court Act Reference*, that the protection offered by the formal amending procedures was intended to capture and protect basic constitutional architecture as it existed in 1982.[38] For example, one could not get a proper sense of the importance and extent of protections for the use of English and French at the national level of government without including the *Official Languages Act*; the scant references in section 133 of the *Constitution Act, 1867* do not in any way convey the subsequent transformation of our national government in this regard.

Nevertheless, caution should be used here, as one could equally say that one cannot understand the basic principles framing the use of English and French in Quebec through section 133 alone, without including the Charter of the French Language. It would be a brave politician outside of Quebec who argued that changes made to Quebec's Charter of the French Language should have had the joint approval of the national parliament as well as the National Assembly under section 43 of the *Constitution Act, 1982*. Such were the realities behind the House of Commons's support in February 2021 for the Quebec National Assembly's right to amend the provincial constitution: this motion was debated in the context of a controversy over whether Quebec legislation could amend the *Constitution Act, 1867* to include a new section declaring French to be the sole official language of Quebec.[39] However, when New Brunswick wished to add a provision to the Constitution that declared French and English to be the official languages of that province, a section 43 procedure was considered necessary. It would be prudent to interpret the constitutional provisions relevant to the unanimity procedures as limited as much as possible to the constitutional documents recognized in the Appendix to the *Constitution Act, 1982*; just because courts may add documents to the list does not mean they should. While more expansive views of the requirement to use sections 41(a) and 41(c) are logical, it is still possible to give substantive meaning to them if their application is focused on whether the proposed changes would fundamentally frustrate or alter the basic provisions on language or the monarchy already found in Canada's formal constitution.

Furthermore, the Supreme Court only became creative in interpreting section 41(d), requiring unanimity for changes to "the composition of the Supreme Court of Canada," because the Court was entirely a creature of federal legislation, under the general authority of section 101 of the *Constitution Act, 1867*. To exclude the *Supreme Court Act* would mean the composition of the court would be entirely at the mercy of unilateral national legislation until such time as the text of the Constitution was amended to add in new provisions. However, this is an entirely different situation from that of the monarchic offices, which are substantively referred to by various documents in the Constitution.

## CONCLUSION

While the drafters of the *Constitution Act, 1982* may have thought that section 41(a) was a relatively straightforward provision protecting the monarchy in Canada, there are a number of complexities and dilemmas that the courts will have to clarify at some point in the future.

Judges will have to determine which legal elements relating to the monarchy in Canada are entrenched in the formal constitution, protected by requirements for federal-provincial consensus before changes are made. They will also have to establish just what is included in the offices of the Queen and her representatives and is deserving of protection by unanimous federal-provincial agreement. It is hoped that the courts will respect the diverse circumstances of each of these offices, a diversity reflecting both Canada's history and the autonomy each government should have to refine the details of its institutions. Of course, that autonomy also has to be balanced against aspects of the monarchy shared by all governments. To exclude certain matters from the "offices" mentioned in section 41(a) should not necessarily leave them vulnerable to unilateral legislative action, as some may still be protected by requirements in sections 38 or 43 for joint federal-provincial action. However, some degree of flexibility should remain, allowing Canadian legislatures to continue legislating on most Crown prerogatives.

# Part Two

## The Canadian Crown and Indigenous Peoples

4

# The Promise of the Crown in Indigenous-Settler Relations

*Keith Thor Carlson*

Does the Crown have more than a symbolic role to play in building and sustaining respectful Indigenous-settler relationships in Canada and in protecting Indigenous rights? History suggests it does. For while the structures of settler colonialism continue to marginalize Indigenous people and alienate them from their ancestral lands, it has been Canada's Crown far more than its democratically elected governments that has served as a check on the excesses of settler colonial power and ambition. Indeed, beyond being a mere check, the promise of the Crown's honour has helped inspire Indigenous people to pursue political and legal strategies to resist oppression from Canada's majority settler population.

Before beginning, I feel it important to explain that I personally have little interest in Britain's and Canada's royal family. I do not follow or even especially care about the men and women in England who carry, or have carried, the hereditary titles of king, queen, prince, and princess. Moreover, I am conflicted over the fact that these people were born with their titles and power and throughout their lives have been showered with privilege.

My ambivalence stems from my belief that the evidence suggests that, despite its shortcomings, the institution of our hereditary constitutional monarchy continues to hold more potential for progressive action on behalf of Indigenous people vis-à-vis a motivated settler majority than an elected head of state who derives authority from the electorate, such as exists within the system adopted by our American neighbours to the south. My personal feelings are, perhaps, not dissimilar to the conflict that necessarily exists in the relationship between Indigenous title and rights in Canada and Crown sovereignty in Canada. The Canadian Supreme Court, for example, has concluded that the "duty of the [Crown's] honour derives from the Crown's assertion of sovereignty in the face of prior Aboriginal occupation."[1] The assertion, therefore, holds within it the contradiction that the Crown's own sovereign position recognizes the *sui generis* nature of Indigenous sovereignty as something derived from Indigenous Peoples' prior occupation of Canadian territory.[2] The Supreme Court has recently clarified what an examination of our history reveals, viz., that *sui generis* Indigenous rights create a special fiduciary obligation on the part of the Crown to "to treat [A]boriginal peoples fairly and honourably, and to protect them from exploitation."[3] It is in light of these legal and political realities, informed by the historical discussion below, that I regard myself as a reluctant monarchist.

Indigenous Peoples' relationship with the Crown is inevitably shaped by settler colonialism. Scholars such as Patrick Wolfe and Lorenzo Veracini have shown that settler colonialism is a distinct form of colonialism characterized by settlers who displace Indigenous people with the goal of opening lands to exploitation and ownership. Colonialism in places like India under Britain, for example, was different. There, a small number of colonists used military force to control Indian labour while they reshaped the diversified Indian economy toward the production of cotton. The cotton was then sent to Britain where it was transformed into wealth via the British textile mills. In settler colonial states like Canada, the United States, Australia, and New Zealand, by way of contrast, settlers arrived in ever-growing numbers and quickly came to regard themselves as distinct and separate from the residents of their countries of origin. Indeed, within a few generations settlers came to think of themselves not as colonizers occupying Indigenous Peoples' lands, but rather as inheritors of land that their forefathers and foremothers had passed to them. Thus, while American and Canadian societies regard 1776 and 1867, respectively, as the dates that marked their transition from British colonists to citizens of independent nations, Indigenous people see and experience these histories differently.[4]

In settler colonial societies Indigenous people are socially, politically, and geographically marginalized. Settlers in settler societies want land and they regard Indigenous people as impediments, as problems that have to be removed. In Canada, Indigenous people were forcibly restricted to relatively small Indian reserves on lands that were typically marginal in terms of their ability to generate wealth for their residents.

Restricted to reserves, Indigenous people in Canada were additionally marginalized by being prevented from purchasing fee simple lands and in other ways from being fully able to engage in the economy as owners and operators of business. What was left as long as there were insufficient settlers to fill settler needs were positions as wage labourers — and typically these were seasonal and therefore unable to provide families with economic security and left them vulnerable to fluctuating commodity prices.

Indigenous people were also denied the franchise until 1962 — by which time they had long since became a minority in their homelands. In all meaningful ways, settler colonialism worked to exclude Indigenous people from the decision-making processes related to both themselves and to their ancestral lands and resources.

As a result, settler colonialism is not simply something that happened to Indigenous people in the past. That is to say, it is not merely an event that Indigenous people should be encouraged to "get over." Rather, settler colonialism is a structure of ongoing oppression. It works to ensure that for as long as Indigenous people resist being assimilated into Canada and becoming just another ethnic and racial minority they will remain socially marginal and economically impoverished and without meaningful control of their ancestral lands and resources. Indigenous people may retain legally protected rights, but these rights have not been meaningfully protected or operationalized. Accordingly, Indigenous people living under Canadian settler colonialism have been left with few economic opportunities, stigmatized by high levels of drug and alcohol addiction, relegated to low educational achievement rates, and over-represented in prisons.

Put another way, as settler Canadians have been building equity in their homes, Indigenous people have been fighting for recognition of their land rights. As settler Canadians have derived benefits from Crown lands and resources, Indigenous people have been confronted by clearcuts and open-pit mines where they used to conduct ceremonies, hunt game, fish, and gather. As settler Canadians have set aside park lands for their aesthetic enjoyment, Indigenous people have been criminalized for hunting, fishing, and gathering on these portions of their ancestral lands. As settler Canadians developed publicly funded local schools to inculcate the skills needed to succeed in Western society, Indigenous people were sent to residential schools where the pedagogical objective was to strip children of their culture while providing them a second-rate academic education that relegated them to the lowest rungs on Canada's economic ladder. And as settler Canadians have built democratic traditions and institutions, Indigenous people have struggled just to be heard.

Settler colonial societies, in other words, elect governments that represent settler colonial interests. Even though Canadian common law (and more recently the *Constitution Act, 1982*, Section 35) guarantees Aboriginal and treaty rights, settler colonial society has systematically worked to undermine and erode those rights. Indeed, in the face of Indigenous political activism in the early twentieth century the federal government even passed legislation that made it a criminal offence for Indigenous people to raise funds toward pursuing claims against the Canadian government.[5]

Given all this, it is perhaps less ironic than it might otherwise first appear that over the past two centuries it has been the Crown, and not Canada's elected governments, that has served as the more effective check on the excesses of settler colonialism. It has been the Crown that has served as a source of power to which Indigenous people have been able on occasion to appeal successfully to have their rights recognized and operationalized vis-à-vis settler interests.

Consider, for example, how in 1763, over strenuous opposition from settler colonists in Britain's thirteen American colonies, it was the monarch

King George III who proclaimed that because of "great Frauds and Abuses" having been committed by settlers against Indigenous people, all remaining unceded Indigenous lands were protected from further occupation by settlers until after nation-to-nation treaties had been negotiated and concluded. Additionally, he proclaimed that the Crown did

> further strictly enjoin and require all Persons whatever who have either wilfully or inadvertently seated themselves upon any Lands within the Countries above described, or upon any other Lands which, not having been ceded to or purchased by Us, are still reserved to the said Indians as aforesaid, forthwith to remove themselves from such Settlements.[6]

While receiving less attention in American popular memory than the supposed insult of taxation without representation in the British parliament, resentment toward the Royal Proclamation of 1763 was among the justifications American settler colonists cited in their decision to rebel in 1776:

> He [King George] has [through the Royal Proclamation of 1776] excited domestic insurrections amongst us, and has endeavoured to bring on the inhabitants of our frontiers, the merciless Indian Savages, whose known rule of warfare, is an undistinguished destruction of all ages, sexes and conditions.[7]

After U.S. independence, Indigenous military allyship with the British was therefore not a simple client-patron relationship, but rather a rational decision on the part of Indigenous people, like Tecumseh, to work with the British Crown against a settler colonial foe.

On the other side of the continent, and nearly a century later, in 1858 (twenty years after the Durham Report had recommended responsible government for the Canadian colonies, and a decade after responsible government was implemented in the Canadas), British Columbia was deliberately established as a Crown colony with no elected legislative body. This was done principally because the large number of American gold miners who had entered the region could not be trusted to be loyal to Britain. Importantly, however, it was also because even the loyal British miners and settlers who had arrived in the region could not be relied upon to respect Indigenous people and their rights. Accordingly, Colonial Secretary E. Bulwer-Lytton explained to the incoming governor, James Douglas, that the apparatus of responsible government would be "temporarily" withheld in British Columbia until "by the growth of a fixed population the materials for those Institutions shall be known to exist."[8]

With specific regard to the issue of Indigenous people, Bulwer-Lytton explained the following to Governor Douglas:

> I have to enjoin upon you to consider the best and most humane means of dealing with the Native Indians. The feelings of this Country would be strongly opposed to the adoption of any arbitrary or oppressive measures towards them.
>
> At this distance and with the imperfect means of knowledge I possess, I am reluctant to offer as yet any suggestion as to the prevention of affrays between the Indians and the Immigrants. This question is of so local a character that it must be solved by your knowledge and experience, and I commit it to you in the full persuasion that you will pay every regard to the interests of the Natives which an enlightened humanity can suggest ... Above all it is the earnest desire of Her Majesty's Government that your early attention should be given to the best means of diffusing the blessings of the Christian Religion and of civilization among the Natives.[9]

Speaking before Parliament, Lytton clarified that "the immediate object" in providing Douglas with his exceptional executive powers was "to establish temporary law and order amidst a motley inundation of immigrant diggers ... of whom perhaps few if any, have any intention to become resident colonists and British subjects."[10]

Similarly, in what became the Canadian prairie provinces, between 1871 and 1921 the Canadian Crown concluded eleven treaties with the

Indigenous people. In signing these agreements Indigenous people understood the Crown (and not the elected Canadian government) to be entering into a covenant that committed the state to intercede to defend Aboriginal rights and interests in the event of conflicts with settlers.[11]

The conviction that the Crown represented a voice distinct from that of the elected provincial and federal governments, and that that voice had genuine agency, was expressed in the aspirations of British Columbia's Indigenous leaders, who empowered a delegation of three regional leaders to represent their interests directly to King Edward VII in Buckingham Palace in 1906.[12]

Led by Chief Joe Capilano, this delegation intentionally chose to bypass the provincial and federal governments and lay their grievances over the lack of recognition of their rights and title directly before the monarch. Their goal was to secure a promise from King Edward VII that he would task someone disconnected and independent from the settler government with looking into their concerns and protecting their rights: "We are sure that a good man, or some good men, will be sent to our country who will see, and hear, and bring back a report to your majesty."[13]

Remembering his participation in the 1906 delegation and his audience with King Edward VII, in 1913 Charlie Isipaymilt of Cowichan told the government agents who visited his community the following:

> I went to the King a few years ago to try to get some settlement from the King, and when I got there, the King gave me this photograph. His Majesty promised to do something for us, and said he would send somebody out to look into the matter. The King told me that I need not feel very sorry about these things, as if there was anything he could do[,] anything for me, he would do it.[14]

Settler hostility to Indigenous aspirations manifested itself both formally (the federal government instructed the high commisioner in London to distract the delegates while delaying the audience with the King and working to ensure that Indigenous politics would not be discussed in the King's presence[15]) and informally in the form of genuine threats of physical violence from local settlers. With regard to the latter, Capilano explained to British reporters in London the message that his white neighbours had provided him prior to his leaving for Britain: "They told me, the white men told me, not to come to the great King ... because he did not like his dusky children. We would never go back to our people alive, they said."[16]

More recently, in 1982, Indigenous people invoked their relationship with the Crown to wrestle from the Canadian settler government formal constitutional recognition of their rights. And in 1995, Indigenous people in Quebec reminded settler Canadians that their relationship with the Crown stood outside the theatre of French-English settler colonial politics. They asserted that their relationship with the Crown prohibited the francophone majority from having the authority to withdraw the lands of the province of Quebec from Canada without their consent.[17]

Perhaps a useful way to frame the Crown in Indigenous-settler relations is to consider how, unlike the United States, where the president is both the head of the government and the head of state, in Canada our prime minister is never more than the head of the settler government. Canada's governors general (who, unlike our elected prime ministers, have in recent years included women of colour from racialized ethnic communities and, indeed, today Mary Simon of Kangiqsualujjuaq) are non-elected officials appointed on the advice of the prime minister by Her Majesty the Queen to protect the honour of the Crown.

Of course the governors general always leave the running of the government to the prime minister, the elected government, and Parliament. But, as the unelected representatives of the Crown, governors general do not answer to, nor are they accountable to, a settler colonial constituency. As the embodiment of a set of principles and ideals, the Crown has been understood by many Indigenous people over time as holding the power to not only transcend, but to challenge settler colonial agendas that are inconsistent with the rights of Indigenous people and the honour of the Crown.

To illustrate my meaning, let us look more closely at the historical relationship between the Crown and the Indigenous people of one particular territory — the Stó:lō of the lower Fraser River watershed.

In 1858, James Douglas, the governor of the new colony of mainland British Columbia, engaged in a lengthy correspondence with senior officials in the Colonial Office, seeking to determine the role Indigenous people would play within a territory that had almost overnight transitioned from an economy anchored in the fur trade into one characterized by industrial mining. Indeed, whereas there had been less than a hundred non-Indigenous people residing along the lower Fraser River in January of 1857, by August of that same year there were over thirty thousand (mostly American) miners scouring the riverbanks for gold.

As governor, Douglas thought deeply about what might, and might not, work to promote positive Indigenous-settler relations. Not only did he speak directly with Indigenous people, he also drew on his lived experience. Moreover, he reflected on lessons that could be learned by looking elsewhere. In the adjacent Washington Territory, for example, a bloody war had just ended that had resulted in Indigenous people being restricted to small collective Indian reservations where they were marginalized from settler society and excluded from settler governance and the settler economy.[18] Indeed, in Washington, as in other American jurisdictions along the Pacific Coast, laws had been passed that made it impossible for a white man to be convicted in court on the testimony of an Indian. And in California, literally thousands of Indigenous people had been systematically exterminated by miners and ranchers who regarded them as impediments to their success.[19]

In British Columbia, Indigenous people petitioned Douglas, imploring him to ensure that they be spared a similar fate. The governor explained to officials in Britain that he had assured the colony's Indigenous population of the Crown's integrity:

They evidently looked forward with dread to their own future condition, fearing lest the same wretched fate awaited the natives of British Columbia [as occurred in Washington and California]. I succeeded in dis-abusing their minds of those false impressions by fully explaining the views of Her Majesty's Government.[20]

Then, over intense opposition from British Columbian settlers, as well as from senior officials within his own administration, Douglas, in the name of the Crown, launched a policy aimed at developing the colonial economy while simultaneously protecting Indigenous rights and securing for Indigenous people a respected, and respectful, position within the new, emerging colony society.

Central to the governor's policy was the protection of large tracts of lands he defined with the term "anticipatory Indian reserves." He called these "anticipatory" because he intended them to protect Indigenous Peoples' anticipated long-term economic interests within the rapidly developing settler economy. Douglas expected that commercial agriculture would become central to British Columbia's future prosperity and so he instructed his agents to work with Indigenous people to collaboratively identify as reserve lands those spaces that consisted of existing villages, as well as burials and cultivated fields. But beyond these, he directed that the reserves include sufficient lands that would facilitate Indigenous people's anticipated future success in commercial farming and commercial ranching.[21]

In the Fraser Valley, giant reserves, such as the 9,600 acre Máthxwi (Matsqui) anticipatory reserve, were mapped and demarcated under Douglas's authority with the active participation of Indigenous people. In the Okanagan and Thompson Rivers regions anticipatory reserves were similarly created. Due to the anticipated differences in land use between the coast and the interior (cattle ranching as opposed to farming), the anticipatory reserves set aside for Secwepmc, Nlakalamux, and Okanagan people were an order of magnitude larger than those in Stó:lō territory (i.e., what is now the Abbotsford and Chilliwack regions). The Kamloops reserve, for instance, was roughly the shape of a triangle, running six miles east-west and twelve miles north-south. Similarly, the reserve at the foot of Okanagan Lake measured twenty square miles.

In addition to anticipatory reserve lands, Governor Douglas also confirmed that Indigenous people would continue to have the right to access and use open and unclaimed Crown lands beyond the boundaries of their Indian reserves:

> I made them clearly understand that Her Majesty's Government felt deeply interested in their welfare, and had sent instructions that they should be treated in all respects as her Majesty's other subjects.... I also explained to them ... that they might freely exercise and enjoy the rights of fishing the Lakes and Rivers, and of hunting over all unoccupied Crown Lands in the Colony.

Douglas went on to note that

> they were delighted with the idea, and expressed their gratitude in the warmest terms, assuring me of their boundless devotion and attachment to Her Majesty's person and Crown, and their readiness to take up arms at any moment in defence of Her Majesty's dominion and right.[22]

Under Douglas's system, fishing and hunting rights on Crown lands would ensure that Indigenous people remained self-sufficient and could continue to practise their cultural traditions despite the pressures associated with the growth of settler communities. Indigenous people who spoke directly with Douglas later remembered him as having said,

> For which land I have surveyed it belongs to the Indians only, that no white men shall intrude on your land. And for all the outside lands Her Majesty Queen Victoria will take and sell to the white people and that which is taken away from the Indians will be like a fruit tree and from this fruit Her Majesty Queen Victoria will give it to the Indians for their lasting support.[23]

Oral histories recorded after Douglas's retirement and still circulating within the Stó:lō community assert that Douglas and his successor, Governor Frederick Seymour, both committed to the future payment of compensation for lands alienated from its use and governance. Significantly, Governor Douglas also ensured that Indigenous people would be able to participate equally with settlers in all other aspects of the emerging society. During his administration he established policies that entitled Indigenous people to pre-empt and own fee simple lands; they were entitled to commercially extract timber and mineral resources, they were entitled to vote (though they were never systematically informed of this right), and they were appointed to government positions, such as magistrates, where they held genuine authority within the structures of the emerging settler society.[24] And, importantly, they were empowered to do all of these things without the accompanying loss of Indigenous status (and rights), as was subsequently incorporated into legislation by the Canadian government in the 1876 *Indian Act*.

It did not take long, however, for the settler government to begin undoing the provisions the Crown's representative had established to protect Indigenous people's rights and secure Indigenous people's future. Mere weeks following his retirement from office in April 1864, voices within the newly created legislative council were denouncing Douglas as having betrayed settler interests, of having "potlatched away" the best lands in the colony by consenting to having them locked up as Indian reserves. And within a few short years all that Douglas had done in cooperation and consultation with Indigenous people to create a relatively respectful and respected place for them within the emerging colonial society had been undone. Indeed, in most cases it had been disavowed.

Consider, for example, that the large anticipatory Indian reserves created to protect Indigenous economic interests were unilaterally reduced by Douglas's successor, without Indigenous consent, by over 90 percent; the right to pre-empt land outside their reserve was repealed; the right to catch and sell fish from the Fraser River was restricted to white men with government-issued licences — and then only to those who fished in nontidal waters downriver of present-day Abbotsford; the ability to hunt was restricted to subsistence hunting and regulated by game laws designed in the interest of non-Indigenous sportsmen; forests were managed under a regime that valued the fibre content of trees and was regulated principally in the interests of large corporations; existing Indigenous magistrates were no longer recognized and no new ones were appointed; legislation was passed explicitly denying Indigenous people the franchise; Indigenous spirituality and ceremony (the "tamanawas" winter dance) were outlawed; Indigenous

governance (the potlatch) was made illegal; and for the next century an informal system similar to the "Jim Crow" laws in the United States ensured
that Indigenous people remained socially marginalized. Indeed, as contemporary Elders today explain, up until the 1960s Indigenous people found
that they were not welcome in most restaurants, they were formally relegated
to certain sections of movie theatres, and of course their community's children were sent to distant residential schools.[25]

Despite the settler colonial juggernaut, the Stó:lō and other Indigenous
groups (like their upriver Nlakapamux relatives and neighbours) continued
to make formal efforts to carve out specific physical, governmental, social,
legal, and economic spaces for themselves *within* Canada. Importantly, for
the purposes of this essay, these proposed spaces explicitly included roles for
the Crown and governor general as buffers between Indigenous governments
and settler provincial and federal governments. In each instance, however,
elected federal or provincial government officials intervened to discredit the
Indigenous spokespersons and to place settler interests above those of the
territory's original inhabitants, thwarting Indigenous aspirations and efforts
at building reconciliation.[26]

More recently (after the 1927 prohibition on raising funds to hire lawyers to pursue Aboriginal rights litigation was repealed in 1951), Indigenous
people have made some progress in operationalizing their rights and in receiving compensation for past harms. This success has largely been tied to
court and tribunal challenges where they have been able to argue that the
honour of the Crown had been breached by settler governments.

Settler society as a whole, and Canadian elected officials in particular,
have not freely and compassionately moved to build reconciliation — to
dismantle settler colonialism. Rather, they have been dragged to the table
by court challenges and Indigenous political activism that appealed to the
honour of the Crown and argued breach of fiduciary obligations. In jurisdictions like British Columbia, governments initiated modern treaty nego-
tiation processes and began working to restore alienated rights and help re-
build injured cultures in meaningful and significant ways only after a string
of court decisions made it increasingly expensive and embarrassing not to
do so. And even then, governments typically only made such moves after

corporate interests pushed them to act in order to establish "predictability" in future resource sector developments.[27]

The above discussion should not be taken, however, to imply that Indigenous people have always had, or necessarily still hold, an unshakable faith in the Crown and its honour. Certainly Indigenous people are not, and have not been, naive about what the Crown is and its role in Canadian parliamentary democracy. Indeed, it is the examples of incidents when Indigenous people were upset with, or disappointed in, the Crown that truly reveal the extent to which Indigenous people regarded the Crown as an active agent and potential ally in their relations with settler society and government.

As early as 1874 Stó:lō and neighbouring Indigenous Peoples boycotted Queen Victoria's birthday celebrations in New Westminster. The reason was outlined in a petition: "We are commencing to believe that the aim of the white men is to exterminate us as soon as they can, although we have always been quiet, obedient, kind and friendly to the whites." Failure to give them "satisfaction," the petitioners warned, would "create ill feelings, irritation among our people, and we cannot say what will be the consequence." And when a year later there had still been no corrective action from the government, Chief Alexis of Cheam penned another letter, this time asserting that Queen Victoria had "not been a good mother and Queen to us." When asked by the provincial secretary to comment on their situation, local Indian commissioner, James Lenihan stated that he was shocked to find within Alexis's letter "language disrespectful of Her Majesty" and "threats of violence towards any white settler who may try to pre-empt lands" that the Indigenous community felt should be included within their reserves.[28]

Consider too, for example, the account from Chief Alexis in 1876 when he told the local Indian agent the following:

> You told us that our great mother the Queen was good and powerful, and we believed you. We know that she has only to speak to this government and our lands must be fixed; we wonder why our great mother does not speak, we want you to tell her that we have said, we were promised 80 acres of land to each

family and now we are treated like children and we are put off with 20 acres, which is not enough if we are to do like the white-man, shall we be obliged to turn to our old ways?[29]

More recently, the scandal surrounding Governor General Julie Payette's alleged abusive behaviour toward her staff and neglect of her viceregal dut-ies tarnished the Crown in many people's eyes, as did her earlier public dismissal of spirituality, even as she made pious statements about the value of listening to Indigenous Elders. It is too early to say whether the recent ap-pointment of Inuit politician and traditional knowledge keeper Mary Simon of Kangiqsualujjuaq will help to restore people's respect for the office.

Indigenous people have been remarkably successful in convincing Canadian courts of the existence of their rights, and of the ways in which settler governments have violated those rights, and by extension, the hon-our of the Crown. But Canada's democratic majority has consistently pushed back against these victories, and our elected governments have often failed to implement new policies and laws that would breathe life into Indigenous people's constitutionally protected Aboriginal and Treaty Rights.

In a way that speaks to contemporary issues as if it had only been spoken yesterday, I close this essay with an invitation to reflect upon the words of Chief Charlie of Máthxwi when he stood before British Columbia's Royal Commission on Indian Affairs more than a century ago and asserted:

In the time of Sir James Douglas he made a lasting promise to us Indians, as all the Indians Reserves lasting support and benefit by the name of Queen Victoria.[30] Also Governor Seymour the second Governor. He also made a lasting promise to us Indians in New Westminster that we will receive or deserving one-fourth from all taxes this money for our support and to improve our land. The promises were never kept. If those good promises was kept up by the British Columbia government the Indians would be all rich, and they would be all living comfortably; be as happy as our white brothers today.[31]

Chief Charlie's statement reminds us that as Canadians we are generally free to oppose, criticize, and even hate our heads of government without fear of being perceived as, or accused of, opposing the Canadian state. Unlike our neighbours to the south, we have never had a parliamentary equivalent to the infamous U.S. House Committee on Un-American Activities.[32] Indeed, as Indigenous people have so ably demonstrated throughout history, opposing and challenging our government's commitment to advancing the interests of settler colonialism has on occasion been a means of bolstering the honour of the Crown, and thereby decolonizing key features of settler colonialism. The monarchy is not the only way to achieve this, but, for all its shortcomings and flaws, I would argue that it has done more in this regard over the years than Canadian democracy.

# 5

# Overturning Royal Monuments: Confronting History, Reconciliation, and the Honour of the Crown

*Serge Joyal*

On July 1, 2021, a group of protesters toppled statues of Queen Victoria and Queen Elizabeth II located on the grounds of the Manitoba Legislative Building.[1] This dramatic act was in response to the recent discovery of hundreds of unmarked graves of Indigenous students who had died while attending residential schools in Kamloops, British Columbia, and Marieval, Saskatchewan. These students, like so many others over the course of decades, had been taken from their families and placed in these institutions of forced assimilation located across much of the country.[2] The discovery of these forgotten and neglected graves was a grim reminder of the cruel treatment of Indigenous students.

In removing the statue of Queen Victoria from its base and dumping its severed head into the Assiniboine River, the protesters were expressing anger at the historic wrongs done to Indigenous and Métis peoples. For more than a century and a half since Confederation they had been forced to endure a system of exclusion and degradation, deprived of their rights to dignity, identity, language, culture, land, and livelihood. In overturning the statue of Queen Elizabeth and pushing her face into the ground, the protesters were dramatically showing their dissatisfaction with the painful process of truth and reconciliation. For them, the statues of the two queens embodied the power structure of an oppressive government, the establishment of a predatory colonial power, and the continuing shortcomings of a legal system that struggled to live up to its professed ideals of rights and justice.

Overturning and despoiling monuments of monarchs or of other figures of authority commemorated for their status and contributions has a long history in Canada and much of the world. A bust of the reigning king, George III, brought to Montreal by Governor Guy Carleton and prominently displayed in the Place du Marché in Montreal was destroyed within years of its installation. A mob of English merchants and townsfolk attacked it in their anger upon learning of the enactment of the *Quebec Act* in 1774, a law that granted rights and recognition to the majority French population, allowing them to speak their language, keep their legal system, and practise their Catholic faith. The monument lost its head in this protest of English Protestant dissent; the rest of it was destroyed soon afterwards by American troops occupying the city temporarily, shortly after the outbreak of the American Revolution.[3] George III was again the target of American anger when an equestrian monument of the king was pulled down in New York City in the buildup to the revolution.[4] A statue of another sovereign, this time Queen Victoria, suffered a similar fate in Quebec City on July 12th, 1963, when a bomb by the FLQ destroyed it. This was part of a violent separatist campaign that targeted royal and colonial symbols, including frequent bombing of mailboxes.[5]

The French also have a history of destroying statues and monuments of royal rule. Many of them were razed once the revolution took hold in 1789. Royal burial sites were desecrated at Saint-Denis and other churches in Paris. The tradition continued, this time under government sanction, with efforts to wipe out reminders of the Napoleonic regime during the restoration of the Bourbon monarchy. It was more violent, though short-lived, during the Paris

Commune of 1871, when the statue of Napoleon I atop a column in Place Vendôme was smashed.[6] The Tuileries Palace burned to the ground following the defeat and overthrow of Napoleon III in the Franco-Prussian war. In the twentieth century, such acts often accompanied successful but often violent struggles in colonies seeking independence. When, for example, independence came to India in 1947 after a long campaign against the Raj, many of the symbols of British rule, statues of royals and their viceroys, were removed from public view and allowed to decay in hidden depots or sold off.[7]

As these recent and more historic events show, aside from anger, the underlying circumstances surrounding the vandalism or destruction of monuments are not always the same, because they do not always have the same goal. In the case of the American and French revolutions, accumulated grievances had turned into outright opposition to the ruling power structure that refused a voice or meaningful representation to the majority of the population. Their anger eventually exploded into outright rebellion. Targeting royal monuments was just one manifestation of the accumulated hostility toward the detested authority. The event in Montreal against the *Quebec Act* was of a different magnitude and purpose. The protest of the privileged minority English community stemmed from a sense of betrayal and disloyalty to their shared Protestant heritage and identity. They were upset that rights were extended to the vanquished majority population, contrary to established norms of their time. Granting such rights to French papists was viewed as an outrageous concession that had been rightfully denied to fellow Catholic subjects in Britain and Ireland. However, the Montreal riot did not fundamentally seek to challenge or overturn the Crown or royal government. The action of the mob was not the beginning of a movement against the colonial administration, but rather a demonstration of their privileged status within the ruling power dynamic.

What happened in Manitoba on July 1, 2021, was altogether different. The Indigenous activists and their supporters were upset at the legacy created by the residential school system, the *Indian Act* (1876) and the underlying racism used to justify it. They were angry that such a policy had ever been put in place and had been maintained for decade after decade. Created in the era of Queen Victoria, shortly after Confederation, the residential schools were the inhumane result of an overt and extended project to erase the culture and identity of Indigenous and Métis peoples. Recognition in recent years of the wrongs perpetrated through the agency of the Canadian government has led to a process of truth and reconciliation. The slow and uneven implementation of policies to provide more just and equitable treatment during the reign of the current Queen as she marks her Platinum Jubilee has led to these outbursts of frustration. However, instead of seeking to overthrow the government, their purpose is to insist that governments live up to their acknowledged obligations. These obligations are identified with the Crown in the person of the sovereign, a concept that gave the Manitoba protest greater meaning.[8]

Recommendations of the Truth and Reconciliation Commission have prompted various measures to openly and frankly acknowledge Canada's shameful history of mistreatment of its Indigenous population. Some of these actions have been voluntary on the part of government and different public institutions; others are the consequence of demonstrations like the one that happened in Winnipeg. More broadly, the results of the Commission's efforts have stimulated a closer re-evaluation of our past, what we have praised and what we have ignored. In Montreal and Halifax, the name of General Amherst and the statue of Colonel Edward Cornwallis have been removed in recognition of their belligerent and destructive policies toward Indigenous peoples. More prominent still have been attacks on memorials to Sir John A. Macdonald. Traditionally admired as the Father of Confederation and its first prime minister, he is now forcefully denounced as the author and instigator of the *Indian Act* and the residential school initiative. Monuments to him across the country in Victoria, Regina, Kingston, Montreal, and Charlottetown have been vandalized, toppled, removed, and stored away.

Colonialism, what it represents and how it is understood in its engagement with the original inhabitants of claimed territories, has undergone a phenomenal reversal. What is now fiercely denounced as shameful racism was once praised as undeniable proof of the superiority of white, Christian, European culture. Representing the vanguard of advanced civilization, the duty imposed by colonialism was to possess and exploit the newly discovered lands with all their riches.

From the earliest days, explorers and settlers in the New World legitimized themselves on lands already occupied by native inhabitants under the old concept of *terra nullius*. Aggressive settlement and expansion displaced the Indigenous peoples, who were derisively and inhumanely dismissed as "savages." The establishments of permanent settlements were acknowledged as historic achievements and those who participated in these efforts were hailed as courageous and brave pioneers and visionaries.[9] They shared in the glory of those kings and queens in whose name they pursued their ambitions. In later years, they became subjects of those many monuments of commemoration that are now under threat. Little consideration was given to the devastating impact these expanding settlements had on the Indigenous population. Indeed, in the rivalry among the European nations for imperial

Commemorative mug of the Diamond Jubilee of Queen Victoria, 1897, distributed throughout the British Empire, with an illustration of the world map and the inscription "the Empire on which the sun never sets."

status, the drive to claim colonies and encourage forceful possession and exploitation was irresistible. The buildup that began in the sixteenth century continued through the nineteenth century and lasted late into the twentieth century.[10]

In this endeavour, Britain was an undoubted leader, creating a global "Empire over which the sun never sets."[11] The maltreatment of the Indigenous peoples, when considered at all, was dismissed as the price to pay in the pursuit of glory, power, and riches and was part of what imperialists saw as their civilizing mission.

It is no surprise that the attitude of the settler colonists became endemic throughout Canada and that it persisted years after Confederation. Ignored out of hand were earlier treaty commitments with the Indigenous peoples made in the name of the Crown. Alliances to support competing French and British claims in their rivalry for possession of Canada were cast aside once they were no longer useful. Treaties signed in the name of the Crown with various Indigenous nations were not honoured or enforced; they became dead letters. Any impediments to Canada's expansionist ambitions to assert dominion over the land from coast to coast to coast were simply crushed.

Growing awareness by the public of the great wrongs done through these policies and programs and mounting protests by Indigenous groups compelled governments to address this reality and take some remedial action. This has been a slow and cumulative process. Certain milestones track how the federal government developed a greater willingness to finally confront the undeniable consequences of racism despite the magnitude of the challenge.

Public opinion and Indigenous protests were not the only factors that led governments to take decisive remedial action. The courts played a significant and determining role in defining the legal and constitutional responsibilities of the federal government and the validity of existing treaty rights of the Indigenous peoples. In fact, the courts' involvement was decisive, since they confirmed the binding legal nature of the government's obligations with respect to the Indigenous peoples.[12] Critical to this judicial determination was the patriation of the Constitution, originally the *British North America Act*, from Westminster in 1982. Included in the patriation package was the

*Constitution Act, 1982* which, through section 35, explicitly admitted and affirmed all existing statutory and treaty rights of the Indian, Inuit, and Métis peoples of Canada, as well as their current and future land claims.

In the landmark decision *Guerin v. R.*[13] of 1984, the Supreme Court of Canada acknowledged the government's fiduciary duty toward the First Nations based on the principle of the honour of the Crown. While this concept has its roots in British traditions, its modern significance is due to the constitutional status accorded to statutory rights as expressed in section 35. As Justice Abella put it, "The unwritten constitutional principle of the honour of the Crown has been affirmed by this Court and accorded full legal force." Abiding by this principle, the court insists that ministers acting on behalf of the government are duty-bound to uphold standards of fairness and justice; the Crown and its agents have to act honourably rather than yield to political expediency.

Legal scholars trace the Canadian history of the honour of the Crown to such early precedents as the Great Peace of 1701, when thirteen hundred representatives of thirty-nine First Nations gathered in Montreal to conclude a treaty to end the war between the Indian confederacy and New France. However, it was the Royal Proclamation of 1763 and the Treaty of Niagara of 1764 that definitively established the continuing legal framework for making treaties between First Nations and the British Crown. Their object was to establish strict procedures for British territorial expansion in North America. This Magna Carta of the First Nations recognized their national status; it would only be through them that the British government could acquire their lands and expand colonial settlement. Acquisition could only be through a treaty with the Crown, thus excluding private individuals or companies. The resulting relationship created an ongoing liaison between First Nations and the Crown that endures "for as long as the sun shines, the waters flow and the grass grows."[14]

Pre- and post-Confederation governments made seventy treaties between the Crown and 364 First Nations, which include eleven numbered treaties made between 1871 and 1921. Though often ignored in the past, the revival of the concept of the honour of the Crown provided the means by which the First Nations could legally assert their treaty rights to their benefit as well as for the Inuit and Métis. As David Arnot pointed out, "Appealing to the honour of the Crown was an appeal not merely to the sovereign as a person, but to a traditional bedrock of principles of fundamental justice that lay beyond persons and beyond politics. It is precisely this distinction that rests at the heart of our ideals of 'human rights' today."[15]

The honour of the Crown has become an effective means by which the treaty relationship between Indigenous Peoples and government can be revitalized. For the Indigenous Peoples, this association with the Crown was originally seen as a form of kinship, a covenant, by which Indigenous people and white settlers would agree to share the land and all its bounty. The treaties themselves were sacred agreements held in equal reverence with the Crown itself.[16] Assent to the treaties formed a lasting relationship between the Indigenous people and the Crown, together with her subjects, as affirmed by the Creator as witness. Now, through the process of reconciliation, the commitments confirmed in these treaties must be effectively pursued and the Crown must do its part through the federal government, which has inherited this duty to operationalize the treaties.

Statements by Chief Perry Bellegarde, past national chief of the Assembly of First Nations, indicate a willingness to negotiate in good faith in the hope that a renewed commitment to the obligations promised in the treaties can over time repair the damage done through colonialism and racism. Moving forward, there is an indispensable need to show mutual respect and understanding. As he explained, "The Crown First Nation Treaty relationship is not founded in colonialism or in rights denial, but rather the equality and sovereignty of people and our agreement to share land without dominating one another."[17] The connection through these treaties to the Crown itself is seen not only as historically important but also as equally significant today. This is clear from "Call to Action 45"[18] of the Truth and Reconciliation report, which would have the Government of Canada, in cooperation with Indigenous people, produce a Royal Proclamation of Reconciliation issued by the Crown in the name of the Queen. Among the commitments to be made through this second Magna Carta, supplementing the Royal Proclamation of 1763 and the Treaty of Niagara of 1764, would be reaffirmation of the nation-to-nation relationship between Indigenous people and the Crown. It would include a conclusive repudiation of claims to sovereignty founded on the European doctrine of discovery and *terra nullius*. Instead, there would be renewal or establishment of treaty relationships founded on mutual recognition, respect, and shared responsibility, acknowledging the full partnership of Indigenous people in Confederation and in its constitutional and legal orders.

Following up on this call to action would be deeply significant. It would better ensure that any future negotiations and settlements would be arrived at honourably. The proclamation would commit the parties to genuine reconciliation so that the actions required from any subsequent agreement would be fully accepted and implemented. It would also confirm the continuing strong attachment of the Indigenous people to the Crown — a reality that has always been present since the time of George III through Victoria and now the present Queen. This attachment is both to the person of the sovereign[19] and to the role of the Crown as the instrument of government. In the person of the current Queen, there is deep respect for the example of a life devoted to service. There is also a sense of reassurance that, as the constitutional source of all executive authority,[20] the Queen acts as the guarantor of the proclamation. The honour of the Crown demands no less. Pursuing the achievement of a Royal Proclamation of Reconciliation during the Platinum Jubilee would be a remarkable way to demonstrate this commitment to mutual respect and understanding, while also marking the unprecedented milestone of the Queen's long reign.

The Royal Proclamation could also provide a key to the approach with respect to the royal monuments. The protest actions of overturning the statues of Queen Victoria and Queen Elizabeth in Winnipeg expressed anger at past injustices and frustration with the slow pace of reconciliation. The past injustices are fully admitted now by governments at all levels and especially by Ottawa. The slow pace is a measure of the scope of work and time it will take to achieve lasting and meaningful reconciliation. Wrapped up in this past, present, and future is the Indigenous connection to the Crown. Reconciliation also presents an opportunity to rethink how past royal monuments can be reimagined and appreciated more honestly by introducing elements that acknowledge a more complete historical reality. While it is still possible to recognize the importance of Confederation achieved during the reign of Queen Victoria and the progress made in subsequent reigns to the present Queen, it is equally important to acknowledge the wrongs perpetrated on the Indigenous population that accompanied the enactment of the *British North America Act*. Only by fully confronting the reality of what happened, by admitting the truth, is it possible to have genuine reconciliation.

Equestrian statue of Queen Elizabeth II on her horse Burmese, a gift from the RCMP in 1969. The statue, by sculptor Susan Velder, was commissioned by the Province of Saskatchewan to commemorate the Queen's Golden Jubilee. Located in front of the Legislative Building in Regina, it was unveiled by Her Majesty in May 2005 during the province's centennial celebrations. The Queen also inaugurated the adjoining Queen Elizabeth II Gardens.

Undertaking such a mature approach requires the ability to properly expose the past, tackling it head-on. Vandalizing royal monuments and other statues is a half-gesture, without a positive impact. It does little to establish the truth or promote its understanding, the necessary precondition to meaningful reconciliation. In the context of the honour of the Crown and the reverence maintained by the First Nations, Inuit, and Métis for the sovereign as the guarantor of treaties, this requires an effort to balance the good with the bad. Even as these memorialized figures are honoured, there must be some recognition of the wrongs that were done and a commitment to remediation and reconciliation. Preserving these monuments is a reminder in the present of the obligation to fulfill this commitment.

Greater awareness and acceptance of the moral obligation to provide information about historic reality by incorporating past and present Indigenous perspectives can lead to a consensus about how royal monuments and the statues to former statesmen should be managed generally. This agreement is one element of a public manifestation of the sincere effort by both government and Indigenous Peoples to move in partnership beyond the pain of the past. By acknowledging how former policies of assimilation and suppression perpetrated on the Indigenous Peoples harmed them and nearly destroyed them, governments are admitting to a truth that was long denied. Accepting this truth and the government's responsibility for it is the first step to achieving meaningful reconciliation. This acknowledgement must form part of the account accompanying the presence of royal monuments and other statues found throughout the country. Many monuments of sovereigns are located across Canada in six different provinces.[21] Success in this would advance an understanding of how praise of celebrated glories owed to a distinct few concealed suffering and pain endured by an invisible many.

Admitting this complexity of our history and incorporating diverse viewpoints into the interpretation accompanying monuments is hugely important. Applying these layers of understanding to the display of royal statues and other public monuments is an open admission of the good and the bad of our history. It permits multiple perspectives that provide an appreciation of how our forefathers thought of their achievements in settling Canada while also promoting an awareness of the impact racist attitudes had on a defenceless minority population, who deserve at long last the recognition of their rights and dignity. It provides an entry into an era that is more deliberately post-colonial, that is set on the path to truth and reconciliation. In parallel to this goal has been the appointment of several prominent First Nations, Inuit, and Métis leaders to fill viceregal positions to represent the Queen. It is not without significance that Her Majesty is now represented by a governor general, Mary Simon, an Inuit from Kangiqsualujjuaq, Nunavik, Québec, and that since 1974 six lieutenant governors have been of Indigenous origin.[22]

It would be a regrettable mistake to remove royal monuments because of the vision of the world carried by our predecessors. It would be equivalent to rewriting history in the context of the present day. Our identity as Canadians is the result of multiple layers of different periods involving various cultural groups — Indigenous, French, and English, as well as wave after wave of diverse immigrants who saw and interpreted the world according to the values and morals of their time. Fortunately, our values have evolved in the direction of a much wider shared humanism that privileges equal dignity for all persons and respect of each identity, wherever and whatever it can be.

Monuments to our sovereigns accompanied with the recital of Indigenous perspectives can promote better understanding. Growing awareness of this complex reality will reinforce the meaning and importance of our shared identity. The monuments of the sovereigns are there to remind Canadians how reconciliation can be achieved in the year of an unprecedented Platinum Jubilee with a highly symbolic Royal Proclamation of Reconciliation.

## APPENDIX 1: PUBLIC ROYAL MONUMENTS IN CANADA

### Alberta

A statue of Princess Louise, Duchess of Argyll, on the Legislative Building grounds, Edmonton.

## British Colombia

A statue of Queen Victoria by Allen Joy (1921) on the grounds of the Legislative Building in Victoria; a statue of King George VI in Vancouver; a bust of Queen Elizabeth II in Beacon Hill Park, Victoria.

In addition to these monuments, one should add those of sovereigns located within private institutions, such as the statues of Queen Victoria on the steps of Victoria College at McGill University, Montreal, or in the entrance hall of the old Royal Victoria Hospital, now in the new CUSUM, a public hospital in Montreal.

## Manitoba

Statues of Queen Victoria by the sculptor George Frampton (1904) and of Queen Elizabeth II by the Canadian sculptor Leo Mol (1970) in Winnipeg on the grounds of the Manitoba Legislative Building.

## Ontario

A statue of Queen Victoria on Parliament Hill in Ottawa (1900), by L.P. Hébert; an equestrian monument of Queen Elizabeth II on her horse Centenial by the Canadian sculptor Jack Harman on Parliament Hill, Ottawa (1992), now located on the roundabout in front of the main gate of Rideau Hall; a statue of Queen Victoria at Queen's Park, Toronto; an equestrian statue of King Edward VII by sculptor Thomas Brock (1919), installed in 1969 on the grounds of the Legislative Building at Queen's Park, Toronto; the Princes' Gates, Exhibition Place, Toronto; the Queen Elizabeth Way monument, Sir Casimir Gzowski Park, Toronto; Princess Margaret Fountain, Exhibition Place, Toronto; a statue of Queen Victoria in Gore Park, Hamilton, and one in Victoria Park, Kitchener; a statue of King George VI in Niagara Falls.

## Quebec

A bust of King Louis XIV at Place Royale,[23] Quebec City; the first statue of Queen Victoria in Montreal, Victoria Square (1869), by the sculptor Marsh Wood; an impressive statue of King Edward VII, Phillips Square, Montreal (1914), by the noted Canadian sculptor Louis-Philippe Hébert; and the Queen Isabella of Castille (1451–1504) Memorial by José Planes (1891–1974), Sir Wilfrid Laurier Park, Montreal.

## Saskatchewan

An equestrian statue of Her Majesty Queen Elizabeth II on her horse Burmese (2005) by Susan Velder, in front of the Saskatchewan Legislative Building in Regina.

# 6

# Treaty Spaces:
# The Chapels Royal in Canada

*John Fraser, Carolyn King, and Nathan Tidridge*

In coming to terms with the long, complicated, and often tragic history between the Indigenous nations and settler communities in what eventually became Canada, the role of Crown-Indigenous relations has often been passed over as insignificant or irrelevant. So much so that when Canada's indefatigable governor general, Lord Dufferin, went to British Columbia in 1876 and chastised elected and appointed officials for ignoring the traditional rights of the Indigenous communities in no uncertain terms, he was utterly disregarded (and never invited back).

Lord Dufferin lectured the local legislators: "The Government of British Columbia has neglected to recognize what is known as the Indian title. In Canada, this has always been done; no government, whether provincial or central, has failed to acknowledge that the original title to the land existed in the Indian nations and communities that hunted or wandered over it."[1]

The implication for the future here is easily discerned, as shown by recent attempts to run the Coastal GasLink Pipeline through unceded Wet'suwet'en territory, with no established treaty relationship with the

Crown, being met with fierce resistance by ancient and enduring Indigenous governance systems that operate outside of those imposed by the Indian Act. Dufferin knew that if we failed to partake in honourable negotiations and forgot that we are all treaty people, we also failed to honour our word, we failed to honour a society built on laws, and thus we broke faith not just with established practice, but also with an equitable future for Canada. There will be a price to be paid down the road, he could have added, and indeed there has been a price, there still is, and it will remain until we get things right. By invoking "the honour of the Crown" in treaty negotiations, the sovereign's representatives set down a marker by which Canadians can still be judged by their actions.

Trying to get things right, or better, between Indigenous and settler relations was the primary motivation nearly a century and a half later in appealing directly to the sovereign to designate the small academic chapel at Massey College in the University of Toronto as Canada's third "chapel royal," named Gi-Chi-Twaa Gimaa Kwe Mississauga Anishinaabek AName Amik ("The Queen's Anishinaabek Sacred Place" in Anishinaabemowin). That Queen Elizabeth did so in anticipation of the country's 150th anniversary of Confederation and more specifically agreed to have it proclaimed on National Indigenous Day of that year (2017) marks it as a very special moment and place in the country's history. Curiously, however, it is one still not widely known or fully appreciated. That is because Indigenous history, and by association "treaty history," was belittled in a similar way that the Canadian Crown has itself been belittled: until relatively recently neither was thought to be intrinsically important by many of our leading constitutionalists, historians, and lawmakers. If at all, Indigenous history, treaty history, and the history of the Canadian Crown itself were presented as footnotes to the main thrust of Canadian history — and seen as merely embarrassing or irrelevant.

Reviving this lost history is still something of an uphill battle because ambivalence about the Crown continues, and when it intersects with Indigenous rights as it has done in the past and continues very much to do to this day, it can arouse something remarkably close to constitutional apoplexy. But the history is, in fact, rich and resonating and pertinent to contemporary reality. Who knew, for example, that four Haudenosaunee (Mohawk) and Mohican representatives — who came to be known fancifully in England as "the four kings of Canada" — travelled to the Court of St. James in 1710 when Queen Anne was on the throne and were received with great fanfare and amicable curiosity as heads of their nations by the sovereign?[2] Who knew that King George III granted land in Canada to Indigenous communities who stayed loyal to the Crown in the American Revolution? Who knew that in 1838 the Chief of the Mississauga of the Credit, Kahkewaquonaby (Peter Jones), and an Elder were honoured by Queen Victoria when they appealed to her directly and in person at Windsor Castle about crucial matters affecting the Mississauga lands along the Credit River in Ontario? Who knew that King Edward VII honoured the Mohawks' house of worship in Brantford with the title of "His Majesty's Royal Chapel of the Mohawks"?

And, actually, who in Canada just a few years ago realized that a small chapel in the heart of the University of Toronto was designated the third chapel royal by Queen Elizabeth II to honour the traditional treaty relationship between the Crown and First Nations? There were a couple of stories in the back pages of newspapers and then, a year or so later, when one of the most extraordinary events in Canadian constitutional history occurred, there were no stories anywhere in the national media. The story? In 2019 the then national chief of the Assembly of First Nations, Perry Bellegarde, came to Massey College and its chapel royal specifically to address the governor general of the day (Julie Payette) and all the provincial lieutenant governors and territorial commissioners about the important and unique relationship between the Crown and its representatives in Canada with First Nations at what is still hoped to be the great turning point of rarely acknowledged and long-delayed reconciliation.

In what was the first meeting of a national chief of the Assembly of First Nations and the viceregal family, Bellegarde reminded the Queen's representatives: "You are the direct representatives of the Queen and therefore the holders of a sacred trust on behalf of the Crown. Each of you must be aware of this history and the significance of Treaty as part of your high office. While the government of the day has a role to operationalize the Treaty obligations held by the Crown, the Queen's representatives are the caretakers and witnesses to this immutable relationship."[3]

Described as "The Council at the Chapel Royal," the meeting was rooted in the traditional meetings between the Crown and its Indigenous counterparts that once happened regularly in these lands. The chapel royal at Massey was the natural place for such a gathering (and similar meetings that have happened since), fulfilling the vision put forward by Giima R. Stacey Laforme in his letter of support for the creation of the chapel: "The establishment of this Chapel Royal — a space to reflect, learn and reconnect — by Her Majesty and the Massey community ... is a profound act of reconciliation. It will become, in effect, a new council fire for our peoples to gather around in love and friendship."[4]

None of this was covered in the local or national media at the time, although an impressive bronze plaque was unveiled. The lack of coverage nevertheless provides a useful lesson in our historic ignorance of Crown-Indigenous relations. It is something that the chapel royal at Massey College hopes to underscore in the years to come. Like the history of the chapels royal itself, the passage of time has brought about a strange but wonderful evolution. Until Tudor times in England, "chapels royal" simply referred to the set of priests and choristers who would accompany the sovereign whenever and wherever he or she travelled beyond the London court. In time, they became housed in specific royal residences. The oldest and most famous of these were at St. James's Palace and Hampton Court, but there were others at other royal destinations in England and Scotland. Canada is the only country that has even one chapel royal outside this definition, and all three here are a sign of special significance to the sovereign and the sovereign's special relationship to the Indigenous nations, stretching right back to that historic visit of 1710 by the four Indigenous delegates to Queen Anne at the Court of St. James.

Like the Mohawk chapels at Six Nations and at Tyendinaga, the Queen's Anishinaabek Sacred Place is rooted in the Covenant Chain, a four-hundred-year relationship first established between the Haudenosaunee and the Dutch before it was assumed by the British Crown in the seventeenth century. Now known as the Silver Covenant Chain of Friendship, this relationship was extended into the Great Lakes region (and beyond) following a Great Council and Treaty at Niagara in 1764. Until the creation of Massey's chapel, no monument existed to remind the Crown and non-Indigenous peoples of the agreements made along the Niagara River. As the College itself states, "With its new designation, the space will be used to acknowledge the history of the Royal Proclamation of 1763 and its ratification through the 1764 Treaty of Niagara. The treaty, through its association with the Silver Covenant Chain of Friendship, represented a relationship of respect between Indigenous nations and the Crown in the Great Lakes Region."[5] The Canadian chapels royal also illustrate a key way that royal traditions in Canada and Britain diverge. In Britain, chapels royal play no role in signifying a relationship between peoples, while in Canada it could be described as the principal purpose.

The story of how Massey College's St. Catherine's Chapel got its royal designation is fairly straightforward. When John Fraser was the head of the college (from 1995 to 2014), he had revived the use of the chapel as a place of regular worship. Subsequently, and at the instigation of his daughter Clara Fraser, who had begun long-term research into Crown-Indigenous relations, he began to study the role of the two Mohawk chapels royal. Through Clara, he was introduced to her mentor, Elder Carolyn King, the former chief of the Mississaugas of the Credit First Nation. This was at the same time that many Canadians were finally trying to come to terms with a tragic part of our story that had been largely obscured or deliberately ignored until the Truth and Reconciliation Committee began its work, although the earlier work of the 1996 Royal Commission on Aboriginal Peoples was instrumental in laying much of the groundwork.

From this emerged an idea that the young graduate students at Massey College who, on the whole, were indifferent to chapel services, might find a useful means of forming relationships with the treaty partners connected to the land on which they studied. It seemed romantic and fanciful to some, but not to Elder King, who embraced the idea with passion. The College was supported in its appeal by the then Secretary to the Queen of Canada in the Privy Council Office, Kevin MacLeod, by Fraser's successor as head of Massey College, Hugh Segal, and by a young high school teacher in Waterdown, Ontario, named Nathan Tidridge, whose seminal study of Crown-Indigenous relations, *The Queen at the Council Fire*,[6] became an important document in the ensuing evolution of the project.[7]

In the background, and unknown at the time to the instigators of the appeal to the Queen, there was another friend, the Reverend Canon Paul Wright, sub-dean of the chapels royals and rector of the chapels royal at St. James's Palace in London, the most senior and most important of the chapels royal. As luck would have it, Canon Wright had served part of his priestly apprenticeship in northern Manitoba, where he saw up close the wisdom and teachings, as well as the challenges, of Indigenous communities. When the appeal for designating St. Catherine's Chapel as the third Canadian chapel royal arrived on the Queen's desk, in addition to Kevin MacLeod, her Canadian secretary, the Queen did not have to look far for advice on the idea.

Canon Paul Wright is gifted Wampum by Rick Hill of Tuscarora Nation, Haudenosaunee Confederacy, at the Mohawk Chapel, Six Nations of the Grand River, Brantford, Ontario, on March 27, 2019. Hill holds the Pledge of the Crown Wampum, while Wright displays a representation of the Covenant Chain. The belts were later presented to the Queen at Windsor Castle.

Canon Wright visited The Queen's Anishinaabek Sacred Place in 2019 as part of a tour that encompassed the other two chapels royal linked with the Mohawk Nation and Haudenosaunee Confederacy. Part of his visit included the gifting of a Bible signed by the Queen to the new chapel, a deeply personal gift from a woman of faith that continued the tradition established by her predecessor Queen Anne two centuries earlier. Canon Wright also brought to each of the Indigenous chapels royal a King George VI edition of *The Book of Common Prayer* (a core text of the Church of England), linking them with the chapel royal at St. James's Palace.

Wright's visit included a meeting with representatives from the Chiefs and Council of the Haudenosaunee Confederacy at the Mohawk Chapel at Six Nations of the Grand River. This was a meeting of allies, as Canon Wright recounted the names of his own ancestors that had fought side by side with the Mohawk against the American rebels. The Queen Anne Bible (filled with royal and viceregal signatures dating back to the 1860 visit by the Prince of Wales) and a set of handbells gifted by Queen Elizabeth II in 2010 to mark the three-hundredth anniversary of the meeting with Queen Anne were laid out by the Council for the Canon to see, each a manifestation of the ancient Covenant Chain relationship with the Crown. At one point Rick Hill of the Tuscarora Nation, on behalf of the Confederacy, asked Canon Wright to convey replicas of the Covenant Chain Wampum (recounting a four-hundred-year relationship between the Crown and his people) to the Queen. As requested, the replicas were safely brought to England and presented to Her Majesty at Windsor Castle.

Wright's visit demonstrated another important mission of Massey's Chapel: honouring the ceremonies and protocols that have bound the Crown in its relationships with Indigenous Peoples across the land. Once a regular occurrence in the lives of members of the Royal Family and their representatives, the ceremonies and protocols that animated treaty and other Crown-Indigenous relationships were largely abandoned following Confederation. Anything that reminded the Crown, and more importantly their governments, of the obligations and responsibilities that are threaded into treaty relationships was quietly pushed aside by a succession of settler administrations. Canadian governments, particularly following Confederation, eroded the honour of the Crown by installing viceregal representatives who were not interested in, or at worst antagonistic toward, anything that did not pave the way for settler access to land and resources.[8] The symbols and relationships used by settlers to enter into treaties were co-opted by their governments and turned over fully to the colonizing enterprise. The honour of the Crown, already tarnished by those entering treaty in bad faith, was abandoned altogether in the hunger for land.

This erosion did not happen without resistance by the sovereigns or their Indigenous partners. The eighteenth and nineteenth centuries were filled with interactions between delegations of Indigenous people and the monarch of the day. King George III's Royal Proclamation of 1763 included its critical references reaffirming Indigenous sovereignty after successful Indigenous lobbying (the King's son, Prince Edward, made a point of visiting the site of the great Council of Niagara where the proclamation was ratified using Indigenous diplomatic practices that created the 1764 Treaty of Niagara). Queen Victoria received numerous petitions, including by Nahneebahweequay (Catherine Sutton) of the Mississaugas of the Credit, highlighting mistreatment by her Canadian government.

In fact, the Queen was so concerned by what she was hearing and reading that she tasked the Duke of Newcastle (organizer of the 1860 Royal Tour of the Prince of Wales) to compile a report on the conditions of Indigenous Peoples in Canada. This report fell victim to the emergence in settler society of a convention of responsible government: that the Queen must take the advice of her elected governments. One month before the Prince of Wales's visit, John A. Macdonald's government passed the *Management of Indian Lands and Property Act*, which removed the role of superintendent of Indian affairs from the Imperial government and handed it to a Canadian commissioner of crown lands. Once Newcastle's report was completed, it would be the settlers that would advise Queen Victoria of its contents. This did not give Indigenous leaders much cause for hope, and their pessimistic expectation was sadly borne out.

Subsequent signatures in the Queen Anne Bible reflect the erosion that Dominion status brought to the Covenant Chain, which nevertheless remains the oldest treaty relationship in these lands. Slowly, Canadian representatives of the Crown stopped adding their names to the ancient book — Vincent Massey was the last governor general to do so, in 1959. The only signatures that appear afterward are those of Queen Elizabeth herself and, of course, the Duke of Edinburgh. (The Haudenosaunee Confederacy presented the Bible to the Queen for her signature on five separate occasions: 1951, 1959, 1977, 1984, and 2010.)

Happily, reflecting the historic Massey College Council at the chapel royal, the Crown's representatives in this country are in the midst of a reawakening with regard to their treaty responsibilities. Ceremonies and protocols, an area still firmly in their jurisdiction, are being restored and even expanded. This is particularly true in the provinces, where lieutenant governors occupy a grey area in treaties as the federally appointed direct representatives of the sovereign in a federation that, according to the *Constitution Act, 1867,* assigns "Indians, and Lands reserved for the Indians" to the exclusive jurisdiction of the national government. Indeed, the evolution of the provincial representatives of the Queen in Canada has led to a type of liberation for those offices in the realm of treaties: neither the federal government nor the respective provinces are on a firm footing to tell them what to do on account of constitutional evolution or issues of jurisdiction. Once this was realized in the twenty-first century some remarkable developments began to arise.

In 2013, for example, the first viceregal signature found its way into the Queen Anne Bible when Ontario's lieutenant governor, David Onley, was invited to sign during a visit to the Mohawk Chapel. His successor, Elizabeth Dowdeswell, followed suit in 2016. And now examples of provincial viceregal engagement with their Indigenous partners can be found right across the country. Massey's chapel is part of this renaissance of ceremony. Since its creation, the chapel royal has grown its own tobacco, sacred in the territory of the Mississaugas, for the Queen and her representatives to gift to Indigenous people who observe such protocols. A description approved by the Giima and Council of the Mississaugas of the Credit explains: "The act of gifting tobacco by the Sovereign or her representatives to Indigenous People is an important protocol supported by the Chapel Royal at Massey College." As Professor Richard Hill

The Chapel Royal Tobacco Badge created by the Canadian Heraldic Authority. The design of the badge includes the use of the royal crown, personally approved by Queen Elizabeth II in March 2020.

reminded participants during his keynote address at the 2019 Chapel Royal Symposium: "The Queen and her representatives are the keepers of [non-Indigenous] protocols."[9]

When Canon Wright toured the Canadian chapels royal he began each visit by gifting tobacco to the delegations that met with him. Similar ceremonies are now being performed across Turtle Island. A few months later, during the historic "Council at the Chapel Royal," sacred tobacco was gifted by all members of the viceregal family, including the territorial commissioners, to the Mississaugas of the Credit and Assembly of First Nations National Chief Perry Bellegarde.

Highlighting the importance of this protocol, the Mississaugas of the Credit sent a petition to the Queen to identify chapel royal tobacco with a unique badge that emphasized its connection to the chapel and her directly. In March of 2020 Her Majesty's approval was given at Windsor Castle, authorizing the creation of the Chapel Royal Tobacco Badge with permission to use the royal crown in its design.

Ensuring that these ceremonies continue well into the future, 2022 saw the planting of Platinum Jubilee gardens by each viceregal representative of the Queen, using tobacco seeds gifted by the keepers of the chapel royal tobacco beds for Massey's chapel royal. As places of ceremony, these gardens embody the kinship relationship rooted in the land between the sovereign and Indigenous Nations.

During her historic address, Mary Simon, Canada's first Indigenous governor general, pledged that she would use her new role "to hold together the tension of the past with the promise of the future, in a wise and thoughtful way."[10] Massey's chapel royal exists to occupy such a space; a place to have the difficult, and critical, conversations that treaties require us to have. If we are to be treaty people, non-Indigenous Canadians must understand their predecessors' use of the Crown to enter, maintain, and — largely following Confederation — allow the erosion of these sacred relationships.

The Crown, due to its history in this land, embodies that tension evoked by Governor General Simon. It is this very tension that makes the Crown — including the spaces and ceremonies it encompasses — not only relevant, but indispensable to the future of Canada. Restored through ceremony by the sovereign and her representatives and made operational by governments acting in her name, the honour of the Crown provides the path to reconciliation but it also holds out the positive possibility of reconciliation through mutually respected symbols, recovered ceremonies, and new ventures.

*Part Three*

---

# Representing the
# Sovereign

# 7

# The Enduring Crown in Canada: Reflections on the Office of Governor General at the Platinum Jubilee

*Barbara J. Messamore*

In 2022, Elizabeth II marks her Platinum Jubilee, her reign unsurpassed in length by any of her predecessors. It would be difficult to identify any other monarch who inspired the respect, affection, and gratitude Her Majesty has won across the Commonwealth and around the world.

Yet, from the perspective of 2021, it was easy to imagine that the jubilee might be a subdued affair. The Queen's energy and commitment appeared unflagging, but at ninety-five some concessions to age must be permitted. The Queen's grief over the death of the Duke of Edinburgh in April of 2021 and more especially the worldwide curtailment of public events amid the continuing Covid-19 pandemic cast a pall over any celebration, as did unsavoury reports that embroiled the royal family in controversy. The year 2021 was a difficult one, and it is impossible to assess the institution of the Crown without acknowledging that. Most of the day-to-day reminders of the royal family's commitment to duty and public service were also a casualty of the world health crisis, with public royal appearances sharply diminished.

From a Canadian perspective, too, the institution of the Crown endured a battering year. In January 2021, Governor General Julie Payette resigned after a third-party report indicated a disturbing pattern of abusive behaviour toward Government House staff by Payette and her secretary and close friend, Assunta Di Lorenzo.[1]

For many months, the weight of allegations about Payette's conduct grew, and earlier media reports, notably by CBC's Ashley Burke, also questioned Payette's demands for expensive modifications to Rideau Hall to meet her needs for privacy, and her apparent unwillingness to fulfil some of the expectations of the role. Payette's decision to choose Di Lorenzo for the senior Government House staff post suggested a failure to grasp the importance of continuity and institutional memory in that role. Di Lorenzo, a corporate lawyer, had no related experience. For months, Prime Minister Justin Trudeau's government did not act to force Payette from office, but rather accepted her inevitable resignation once a full report on the allegations of abuse had been made by expensive consultants. Evidence also emerged of Payette's unwillingness to work with her RCMP security detail and refusal to follow designated procedures. There is no clear evidence that the prime minister insisted on the governor general's resignation, but it would have been surprising had he not, if she had been reluctant to step down. There was no other way forward, given the seriousness and pervasiveness of the allegations and the need to preserve the dignity of the office.

For Trudeau's government, the episode was undoubtedly even more embarrassing because Trudeau had opted not to use the mechanism of an advisory selection panel devised by his Conservative predecessor to make the 2017 appointment, but rather jumped at the opportunity to appoint someone with Payette's dazzling resumé. The multilingual Payette, an astronaut, scientist, and engineer, with what appeared to be a strong record of public service, seemed precisely the sort of standout any government would be delighted to showcase. But a clear failure to vet the candidate was revealed when journalists uncovered troubling elements in Payette's background. In 2011, she had been charged in Maryland for domestic assault, although the charges were dropped and expunged. It was also discovered that in 2011 she had struck and killed a pedestrian while driving, but was not deemed to be at fault.[2] The procedural flaws in the appointment process also apparently left the Prime Minister's and Privy Council Offices unaware that Payette had left earlier high-profile positions under a cloud. In 2016, she received a generous severance from the Montreal Science Centre when employee complaints forced her from her position. In 2017, the Canadian Olympic Committee also parted company with Payette after two internal investigations into verbal abuse of staff.[3]

Amid mounting concerns in the fall of 2020, Trudeau denied any immediate plans to replace the "excellent" governor general and implied that to do so would trigger a constitutional crisis.[4] The government of the day must always accept responsibility for any actions by the representative of the Crown, as tradition demands that the governor general refrain from controversy or offering her own defence, even if criticism is baseless. Payette seemed disinclined to leave voluntarily when damaging reports first surfaced, although it is tempting to speculate that she must have known what third-party inquiries would ultimately reveal.

The challenges posed to the institution of the Crown during 2021 were profound, and remind us that at other times in history the Crown has been touched by controversy and even scandal. In the early nineteenth century, the supposed adultery of Queen Caroline, consort of George IV, sullied the dignity of the monarchy. Queen Victoria's prolonged and arguably self-indulgent mourning after the death of Prince Albert prompted a withdrawal from public life that was much criticized. Press coverage of Edward VIII's 1936 abdication was accompanied by lurid details about Wallis Simpson's marital history. Queen Elizabeth II famously described 1992, the fortieth anniversary of her reign, as a horrible year, an "annus horribilis," one which included the public airing of details surrounding the disintegrating marriages of three of her children.

The term *annus horribilis* might equally apply to the Crown in 2021. To the global tragedy of the pandemic and the death of the Queen's long-serving consort must be added the distressing news story of Prince Andrew's association with the notorious American financier Jeffrey Epstein. The highly publicized withdrawal from royal duties of Prince Harry and Meghan Markle, the Duke and Duchess of Sussex, amid vague allegations of racism, brought further damage. In an Oprah Winfrey interview, Markle shrank from offering specifics on the grounds that "that would be very damaging to them," thus accusing no one and everyone. Her passive phrase — that "there were conversations" about race — left a free-floating allegation of racism to taint the entire royal household.[5]

Nevertheless, the institution has proved resilient, weathering periodic storms. Queen Elizabeth II herself remains personally more admired than ever, even if Buckingham Palace's response to some incidents involving others has prompted disapproval.

Where the office of governor general of Canada is concerned, for all the fears of a constitutional crisis stemming from the unsuitability of Payette to her role, the functions of the Crown remain unshaken after her resignation. Canadians who had not before taken notice of the procedure learned that the chief justice of the Supreme Court would act in the governor general's capacity until a successor could be named. Chief Justice Richard Wagner ably performed the core constitutional duties, and Covid-19 dictated the curtailment of other traditional viceregal social and cultural functions. In earlier years, Chief Justice Bora Laskin had similarly acted as administrator for six months when, shortly after his 1974 installation, Governor General Jules Léger suffered a stroke. While some media commentators feared that Wagner's stint as administrator might be a fraught one, given the minority government situation in 2021, the chief justice was well prepared to deal with any controversy that might develop over who had the right to form a government, and in the event no such issue arose.

Inevitably, criticism of Payette raised wider questions about the utility of the office of governor general and, indeed, of Canada's adherence to a shared monarchy. The silver lining, perhaps, was the opportunity the episode afforded to reflect on these very questions. Should Canada ever decide to change its constitutional monarchy — and the hurdles standing in the way of that are admittedly substantial — such change should not be contemplated without a full appreciation of the evolved system we now enjoy. Canada's good governance and adherence to the rule of law are a model to the world and represent not the fruit of single scheme, but rather the accumulation of generations of tradition, with all the obscurities, ambiguities, and even incoherencies that necessarily involves.

The Crown is at the functional heart of the constitution of Britain, Canada, and other Commonwealth realms, and its deep symbolic importance is wrapped up in the person of the monarch. All the trappings of the monarchy — "the balm, the scepter, and the ball / The sword, the mace, the crown imperial, / The intertissued robe of gold and pearl," — all of Shakespeare's "thrice-gorgeous ceremony"[6] centre around the person of the sovereign. This encourages us to regard the monarch as a kind of synecdoche — a part for the whole, in other words — and makes the Crown in our constitution concrete. The tendency to conflate the person of the monarch with the function of the Crown in the constitution is not new and is perhaps even more pronounced when we enjoy the sort of continuity experienced during Elizabeth II's long reign.

This conflation can produce a kind of ambiguity with respect to realms outside Britain. The functions of the Crown are carried out by different individuals in different realms, with the governor general normally fulfilling the Crown's function at the federal level in Canada. The core constitutional duty is to facilitate the continuity of legitimate government by ensuring that a ministry is in place that has the support of the elected House of Commons, and, when it does not, by providing for a peaceful transition to another that does. Summoning, proroguing, and dissolving Parliament on ministerial advice, and appointing an executive council that enjoys the confidence of the elected legislature are chief among these duties. In addition, the Crown possesses emergency reserve powers, independent of ministerial advice, for use in grave emergencies, and these ensure that legitimate government is upheld. For example, the governor general might refuse the advice of a prime minister who had lost the confidence of the elected house and refused to accept that verdict, or one who attempted to evade that test of confidence. The governor general also gives royal assent to legislation passed by Parliament and signs government orders, writs, and proclamations

The Queen is of course Canada's head of state. On some occasions when present in Canada, Her Majesty has personally performed the executive duties of head of state, as did her father, George VI, the first reigning monarch to travel to Canada, when he made an extended tour in 1939.[7] The most high-profile example of the Queen's personal exercise of these duties in Canada was the proclamation of the newly patriated *Constitution Act* in April 1982. The proclamation carried with it the important symbolic message that Canada's complete legislative autonomy — notably legislative control over Canada's own constitution — was entirely compatible with adherence to a shared monarchy.

In 2009, Governor General Michaëlle Jean described herself as the "head of state" in a speech. "Just who does Governor-General Michaëlle Jean think she is?" demanded a media commentator.[8] A Government House elaboration that the governor general was the "de facto" head of state did not appease monarchists who were watchful for any creeping attempts to diminish the importance of the Queen in Canada's constitution. The term *de facto*, of course, means "in effect"; in contrast to *de jure*, "in law." But because the distinction is murky and the phrase often taken to mean something like "in fact," the use of the phrase in Jean's speech was probably ill-advised. But to defend the institution of the monarchy does not require a denial of this Canadianization of the Crown's function. The governor general in all but rare circumstances performs what Walter Bagehot called the "efficient" functions of the Crown. The Queen's activities with respect to Canada fall almost entirely within what Bagehot called the "dignified" parts of the role.[9] This is not to say that the governor general does not also carry out many, indeed most, of the "dignified" ceremonial duties under normal circumstances. But the core constitutional aspect of the role — the business of ensuring that a government is in place that has the confidence of the elected legislature — is a duty typically performed by the resident representatives of the head of state.

———

It is not always fully appreciated that the Queen does not personally direct the Crown's representatives in Canada. There is no chain of command. At no period in our post-Confederation history, or indeed even well before, did the sovereign seek to personally manage governors in the exercise of their duties.

Some viceregal representatives have corresponded with the monarch at regular intervals, but it is important not to draw inferences from this about the constitutional function of the Crown's representative. In an earlier age, when many of the governors general were drawn from the innermost ranks of Britain's aristocratic elite, personally acquainted with, or even related to, the sovereign, they in effect personalized their role as his or her representative. For others, periodic dutiful missives were meant to keep the sovereign abreast of Canadian events. But, in either case, the limits of constitutional monarchy meant that they did not operate under any direct guidance from the palace. Lord Dufferin, for example, Canada's governor general between 1872 and 1878, had once been a lord-in-waiting to Queen Victoria and his letters to her were not sent with a view to seeking instruction, but to inform Her Majesty. Dufferin was never economical in his communications; his successive chiefs at the Colonial Office were apt to be on the receiving end of what Dufferin admitted were "monster dispatch[es]" on Canadian affairs, with fulsome private letters as a supplement. Some of these missives were organized into chapters.[10] The motive was often personal vindication, not least because the Colonial Office held the key to future opportunities, notably the plum of the viceroyalty of India, which Dufferin eventually won.

For all that, the evidence strongly discounts any eagerness either on the part of the monarch or on the part of the British government to plunge into Canadian domestic governance. Even the incontinent communications of Lord Dufferin were tempered by his admitted realization that Canada could not be governed from Downing Street.[11] Dufferin's successor, the Marquis of Lorne (1878–83), was a son-in-law of Queen Victoria, and his letters sometimes include colourful accounts of Canadian life to be shared with the family; there is no suggestion of interference in the viceroy's constitutional duties.

The matter is muddied by the fact that, even after Confederation, the governor general remained in certain respects answerable to the British government. The Queen's role as a constitutional monarch who reigned but did not rule was clearly established by 1867. But the precise extent of Canada's freedom of action vis-à-vis Britain's *government* was not. While Canada had enjoyed self-government with respect to internal matters since the 1840s, autonomy over external affairs was only won incrementally in the post-Confederation era and was formally recognized only with the 1931 *Statute of Westminster*. Before this, the governor general was in the awkward position of being advised by two sets of ministers, one in Canada and one in Britain. And even those at the top were frequently unclear about the chain of command.

Moreover, the limits of Canada's autonomy were clouded by a tendency of Canadian statesmen to use the Imperial government as a shield to protect them from politically sensitive decisions. When, in 1879, John A. Macdonald was facing pressure from his Quebec Conservative caucus to dismiss that province's meddling lieutenant governor, Luc Letellier de Saint-Just, a Liberal party stalwart appointed in 1876 by Alexander Mackenzie, Lorne innocently allowed Macdonald to manipulate him into referring the matter to the Imperial government, thus delaying and deflecting responsibility. Lorne triumphantly reported to his Colonial Office chief that Britain's government would thus have "the opportunity" to advise against Letellier's dismissal.[12] In reply, Lorne received a scolding from the crusty colonial secretary, Sir Michael Hicks Beach.[13]

At the same time, Macdonald was apt to exploit the imprecision around Canada's freedom of action and sometimes drew the governor general into his machinations. Based on his prime minister's assurances, Lorne had advised the Colonial Office late in 1878 that Macdonald planned to introduce tariffs that were strictly revenue focused, and not protective in nature. Once the truth came out — only as the budget was put before Canada's parliament — Hicks Beach recognized that it would be "useless" for Britain's government to attempt to overrule Canada's new protectionist National Policy, even though Britain ostensibly still maintained control over tariffs.[14] Macdonald expanded the bounds of Canadian powers by keeping his own governor general in the dark until it was too late for him to act without provoking a crisis.

Most often, the link between the governor general and the British cabinet in these early decades after Confederation was a channel for informal suasion and not heavy-handed imperial control. Indeed, the very scope of empire, coupled with chronic discontinuity in the Colonial Office, meant that administration by remote control would have been impossible, even if it had been the goal. Hicks Beach, for example, was among six secretaries of state for the colonies to serve between 1880 and 1886.

Perhaps the most conspicuous examples of the use of this informal suasion in the past can be found in military matters; but even here the effect was negligible. The governor general was, and remains, the nominal commander-in-chief, but from the earliest days the governor general's ability to encourage more effective defence planning was strictly limited. Britain in 1871 withdrew its garrison from Canada in the vain hope that Canada would remedy the deficiency; a succession of governors general remarked on what Lord Lorne in 1883 called Canada's "charming confidence in perpetual peace."[15] Lord Stanley (1888–93), who had once been Britain's secretary of state for war, warned Prime Minister Macdonald about the risks of "a bitter awakening some day."[16] In the Boer War era, Lord Minto tried to encourage a Canadian commitment, but recognized that Canada resented "unjustifiable imperial pressure."[17]

A later governor general, Prince Arthur, Duke of Connaught (1911–16), a son of Queen Victoria and uncle to the then-reigning George V (1910–36), had come to Canada after a wide-ranging military career. His daughter's link to Canada is commemorated in the Princess Patricia's Canadian Light Infantry Regiment. During the Great War, however, Connaught's literal interpretation of his role as commander-in-chief caused some consternation. R.H. Hubbard notes that the Duke "donned his Field Marshal's uniform, mounted his charger, and actively participated in raising contingents," prompting criticism that he failed to understand the limitations of his role.[18] When Lord Byng, who had commanded the Canadian Corps at Vimy Ridge, was proposed as a viceregal appointee in 1921, his very popularity with Canadian Great War veterans was a potential stumbling block. Jeffery Williams suggested that Canadian politicians feared the proverbial "man on horseback" who might "turn popularity to political advantage."[19] Military men frequently filled the viceregal role. During the Second World War, Major General Alexander Cambridge, Earl of Athlone (1940–46), became "an ideal war-time Governor General," according to one observer. Athlone's itinerary of visits to military camps, munitions plants, and other war industries in Canada was "grueling," according to Hubbard,[20] but not controversial, as this activity was in support of Canada's wartime objectives and not undertaken at Britain's behest. Athlone was official host to the 1943 and 1944 Quebec Conferences held to bring together Winston Churchill, Franklin Roosevelt, and Mackenzie King to discuss Allied strategy.

By this time, Canada's autonomy had been clearly established. The 1931 *Statute of Westminster* recognized that the parliaments of the Dominions — which then included Canada, Australia, New Zealand, South Africa, the Irish Free State, and Newfoundland — had "full power" to legislate extra-territorially. It was a codification into law of the 1926 Balfour Report, a report that encapsulated the ideas arrived at in the 1917 and 1926 Imperial conferences. The 1931 act stated that it was "in accord with the established constitutional position that no law hereafter made by the Parliament of the United Kingdom" would extend to any Dominion, except by the request and consent of the Dominion. The *Statute of Westminster* is rightly recognized as an important constitutional milestone, but, as the act itself acknowledges, it was in effect a codification of a long-evolved state of things.[21] Canada's Prime Minister Mackenzie King recognized that the 1926 report on which the legislation was based, like other landmark documents in British history, "did not 'introduce anything new or revolutionary.'"[22]

The British government's recommendations to the sovereign about vice-regal appointments were to a growing extent guided by Canadian wishes, and the 1930 Imperial Conference established that the Dominion prime minister would henceforward be the one to tender advice to the sovereign about future appointments after informal consultations had taken place.[23] Further, it was now clearly understood that the governor general was advised by his Canadian ministers alone and had no duty to police the lines of Canadian autonomy by reserving or refusing assent to bills that had previously fallen under Imperial jurisdiction. Legal challenges to legislation could still go beyond Canada's Supreme Court to Britain's Judicial Committee of the Privy Council, which remained the highest court of appeal until 1949, but that was a different matter, not touching the function of the Crown.

Mackenzie King's acknowledgement that the 1926 Balfour Report (and thus the 1931 *Statute of Westminster*) did not mark a new departure in constitutional practice is significant, insofar as it offers a clear demonstration that this articulation of Canadian autonomy was not a product of King's own conflicts with the governor general. As prime minister, Mackenzie King had earlier in 1926 clashed with Lord Byng over the latter's refusal to follow his advice to dissolve Parliament. King subsequently exploited the episode for electoral advantage, reveling in the image of a champion of Canadian autonomy fighting against British domination. Yet in his clash with Byng, it was King, ironically, who unsuccessfully urged the governor general to involve the British government in the purely Canadian constitutional dispute. Byng himself recognized that, as tempting as it might have been to deflect responsibility, the matter was in his hands alone. He acted, not as an imperial functionary, but in a wholly domestic Canadian capacity. Byng — "Bungo," to the sovereign — had a long-standing friendship with George V and with the King's private secretary, Lord Stamfordham, and wrote accounts of the developing events to each.[24] But it was clearly understood that Byng was not seeking to be guided by either George V or the British cabinet in making his decision.

Byng's successor, the Marquis of Willingdon (1926–31), was equally connected. He had served as the King's lord-in-waiting and favourite tennis partner, and George V reportedly added Willingdon's name to the list of prospective viceregals being considered by the Dominions Office. Willingdon had also been an MP before his accession to the peerage, had been governor of Bombay and Madras, and would crown his career with the Indian viceroyalty after his tenure in Canada.[25] As Willingdon's time at Rideau Hall drew to a close, he wrote to Stamfordham to argue that, where his replacement was concerned, "His Majesty should send out from England his own personal representative, or a man with whom he has some personal acquaintance, and to whom he can communicate freely, a man, in fact, whom he could trust to be his personal liaison officer in the particular part of the Empire where he is sent."[26]

This personalized view of the relationship between sovereign and viceregal representative persisted. Indeed, Vincent Massey, the first Canadian appointed, described himself as the Queen's personal representative in his installation speech.[27] This did not, however, mean that the sovereign who reigned over Canada was the final arbiter in any constitutional sense. Sir Shuldham Redfern, secretary to two successive governors general, Tweedsmuir (1935–40) and Athlone (1940–46), explained that, while it was often said that the governor general represented the king, it would be "more correct" to say that he is "the official representative of the Crown, for there is a difference between representing a person and representing an Office held by a person."[28]

John Buchan, Lord Tweedsmuir, appointed by George V in 1935, was well acquainted with the King. Years earlier, when director of information with Britain's Intelligence Bureau during the First World War, he was "occasionally summoned to discuss with him public opinion in foreign nations." Buchan recalled the sovereign's "eager interest, his quick apprehension and his capacious memory."[29] In 1935, Buchan published *The King's Grace*, a commemorative work celebrating George V's Silver Jubilee.[30] Upon his Canadian appointment, George V gave Buchan "wise advice ... to be sympathetic to the French people of Canada, and jealously to respect their traditions and their language." Once in Canada, Buchan received less weighty advice that arrived on the very day of George V's death on January 20, 1936: the King cautioned him to "remember that skiing was not a safe pursuit for a middle-aged man!"[31] Such a message suggests a relationship of affection and personal regard.

A former Member of Britain's Parliament, Buchan was also on terms of intimacy with members of the political elite: both prime ministers Stanley Baldwin and Ramsay MacDonald, representing the Conservative and Labour party, respectively, were close confidants and correspondents.[32] Tweedsmuir was unique in that his appointment spanned three royal reigns, including the short and troubled one of Edward VIII. During that time of crisis, Tweedsmuir and his friend Prime Minister Baldwin exchanged letters, phone calls, and telegrams, and Tweedsmuir also provided insight into Canadian public reactions for the private information of the King's secretary, Sir Alexander Hardinge. Tweedsmuir understood Mackenzie King well enough to discreetly avoid any mention of his personal communications with Baldwin, although he let the Canadian prime minister know about his communication with the King's secretary. He told Baldwin that any "official" communication about Canada's views would have to come from Mackenzie King. Nevertheless, frequent telephone and telegraph communications over those strained weeks between Baldwin and Tweedsmuir carried risk for the governor general's relationship with King, and his own situation was, Tweedsmuir admitted, "horribly delicate." Always suspicious about British attempts to impinge on Canadian autonomy, King would not have been pleased to hear that Tweedsmuir had hardly been "off the telephone or cable with Mr. Baldwin" over the course of the several days leading to the abdication. The reverence for the Crown that Tweedsmuir had exhibited during George V's reign gave way to private fears that the institution was becoming "shabby, shoddy, [and] raffish" under the weight of the 1936 scandal.[33]

The accession of George VI to the throne offered the opportunity to repair the damage, and Tweedsmuir, working toward an objective he shared with his Canadian prime minister, pursued the idea of a royal tour of Canada with the self-described "persistence of a horse-leech." He had personal meetings with the King, and even wrote a speech for George VI during his supposed convalescence at a medical clinic in Wales. Before Tweedsmuir returned to Canada, His Majesty summoned him to a meeting at which he agreed to the proposed tour.[34] The 1939 tour was especially important as a way to promote Commonwealth ties, given the uncertainty of Canadian military support during the looming war in Europe. Mackenzie King characteristically locked horns with palace officials who believed the governor general ought to have been the one to welcome the royals to Canada; he had been assured by the dead George V in a seance that "the visit is due to their affection for you."[35] Tweedsmuir interceded with the palace to ensure that King's wishes prevailed, and the governor general went fishing once the tour commenced: "I cease to exist as Viceroy, and retain only a shadowy legal existence as Governor-General in council," he explained.[36]

It is tempting to speculate that Tweedsmuir's close acquaintance with many in the corridors of power in Britain may have added a dimension of complexity to his already-challenging Canadian tenure. The line between

Canadian and British foreign policy objectives had to be closely observed in a climate when the members of the Commonwealth were now autonomous. In an earlier era, the fact that the governor general was a British aristocrat, removed from any taint of partisan Canadian politics, was often lauded as an asset, something that would enable him to be a disinterested arbiter in any constitutional dispute. But with the acknowledgement of Dominion autonomy, the fact that Tweedsmuir was an Imperial "insider," someone in regular communication with powerful figures in London, potentially threatened Canada's independent foreign policy. His intelligence background also made him acutely attentive to world affairs, and he was aware of how valuable any assurance of Canadian support would be to Britain in the dangerous climate created by the rise of Nazi Germany. Mackenzie King's initial insistence that any Canadian aid to Britain would be limited to food and materials and that obligations extended only to a defence of Canada sent a chill, especially since it seemed that King was hard pressed to devote enough attention to the rising threat. Acting as his own Minister for External Affairs, King was overburdened with work and sometimes suffered ill health. In 1938, Hardinge, George VI's secretary, confided in Tweedsmuir that he thought it unwise to have the prime minister also handle the External Affairs portfolio. Hardinge sent regular secret telegrams and letters to Tweedsmuir about the rising Nazi threat.[37] It simplified matters that both Tweedsmuir and Mackenzie King approved of the British government's initial policy of appeasement, but Canada's prime minister did not offer any relief to British anxieties by pledging Canadian military assistance as tensions rose.[38]

Tweedsmuir's successor in Canada, the Earl of Athlone, Carolyn Harris notes, was the last close relative of the monarch to serve as governor general.[39] He was born Prince Alexander of Teck; his mother was a granddaughter of George III, and his sister, Mary, was Queen Consort to George V. His wife, Princess Alice, was a granddaughter of Queen Victoria, and the couple were thus aunt and uncle to George VI.

Viscount Alexander, Canada's governor general from 1946 to 1952, was also on intimate terms with the monarch. He had earlier served as aide-de-camp to George VI[40] and had hosted the King for a week in the summer of 1944 at his caravan headquarters on the shores of Italy's Lake Bolsena while

Alexander was in command of the Allied 15th Army Group. Alexander recalled that they enjoyed pleasant walks along the lake; the King "behaved as if he were on holiday," was "very relaxed and seemed to enjoy it all." The King used a bath made of a barrage balloon and made a gift of it to his host when he left.[41]

The Canadianization of the Crown accelerated in the post–Second World War era. The 1947 *Letters Patent* — an updated version of the 1931 document issued by the monarch defining the office of governor general — "authorize[d] and empower[ed]" the governor general to "exercise all powers and authorities lawfully belonging to Us in respect of Canada."[42] This represented a delegation of the sovereign's day-to-day constitutional function as head of state — something that had long been the practice — which would now also include the sealing of documents under the Great Seal of Canada, a power specifically referred to in the new letters patent. Constitutional legal scholar Peter Hogg observed that, since 1947, "it has become possible to conclude all formalities in Canada" without the need to send treaties in head of state form to London to be sealed. Hogg also noted, however, that, since international treaties in head of state form are now rare, Canada has had no occasion to use these new formal powers in the conclusion of treaties.[43]

The 1952 appointment of Canadian Vincent Massey as governor general was likewise an important milestone, although Massey's many connections with Balliol College, Oxford, and his intimacy with Britain's elite, including the Royal Family, that was nurtured during his long tenure as Canada's High Commissioner to the United Kingdom (1935–48) meant that he was arguably as steeped in the environment of British elite power as any of his predecessors. He had long been a friend of Prime Minister Harold Macmillan, a Balliol contemporary who had also served as an aide-de-camp to Governor General the Duke of Devonshire. Massey's family connections facilitated his own acquaintance with Devonshire and other governors general, notably Grey and Byng. Massey's secretary at Canada House, Georges Vanier, would later be his successor as governor general (1959–67).[44] Oxford seemed to be an especially fertile source of Ottawa talent. Roland Michener, who followed Vanier as governor general, had formed a close friendship with Lester B. Pearson as part of the Oxford University Ice Hockey Club in the

1920s, and "Mitch" and "Mike" helped the club win lopsided victories.[45] Michener later continued his Oxford affiliation as general secretary of the Rhodes Foundation in Canada.

Vanier's own ties to the viceregal office included service as aide-de-camp to Lord Byng, and he and his wife Pauline lived at Rideau Cottage, the home on the grounds at Government House later occupied by Prime Minister Justin Trudeau. The affable Byng assured his aides-de-camp that "Now you're members of the family."[46] Byng served as godfather to Vanier's son Georges, who bore the nickname "Byngsy," and Byng even began an education fund for the boy. It seems to have been Byng who engineered an invitation for Vanier to meet and dine with George V in the early 1920s. In the course of a long military and diplomatic career, Vanier built connections to numerous prominent world figures.[47] But as governor general, Vanier emphasized the Canadianization of the Crown,[48] something that had long been the reality in a constitutional sense. His term began in 1959, and his consciousness of a re-emergent Quebec separatist movement may have led Vanier to downplay the fact that the Queen was Canada's head of state. In his 1959 installation speech, Vanier described Elizabeth II's bond with Canadians as "personal rather than formal," which rather overstates the case. Somewhat ambiguously, he invoked Shakespeare's Henry VI to describe the Queen's relationship with Canada: "The Crown is in my heart, not on my head."[49]

––––––––––

In Canada, the difficult year of 2021 also marked a more positive milestone. After several months of careful consideration and consultation with an advisory committee formed for this purpose, in July 2021 Prime Minister Justin Trudeau announced the appointment of Mary Simon (Ningiukudluk) as governor general, and Simon was sworn in later that month. Simon is Inuk, from Kuujiuaq in northern Quebec. Her name had long been mooted as a promising candidate for the role,[50] although her lack of fluency in French was perceived as a potential barrier. Simon speaks English and Inuktitut. If we are indeed sincere in a wish to attract an inspiring Indigenous appointee to the viceregal role, it seems a necessary corollary that we must be open to someone who has mastery of only one colonial language as well as an Indigenous one. Simon's career has been one of impressive public service. In 1975, she helped to negotiate the historic James Bay and Northern Quebec Agreement, a comprehensive land claim agreement made between the Cree and Inuit of Quebec, the governments of Canada and Quebec, Hydro Quebec, and other parties. Simon was also a representative of Inuit interests in the negotiations leading to the 1982 patriation of the Constitution and the entrenchment of Indigenous treaty rights in the Charter of Rights and Freedoms. Additionally, she led the Inuit Circumpolar Conference, was in 1994 named ambassador for circumpolar affairs, negotiated the creation of the Arctic Council, and served as ambassador to Denmark.[51]

In a climate where efforts toward reconciliation with Canada's Indigenous Peoples have sometimes fallen short, the appointment of Canada's first Indigenous governor general is a hopeful sign. Provincial lieutenant governors and territorial commissioners have occasionally been drawn from Canada's Indigenous Peoples, but Mary Simon's appointment at the federal level is a first. Just as the Queen is the most visible symbol of the essential functions of the Crown in our constitution, the monarch is also the personal embodiment of the treaty relationship between the government of Canada and Indigenous Peoples, and the honour of the Crown is equally important to those Indigenous Peoples that are not parties to treaties. The governor general, as the on-the-scene Crown representative, is part of that chain of continuity, something that transcends the shifting winds of electoral politics. Elected politicians, after all, respond to the views of their constituents, while the treaty relationship and historic recognition of Indigenous land rights are rooted in law.

This has been a difficult time for the institution of the Crown in Canada and the wider Commonwealth. But there is clearly also much to celebrate. This enduring, flexible institution has weathered difficult times before, and will continue to do so. The Queen's tireless public service and devotion to duty stand as an example, and in her embodiment of the enduring Crown we can see an outward symbol of so much that is good in our constitution.

# 8

# The Lieutenant Governors —
# Second Fiddles or Coordinate Viceregals?

*D. Michael Jackson*

At Confederation in 1867, Canada was conceived as a largely centralized state, with the provinces regarded as junior partners. The Crown had been an institution of a unitary state, the United Kingdom in the nineteenth century. It was viewed as indivisible for purposes of the British Empire and the same model was expected to apply within the new Canadian federation. Thus the lieutenant governors were appointed not by the Queen but by the governor general on the advice of the prime minister and were deemed to be federal officers instead of royal surrogates.

This was to change dramatically as the Crown adapted to the realities of federalism. Provincial jurisdiction and identity soon asserted themselves against the domination of Ottawa. In that context, the subordinate status of the lieutenant governors, their nominal chief executive officers, was transformed by court decisions into one coordinate with that of the governor general. In the pivotal *Maritime Bank* case of 1892,[1] the Judicial Committee of the Privy Council in London ruled that "a Lieutenant-Governor, when appointed, is as much a representative of Her Majesty for all purposes of provincial government as the Governor General himself is for all purposes of Dominion government."

Over the following decades, the status of the provincial Crown was further clarified and reinforced. For example, the Supreme Court of Canada stated in 1948 that

> the nature of the federal and provincial legislative and executive powers is clearly settled, and a Lieutenant-Governor, who "carries on the Government of the Province," manifestly does not act in respect of the Government of Canada. All the functions he performs are directed to the affairs of the Province and are in no way connected with the Government of Canada, and it is the functions that he performs that must be examined in order to determine the nature of his office.[2]

While the lieutenant governors are still appointed by the governor general, effectively they are no longer federal officers but the Queen's representatives in their own right, personifying the Crown in their provinces. Canada is now what scholar David E. Smith calls a "compound monarchy," with federal and provincial Crowns reflecting the nature of federalism.[3] The institution of the Crown has thus been an instrument for the assertion of provincial autonomy.

Theory and practice, however, do not always coincide. Political scientist Andrew Heard notes that "despite the judicial infusion of the Crown into provincial government in Canada, little has changed in the hierarchy of Canadian governments and their relations with the sovereign. Canada has never had a condition where all federal and provincial crowns are coordinate." "There are myriad ways," he says, "in which lieutenant governors are subordinated to the governor general and the federal government."[4]

These "myriad ways" are nineteenth-century colonial relics — the continued appointment of the lieutenant governors by the federal government without any requirement to consult with the provincial governments concerned; the payment of their salaries and a modest entertainment and travel allowance provided by Ottawa; the inability of the lieutenant governors to officially communicate directly with Buckingham Palace, unlike the governor general — and the governors of the Australian states;[5] the second-rate appellation of "Your Honour" compared to the title of "Your Excellency" for the governor general (and again for the governors of the Australian states); fifteen-gun salutes instead of the twenty-one accorded to the governor general (and nineteen to the prime minister); a place well down in the national table of precedence, below foreign ambassadors, the federal cabinet, and the leader of the opposition.[6]

Yet Heard also asserts that "there is much potential to build on the status and prestige of the provincial Crown and lieutenant governor."[7] Indeed, historian Christopher McCreery, himself a viceregal private secretary, titled a book chapter "The Provincial Crown: The Lieutenant Governor's Expanding Role."[8] The original role of the lieutenant governor as a federal officer, he says, has long been obsolete and the provincial viceregal representative is increasingly seen as promoting not only the Crown, but the identity and status of the province domestically and even on occasion abroad. McCreery recognizes, however, that the office of lieutenant governor faces major challenges and has inherent weaknesses.[9] The situation is, as might be expected in the Canadian federal state, varied and uneven across the country.

## APPOINTMENT OF LIEUTENANT GOVERNORS

Traditionally, lieutenant governors had been viewed as patronage opportunities for the federal government that appointed them. The Prime Minister's Office would consult with party loyalists in the province to find a suitable candidate. Not surprisingly, stalwarts of their own party were frequent choices: senators and members of Parliament, members of the provincial legislatures, fundraisers, constituency presidents. Such appointments were often problematic, especially when the provincial government was of a different political stripe than the one in Ottawa. McCreery notes that from

Confederation to 1988, 138 of 211 lieutenant governors had campaigned for or served in elected office, federally or provincially.[10]

Starting in the 1970s, however, federal governments began drawing their appointees from more varied backgrounds and not necessarily with ties to the governing party — the first women and Indigenous lieutenant governors were among them. The profile, prestige, and credibility of the provincial viceregal offices gradually increased as the incumbents were perceived to be more qualified and impartial. This trend was enhanced by an advisory committee process instituted in 2010 by Prime Minister Stephen Harper for the appointment of Governor General David Johnston and extended in 2012 to the selection of provincial lieutenant governors and territorial commissioners.[11] The advisory committee, with added representation from the province and territory concerned, canvassed opinion from political parties and civil society in preparing a short list of candidates for the prime minister. The outcome was excellent choices like Elizabeth Dowdeswell in Ontario, Janice Filmon in Manitoba, and the late Jocelyne Roy-Vienneau in New Brunswick. At last there appeared to be a workable method of provincial consultation on viceregal appointments.

It was therefore disappointing that in 2017, Prime Minister Justin Trudeau abandoned the advisory committee process when he named Julie Payette as governor general, reverting to the discredited practice of patronage through the Prime Minister's Office. While Trudeau hastily revived the advisory process in a different form for the selection of Mary Simon as governor general in 2021, nothing similar was done for the provincial and territorial equivalents. As Andrew Heard remarks, "The result has been the return of partisan patronage, with three of the six individuals appointed by mid-2019 having donated to either the federal or provincial Liberal parties; one was even a member of Prime Minister Trudeau's cabinet. Unfortunately, allegations of continued partisan connections later surfaced in connection with at least one of these appointees." Heard goes on to point out that "in their constitutional role, lieutenant governors can only act effectively if the political actors involved, as well as the general public, have confidence in their political neutrality."[12]

What steps can be taken to reform the selection process for lieutenant governors? A theoretical possibility is adopting the Australian system, where state governors are appointed by the Queen on the advice of the state premier. But while this appears to work well in Australia, it might be seen in Canada as simply replacing federal by provincial political patronage, not to mention the awkward situation in Quebec, where governments tend to be hostile to the viceregal office. And it would require a constitutional amendment, which is a non-starter. Another possibility is a federal policy commitment to formal consultation with the provinces, even to the point, Andrew Heard suggests, of inviting nominations from them, based in turn on recommendations from provincial advisory committees.[13] An alternative would be to return to the short-lived (2012–2015) advisory committee process, which proved clearly superior to untrammelled prime ministerial patronage.

## LIEUTENANT GOVERNORS IN OFFICE

How do lieutenant governors fare once appointed and installed? The pattern ranges from influential and well-resourced viceregal offices, such as those of Nova Scotia, Ontario, and British Columbia, to Quebec, where the lieutenant governor is effectively marginalized by the provincial government. Despite the theoretical arm's-length distance between the non-partisan offices of the Queen's representatives and the partisan governments of the day, these offices are dependent on their governments for operational funding. McCreery points out that the "subtle threat of withdrawal of resources has the potential of encroaching on the governor's independence from the government of the day, and by extension of impinging upon the prerogative powers exercised by the Crown's representative."[14] The lieutenant governors do, however, have one important safeguard of their independence: the payment of their salaries and some allowances by Ottawa.

The provinces are responsible for providing accommodation, office staff and facilities, and reception/event space for their lieutenant governors. This should not be just a matter of standard civil-service issue: as the highest-ranking person in the province, its constitutional chief executive officer, and the representative of the sovereign, the lieutenant governor deserves to be housed appropriately. From pre-Confederation days, a prominent and imposing "Government House" in the provincial capital was the location of the viceregal residence, office, and entertainment venue.[15] But the perception of the lieutenant governor as an officer imposed on the province by Ottawa sometimes resulted in frosty relations between the provincial government and the appointee. In several instances, viceregal accommodation was targeted in retaliation. New Brunswick closed its Government House in 1893, Alberta did the same in 1937, Ontario in 1938, and Saskatchewan in 1945 (under a Parti Québécois government, Quebec closed its facility much later, in 1997). As McCreery has said, "The closure of a Government House naturally results in a reduction of office resources, prestige, and the presence of the Crown and its representative. This erodes the dignity of the office in a tangible manner."[16]

The period from the late nineteenth to mid-twentieth century, during which four Government Houses were closed, was one in which the provincial viceregal offices were at a low ebb, due particularly to their partisan

Government House Halifax.

tinge. With this came a lack of resources and a commensurate lack of prestige, given that the offices were restricted in their public duties and profile. But as they regained their lustre, provincial governments looked more kindly on them. The best-served lieutenant governors today are those occupying historic Government Houses: Nova Scotia (1805), New Brunswick (1828, closed in 1894 but restored to viceregal use a century later), Newfoundland and Labrador (1830), Prince Edward Island (1834), Manitoba (1883), British Columbia (1959 — replacing earlier structures dating back to 1865), and Saskatchewan (1891, closed in 1945, restored to viceregal use in 1984).

Nova Scotia's historic Government House, the oldest of them all, continually occupied by the lieutenant governors since 1805, benefited from a superb $6 million, three-year restoration in 2006–2009, evidence of the province's esteem for both the building and the viceregal office.[17]

Saskatchewan's Government House, built in 1891 for the lieutenant governors of the Northwest Territories and occupied by those of Saskatchewan from 1905, was closed by the first CCF government of Tommy Douglas in 1945. But it was elegantly restored in 1980 by the NDP government of Allan Blakeney, first as a museum and event facility. The subsequent Conservative government returned the lieutenant governor's office (but not residence) to Government House in 1984. Since then, governments of all stripes have enhanced the facility, notably with another NDP administration constructing a $6.2 million additional wing — named in honour of Queen Elizabeth II and formally opened by her in 2005, the province's centennial year.[18]

New Brunswick, the first province to close its Government House, in 1894, was a latecomer to restoration in 1999. But it did so with aplomb, spending $5.5 million on a first-rate reconstruction, including the lieutenant governor's residence and office as well as public spaces for events and exhibits. Alberta restored its Government House in 1976, but only as a conference facility; subsequent plans to restore it to viceregal use did not materialize. Parsimonious Manitoba has neglected its Government House, located adjacent to the Legislative Building and badly in need of renovation. Ironically, Ontario, Canada's wealthiest and most populous province, citing costs, has never replaced the Government House closed in 1938, despite an offer in the 1960s to donate a residence; the lieutenant governor's offices and reception area are housed instead in a large suite in the Legislative Building. Ontario, Manitoba, and Alberta are the only provinces to place the viceregal offices in the same building as the executive and legislative branches — a practice frowned on by those who emphasize the autonomy of the Queen's representative vis-à-vis the government of the day. The office of the lieutenant governor of Quebec is located in a building near that of the *Assemblée nationale.*

## THE VICEREGAL ROLE

The duties of the Crown's representative are described as dual in nature: "efficient" — the constitutional role; and "dignified" — the ceremonial or symbolic dimension. Both are equally significant ingredients of the provincial viceregal positions as well as of their national equivalent.

### The "Efficient"

A challenge facing lieutenant governors in their "efficient" dimension is their relationship with the premier. The traditional right of the sovereign or her representatives to be consulted, to encourage, and to warn is a dead letter if the viceregal person does not have regular private meetings with his or her first minister. As with resources, there is a checkered pattern across the country. Much depends on the personal relationships between the viceregal person and their head of government, further complicated when there is an evident partisan divide. In 2021, lieutenant governors met monthly or close to monthly with their premiers in Nova Scotia and Ontario, every two months in Alberta, and quarterly in Prince Edward Island. Such meetings apparently did not occur in the six other provinces. Most viceregal offices cite cordial relationships with premiers, informal conversations at events, and support for their initiatives. Welcome and positive as these may be, however, they are not substitutes for regular private meetings. Given that lieutenant governors are usually senior, experienced people from a variety of backgrounds, normally detached from the political fray, premiers who fail to consult them are missing a valuable opportunity for impartial advice.

Essential to the functioning of political institutions in the Westminster parliamentary system is the viceregal constitutional role.[19] A large part — in fact, most — of this is routine in nature: giving royal assent to legislation; summoning, proroguing, and dissolving the legislature; formally appointing first ministers and swearing in their cabinets; signing executive orders; issuing proclamations and writs; authorizing order-in-council appointments. By convention, this "royal prerogative" is exercised for actions that are not statutory in nature, normally on the "advice" of the first minister. Nonetheless, the viceregal imprimatur is required for all such actions to be legitimate.

Certain uses of the royal prerogative are termed "reserve powers," because the viceregal incumbents retain some discretion in exercising them. The reserve powers, although rarely invoked today, are no rubber stamp. In the early decades of Confederation, lieutenant governors refused dissolution of the assembly to premiers three times and dismissed premiers and governments on five occasions. Up until 1945, royal assent to bills was refused thirty-eight times by lieutenant governors (royal assent has never been refused by a governor general of Canada and not by a British monarch since Queen Anne in 1707!). "Reservation" of bills by the lieutenant governor for the consideration of the governor general, usually on instructions from the federal government, occurred sixty-nine times, with one final outlier case in Saskatchewan in 1961. These powers, apart from dissolution, have not been used since then and have effectively lapsed.[20]

Reserve powers may, however, still come into play in minority-government situations. On occasion, lieutenant governors have intervened to select a premier from another party on the defeat in the legislature of a government following an inconclusive election. Examples are Saskatchewan in 1929, Ontario in 1985, and British Columbia in 2017. The latter was a particularly appropriate exercise of viceregal discretion. The incumbent Liberal premier, defeated in the legislature shortly after being reduced to minority status in an election, declined to resign and asked Lieutenant Governor Judith Guichon to dissolve the assembly and call another election. The lieutenant governor refused, instead inviting the NDP leader, backed by the Green Party, to form a government.[21] Here we see the viceregal position functioning as a constitutional backstop, a safeguard in situations of political uncertainty or potential crisis.

## QUEBEC — ALWAYS A SPECIAL CASE

After Britain gained control over New France following the 1763 Treaty of Paris, *Canadiens* adapted to the British monarchy. Many *Canadien* leaders proclaimed their loyalty to the Crown. Sir George-Étienne Cartier said in the 1865 Confederation debates, "[if French-Canadians] had their institutions, their language and their religion intact today, it was precisely because of their adherence to the British Crown." *Québécois* enthusiastically welcomed members of the Royal Family. Successive governors general, notably the first francophone, Georges Vanier, made their mark on the province through their official residence, *la Citadelle*, in Quebec City. But the rise of the sovereigntist movement from the 1960s cast doubt on Quebec's historic links with the Crown, now viewed by many as a symbol of colonialism rather than a vehicle for francophone particularity.[22]

And yet, paradoxically, as we have seen, the Crown has been instrumental in defining and asserting provincial autonomy in Confederation, including that of Quebec. Laval University scholars Julien Fournier and Amélie Binette, in an intriguing article, "La Couronne: vecteur du fédéralisme canadien" ("The Crown: Vector of Canadian Federalism"), assert that "the unwritten rules and conventions regarding the Crown in the Westminster system, in general, and the rules of the indivisibility of the Crown, in particular, have increased the prestige and the powers of provincial executive power in the Canadian federation, even if the text of the Constitution appears to rank the federal government over the provinces."[23]

For Fournier and Binette, "*véritable trait d'union du fédéralisme canadien, la Couronne est l'institution par laquelle la souveraineté canadienne*

*peut se partager entre deux ordres de gouvernement, tout en demeurant indivis-*
*ible.*" Whereas most writers on the subject have identified the *divisibility* of
the Crown as the rationale for its provincial manifestation, Fournier and
Binette see its *indivisibility* as key. In their view, the lieutenant governor
draws on the powers of the Queen incorporated in the single Canadian
Crown to exercise executive authority in the province. They resolve the para-
dox thus: "*La Couronne canadienne connaît ainsi une forme de « divisibilité
fonctionnelle ».*"[24] As examples, they cite the use of royal prerogative powers
rather than legislation for purposes as diverse as the adoption of the Quebec
flag in 1948, the establishment of diplomatic missions abroad, and the creation of lieutenant governor's medals.

Despite this underlying, though underappreciated, role of the Crown
as a "vector" of its autonomy, the office of lieutenant governor is largely
ignored, dismissed as irrelevant, or even resented in Quebec. In February
2021, following the debacle of the Julie Payette incumbency at Rideau
Hall, the *Assemblée nationale du Québec* debated a motion by the *Parti
Québécois* — the third opposition party in the Assembly — to "abolish the
office of lieutenant governor, as well as other symbols of the British monarchy in Quebec." The motion was supported by the fourth opposition
party, *Québec solidaire*. The governing *Coalition avenir Québec* (CAQ),
however, while stating its lack of enthusiasm for the monarchy, took the
stance that abolishing the office of lieutenant governor was impractical for
constitutional reasons (it is protected by the *Constitution Act, 1982*[25]) and
was a distraction from the major issues facing Quebec. The main opposition Liberal Party took a similar approach to that of the CAQ, agreeing
that the appointment process for lieutenant governors lacked legitimacy
and Quebec should be consulted on the choice of its viceregal representatives. A Liberal member of the *Assemblée* decried the move by the federal
Liberals to discontinue the viceregal appointments committee established
by Stephen Harper.[26]

Various ideas have been floated in Quebec to rename the office of lieutenant governor. Laval law professor Patrick Taillon suggested pursuing "the
great work of the Quiet Revolution" in changing the title of the lieutenant
governor to "less prestigious terminology." Scholars Hugo Cyr and Philippe

Lagassé, more sympathetic to the viceregal office, have proposed something like "*titulaire de l'autorité de l'État Québécois*," which, they say, would be "a better reflection of the real functions of the office."[27]

Interestingly, all parties in the National Assembly debate on February 10, 2021, praised the incumbent lieutenant governor, J. Michel Doyon. [28] "A brilliant, committed, and humane man," said a *Québec solidaire* member of the *Assemblée*.[29] Doyon was among the lieutenant governors chosen through the viceregal advisory committee mechanism in 2015. He ventured into policy matters in 2020 at the beginning of the pandemic crisis. "Québec's Lieutenant-Governor J. Michel Doyon is worried that the Covid-19 crisis may lead to abuse of power by governments and law enforcement agencies," reported *La Presse*. "The Covid-19 crisis 'will certainly be dangerous for democracy,' Mr. Doyon said straightforwardly, 'because governments are exercising very strong powers.'"[30] Doyon instituted Lieutenant Governor's Medals for youth, seniors, and Indigenous Peoples. Despite all the constraints faced by the Quebec viceregal office, the lieutenant governor can have a positive influence.

## The "Dignified"

The "dignified" or ceremonial and symbolic dimension of the provincial viceregal offices has become more prominent in recent decades. While lieutenant governors traditionally were patrons of worthy causes and charitable organizations, their enhanced stature in the twenty-first century has been manifested in a wider range of community activities. McCreery suggests that the most significant development has been what he calls a "dignified federal role," where lieutenant governors promote the Crown and the nation as well as their own provinces.[31] Although this may at first seem counterintuitive, it must be recalled that the provincial viceregals represent the *Canadian* Crown and the Queen *of Canada* in their jurisdictions. They are thus instruments of national unity as well as symbols of the diversity of the federal state.

Though it had always been visible at events such as Canada Day or Remembrance Day, this national aspect became more noticeable from the

1970s. When some governors general, reflecting the tendencies of the federal governments of the day, minimized the role of the monarchy and the Queen, lieutenant governors stepped in to fill the breach as promoters of the Crown. More recently, the provincial viceregals have expanded their involvement in two areas hitherto primarily national in scope: citizen recognition and Crown-Indigenous relations.

## CITIZEN RECOGNITION

### Awards

The viceregal offices in Canada, national and provincial, are natural channels for recognizing citizens through various awards, some sponsored by academic, professional, cultural, or voluntary organizations, others instituted by the viceregal offices themselves. By 2021, there were 130 viceregal awards across the country. Nova Scotia was the champion, boasting no fewer than seventeen lieutenant governor's awards, among them those for culinary excellence, conservation, volunteerism, and francophone contributions. Ontario's lieutenant governor confers awards for student volunteers, architectural design, excellence in wines, heritage, and marketing excellence. Manitoba's viceregal awards include those for community contributions, interreligious understanding, and heritage preservation. Among British Columbia's are a medal for inclusion, democracy, and reconciliation, and awards for literary excellence and excellence in education. Given the low profile of the Crown in Quebec, it is gratifying to see the vigour of its viceregal award program: *La Médaille du lieutenant-gouverneur du Québec pour les Premiers Peuples (catégories Premières Nations et Nation Inuite)* and *les Médailles du lieutenant-gouverneur du Québec pour la Jeunesse, les Aînés, et le Mérite exceptionnel.* As can be seen, viceregal awards increasingly emphasize social diversity, inclusion, and the Indigenous Peoples.

## Provincial Honours

The establishment of Canada's national honours, starting with the Order of Canada in 1967, the centennial of Confederation, renewed interest in official recognition across the country. Since the Canadian provinces were not in any way involved in the national program, it was perhaps inevitable that they should eye their own honours. Ontario was the first, introducing a medal for good citizenship in 1973, followed by other medals. Quebec established the first provincial order, *l'Ordre national du Québec*, in 1984. Saskatchewan created its order in 1985, Ontario in 1986, and British Columbia in 1989. By 2001, all ten provinces had orders and some had instituted decorations and medals as well. Although at first these were not recognized by Ottawa, an agreement was reached in 1991 to give most of them status in the national precedence of official honours.[32]

As the governor general does for national honours, the lieutenant governors present the insignia of provincial honours to recipients and serve as chancellors of the orders in all provinces except Quebec, where there is no chancellor and the premier presides over investitures. Lieutenant governors, like the governor general, do not take part in the deliberations of the advisory councils that recommend recipients of honours, and proceed to make the presentations to those whose names are submitted to them.[33] A drawback to provincial honours, however, is potential political involvement in the process. Whereas Canada's national honours are housed and staffed at Rideau Hall, the office of the governor general, provincial honours are managed by executive government. The councils' recommendations are channelled through the premier, who approves them and requests the lieutenant governor to make the presentations (Ontario and Quebec appoint the recipients through order-in-council). There have been instances in Newfoundland and Labrador and Prince Edward Island where premiers unilaterally announced the awarding of the provincial order to Olympic medal winners without nominations going through the advisory committee process. Through their appointments of advisory council members, premiers can influence the selection of honours recipients. Ontario came under fire in 2020 when two former premiers and others with connections to the governing party were named to the Order of Ontario.

To avoid perceptions of partisan partiality, it would be preferable that recommendations for provincial honours be submitted directly to the lieutenant governor by the advisory council. Similarly, councils should recommend termination of membership to the lieutenant governor. It would be in the best interest of provincial governments to entrust more responsibility to the offices of the lieutenant governors, staying at arm's length from the selection and revocation processes and thus enhancing the integrity and prestige of their provincial honours. It would be an appropriate use of the viceregal "reserve power" to challenge nominations or revocations in the very rare cases where these might be called into question.

## National Honours

From their inception in 1967 the national honours of Canada accorded no role to the provinces and their lieutenant governors, despite repeated attempts made in the 1970s and 80s.[34] By contrast, the Australian honours system established in 1975 provides for representation of all the states and territories on the council of the Order of Australia; furthermore, the governor general delegates to state governors the authority to invest recipients of the Order of Australia except those at the companion level. Eventually, Canadian lieutenant governors began presenting some lesser national honours, such as long-service medals. And when recipients of the Order of Canada were for health reasons unable to travel to Ottawa for their investiture, lieutenant governors might be asked to invest them on behalf of the governor general.

A major shift occurred after 1996, when Governor General Roméo LeBlanc created the Caring Canadian Award to celebrate volunteerism and lieutenant governors were invited, on occasion, to make the presentations on his behalf. In 2015, the award was replaced by a new honour of the Crown, the Sovereign's Medal for Volunteers, on the initiative of Governor General David Johnston and with the blessing of Queen Elizabeth II.[35] Provincial viceregal offices are among those who can submit nominations and it is now routine for lieutenant governors to present the medals in the name of the governor general. Not only does this make practical sense, it enhances the stature of the provincial viceregal offices and demonstrates the underlying unity of the Canadian Crown.

## THE PROVINCIAL CROWN AT THE JUBILEE — INTO THE BREACH

Early in 2022, the federal government made public what had been expected by many observers: breaking with decades-long Canadian practice, there would not be a national commemorative medal for the Queen's Platinum Jubilee.[36] Anticipating this decision, several provinces had prepared plans for their own medals. In February 2022, Alberta announced "a one-time Platinum Jubilee Medal to recognize 7,000 Albertans who have made significant contributions to society." Saskatchewan and Nova Scotia unveiled similar projects the following month. In announcing the establishment of the Nova Scotia Queen Elizabeth II's Platinum Jubilee Medal, Lieutenant Governor Arthur J. LeBlanc said, "The medal program marks the unprecedented 70th anniversary of the Queen's accession to the throne in 1952 and honours significant contributions and achievements by Nova Scotians." Manitoba, New Brunswick, and Prince Edward Island followed suit, with all provinces using a common template for their medal and ribbon designs and replicating the image of Queen Elizabeth II found on the national Diamond Jubilee Medal of 2012. Thus, six of the ten provinces would step into the breach of Jubilee recognition vacated by their national counterpart.

What was the implication of this unprecedented interprovincial move? Was it an intrusion into federal protocol jurisdiction? Saskatchewan's announcement set the context: "This is Saskatchewan's second provincial commemorative medal. The first, the Commemorative Medal for the Centennial of Saskatchewan, was created to mark the centenary of the province in 2005." Saskatchewan's Centennial Medal of 2005, like its equivalent in neighbouring Alberta, was granted status by Ottawa in the national precedence of honours. It would be appropriate that the same be done with their

Platinum Jubilee medals. Regardless of the outcome, the provincial Crown had stepped in where its federal manifestation chose not to tread.[37]

## THE PROVINCIAL CROWN AND INDIGENOUS PEOPLES[38]

"The Crown–First Nations treaty relationship," said National Chief Perry Bellegarde of the Assembly of First Nations in 2019, "is not founded in colonialism or in rights denial, but rather the equality and sovereignty of peoples and our agreement to share the land without dominating one another."[39] This treaty relationship was at first with the British Crown. King George III's Royal Proclamation of 1763 and its ratification by the Nations of the Great Lakes Region through the 1764 Treaty of Niagara affirmed Indigenous sovereignty in their lands. Following Confederation and under the *British North America Act* of 1867, responsibility for those who were then called Indians passed to the Crown in right of Canada in its federal incarnation, although First Nations have continued to emphasize their direct link with the sovereign.

How can the provinces be involved in what appears to be federal jurisdiction over Indigenous affairs? Julien Fournier and Amélie Binette, citing a 2014 Supreme Court ruling,[40] assert that the indivisible Canadian Crown provides the basis for recognizing provincial governments as interlocutors with First Nations in areas of provincial jurisdiction.[41] For their part, the lieutenant governors, as they gained a larger profile and expanded their role of community leadership, paid more attention to relationships with the First Nations in their provinces. For example, Saskatchewan Lieutenant Governors Sylvia Fedoruk (1988–1994) and Lynda Haverstock (2000–2006) in their travels and projects emphasized the province's north with its large Indigenous population and attended First Nations treaty days. The first Indigenous lieutenant governor of Ontario, James Bartleman (2002–2007), promoted literacy among Indigenous youth in northern Ontario, spearheading a province-wide campaign to collect books for them.

Pow Wow at Cowessess First Nation, Saskatchewan, August 13, 2019. This was the first event in an Indigenous community attended by Lieutenant Governor Russ Mirasty following his swearing-in. On the left is Chief Cadmus Delorme of Cowessess First Nation; on the right, Vice-Chief Dutch Lerat of the Federation of Sovereign Indigenous Nations.

Crown-Indigenous relations came increasingly to the fore with the report of the Royal Commission on Aboriginal Peoples in 1996, the Idle No More movement from 2012, and the residential schools issue leading to the Truth and Reconciliation Commission's report in 2015. The lieutenant governors — and territorial commissioners — rose to the occasion, placing Indigenous peoples at the forefront of their agendas. The 2021 report of the Ontario lieutenant governor is illustrative of their approach: "The Lieutenant Governor engages with representatives of Indigenous communities, ensures Indigenous representation at viceregal events wherever possible, and creates opportunities for meaningful dialogue between Indigenous and non-Indigenous people in the spirit of reconciliation."[42]

The close relationships developed between the Office of the Lieutenant Governor of Ontario and Indigenous Nations through James Bartleman were deepened by his successors David Onley and Elizabeth Dowdeswell.

Dowdeswell gifted sacred tobacco to the Indigenous Nations in Ontario and was awarded an Eagle Award (Friend of the First Nation Award) by the Mississaugas of the Credit. Her office supported the creation of the first non-denominational chapel royal at Massey College in Toronto.[43] In 2019 the lieutenant governor of Prince Edward Island hosted a council, convened by the Crown, bringing together the province's Indigenous and non-Indigenous leadership. The Office of the Lieutenant Governor of British Columbia highlights reconciliation on its website as a key pillar of its role.[44] In 2018 Nova Scotia's Government House hosted the annual Grand Council of the Mi'kmaq. Saskatchewan's viceregal office has been growing its own sacred tobacco at Government House to gift to Indigenous dignitaries since 2019.

In 2021, Saskatchewan's first Indigenous lieutenant governor, Russ Mirasty, from Lac La Ronge Cree First Nation, proposed to the premier that a memorial for former students of residential schools be built in the grounds of the province's Government House. This was readily accepted by the provincial government, providing an example of how viceregal representatives can accomplish a great deal through influence and persuasion. The notion is now widespread of Government Houses serving as venues for Crown-Indigenous dialogue, with appropriate protocols and dedicated spaces.

At the beginning of 2019, John Fraser and Nathan Tidridge, respectively founding president and first vice-president of the Institute for the Study of the Crown in Canada, submitted recommendations to Governor General Julie Payette about the role Rideau Hall could play in "opportunities for nation-building and fostering reconciliation."[45] There was no reply. The notable absence of the governor general from Crown-Indigenous initiatives in 2017–2020 was an incentive to turn to the provincial viceregal offices for support. The authors made their recommendations public a year later, noting that "excellent models of this relationship can already be found in most provinces, including British Columbia, Saskatchewan, Ontario, Nova Scotia and Prince Edward Island."[46] The appointment of the first Indigenous governor general, Mary Simon, in 2021 reassured observers that Indigenous relations were back on the agenda of Rideau Hall. The offices of the lieutenant governors and territorial commissioners undertook to create "treaty gardens" in each of their jurisdictions in 2022 to honour the Queen's Platinum Jubilee. Each of the twelve gardens includes plants and medicines suited to the local climate. Viceregal offices received tobacco seeds from plants grown for the chapel royal at Massey College in Toronto, which is called Gi-Chi-Twaa Gimaa Kwe Mississauga Anishinaabek AName Amik (The Queen's Anishinaabek Sacred Place). The inclusion of tobacco, where climates and protocols allow, represents the enduring relationship between the Crown and Indigenous Peoples.[47]

Such joint approaches by the viceregals signal the importance of the issues and underscore the intrinsic value of what has been called the "team of governors" characterizing the collective Canadian Crown.[48]

# CONCLUSION

This Crown, reconciling unity with diversity in the Canadian federal state, has the potential to exercise considerable moral authority and a positive influence on society. The Crown's vocation of transcending differences through political neutrality and embodiment of public ideals is particularly appealing in an age where partisan, ideological, and regional divisions are acute. In addition to their formal and informal constitutional roles, the viceregal representatives are uniquely placed to recognize and promote social solidarity. Treaty relationships and fostering reconciliation with Indigenous Peoples are now among their most significant tasks. And they substantially enhance the nation's social fabric by impartially conferring honours and awards and lending their support to charities and organizations of civil society.

A number of steps can and should be taken to fully realize this potential.[49] First and foremost, the method of selection of lieutenant governors must involve consultation with, and genuine input from, the provinces, either by resuming the advisory committee process in effect from 2012 to 2015, or by adopting an arrangement similar to that agreed between Ottawa and Quebec in 2019 for nominating justices of the Supreme Court of Canada from that jurisdiction.[50] A reformed appointment process is essential to the legitimacy and credibility of the Queen's provincial representatives.

National protocol can be adjusted to recognize the position of the lieutenant governors as coordinate viceregals in the Canadian federation. They should be granted status in the federal table of precedence after the governor general, entitled to a twenty-one-gun salute on official occasions, and accorded the title "Excellency." These measures require no constitutional amendment — they are simply administrative changes that are fully within the purview of the Government of Canada. The Office of the Governor General can do its part by firmly backing in word and practice the notion of the collective Canadian Crown, well described as "the Canadian viceregal family" by David Johnston, governor general from 2010 to 2017. By functioning as integral components of a composite institution, governor general and lieutenant governors can be more effective; for example, in Canada's relationship with Indigenous communities. Similarly, increased participation by lieutenant governors in conferring national honours reinforces the concept of a single Canadian Crown localized through its provincial components.

The provinces for their part have every interest in supporting their viceregal offices, especially if they have a voice in the appointment of the incumbents. The provincial embodiment of the Crown is at the root of their constitutional existence and cements their status as co-sovereign partners in Confederation. Provincial governments should provide adequate resources to their lieutenant governors in terms of budgets, facilities, staff, and bureaucratic support. They should ensure that protocol norms for the viceregal person are respected; for example, in openings of the legislature, granting of royal assent, international visits, and royal tours. Premiers would do well to meet regularly with their lieutenant governors to tap into their experience and benefit from their impartial advice. And they would also do well to insulate provincial honours from the taint of partisanship by ensuring a more substantive role for their lieutenant governors.

At the Platinum Jubilee of Queen Elizabeth II, it is time that the provincial dimension of the Canadian Crown came fully into its own. Lieutenant governors are no longer second fiddles. They are, and should be recognized as, coordinate viceregals in Canada's federal monarchy.

# 9

# The Spare Fire Extinguisher: The Administrator of the Government of Canada

*Christopher McCreery*

Following the unceremonious departure of Julie Payette and the termination of her commission as governor general and commander-in-chief on January 22, 2021,[1] Canadians rapidly became more familiar with Chief Justice Richard Wagner. Sworn in as administrator of the government of Canada on January 23, in the presence of the clerk of the Privy Council at the Supreme Court of Canada, Wagner's tenure of 182 days became the longest tenure of a single person to continuously serve as administrator in the country's post-Confederation history.[2] It also marked the lengthiest vacancy in the office of Canada's governor general — one day short of half a year.

In *The Crown in Canada*, Frank MacKinnon described the role of the governor general and lieutenant governors in Canada's system of parliamentary democracy as being akin to a fire extinguisher.[3] Although not frequently required, it is ever-present and at the ready to extinguish a fire — albeit in this context a constitutional fire. Building upon MacKinnon's analogy, the administrator is analogous to a spare fire extinguisher.

This chapter will focus on the largely unobserved, yet constitutionally significant, position of the administrator of the government of Canada (the administrator) and the origins, history and development of the role in the post-Confederation period. In the federal sphere, the governor general is aided by a team of "deputies of the governor general" who routinely exercise certain elements of the governor general's legal and constitutional authorities; however, they are not authorized to exercise all of them, and they may only act when there is a governor general in office.[4] Just as their ability to carry out the governor general's constitutional duties is limited, they have not acted in a ceremonial capacity, what Walter Bagehot called the "dignified" function of the Crown. In the event the incumbent governor general dies in office, is incapacitated, or goes on an extended visit outside the realm, it becomes necessary for there to be an officeholder who can exercise all the governor general's powers, legal, constitutional and symbolic. To this end, the *Letters Patent Constituting the Office of the Governor General, 1947* allow for the appointment of an administrator, who is able to exercise "all and every the powers and authorities herein granted"[5] to the governor general.

In the provinces the situation is different, as there is no equivalent "deputy of the lieutenant governor"; rather, when a lieutenant governor is absent or incapacitated the administrator of the province automatically takes office with what is a dormant commission.[6] This commission empowers the administrator to exercise all the authorities and powers of a lieutenant governor for the duration of the absence or incapacity. Because of a bizarre constitutional quirk, the authority of the administrator lives vicariously through the physical person of the lieutenant governor and not the state office.[7] When a lieutenant governor dies in office and a viceregal vacancy occurs, the authority of the administrator of the province evaporates. On these occasions, which effectively occur only when a lieutenant governor dies in office,[8] the government of the day is left with no ability to pass orders-in-council; issue special warrants, commissions of appointment, and proclamations; or obtain royal assent to legislation. Unfortunately, this debility is not an extraordinary constitutional conundrum devised by the mind of a creative legal scholar; it is something that happened twice in four years.[9]

The administrator's primary function has always been legal and constitutional in nature, ensuring the continuity of executive government and the ability for the government of the day to proceed without let or hindrance, as though the Crown's normal representative were present. This responsibility was particularly important in the pre-Confederation period when governors would be recalled to Britain and the voyage across the Atlantic was lengthy or when they would die in office. Following Confederation, some governors general would take a month or more leave to return to Britain for a holiday, normally during the summer months. There is little indication that early post-Confederation administrators or their predecessors undertook much in the way of exercising the dignified function of the Crown — aside from the events surrounding a speech from the throne. As we will see, this restricted approach, fostered by the father of protocol in Canada, Sir Joseph Pope, would be abandoned by Sir Lyman Duff during his periodic service as administrator in the 1920s, 1930s, and 1940s, and later when Bora Laskin took office as administrator in June 1974.

## ORIGINS

The office of the administrator traces its roots to the inauguration of non-Indigenous government in North America following the arrival of the French and English. The office and position of the administrator find their origins and function in the sunny climes of the Royal Province of Virginia and the colony of Barbados.

British colonial governors general, governors, and lieutenant governors received letters patent constituting their office, a commission of appointment, and royal instructions. While the commission came from the sovereign to his personal representative and emissary, the royal instructions were part of a general format eventually adopted by the Board of Trade, which had responsibility for most of Britain's overseas territories prior to the establishment of the Colonial Office. Contentious questions would arise about how much of the governor's authority could be exercised in the event of his death; however, during periods of absence the governor would typically instruct his lieutenant governor and the council on his expectations and limitations on exercising his authority.

Following the establishment of Virginia as a royal colony by James I in 1624, a definitive approach to the continuity of the governor's authority was adopted, one that no longer relied on the governor's council to elect one of their own to serve in place of the governor.[10] In the event of the death or absence of the governor, the lieutenant governor would act,[11] and if the lieutenant governor was also absent or deceased then the "member of the Governor's Council with the most seniority was designated as President and he would serve in the Governor's stead."[12] The use of the senior member of the council would eventually become a standard feature of colonial governance throughout the non-self-governing territories of the British Empire.

Following the conquest of Quebec, a hybrid of the New France model was adopted in the instructions provided to James Murray on December 7, 1763, for that jurisdiction. In the absence of Governor Murray as governor of Quebec, the lieutenant governor of Montreal would act, followed by the lieutenant governor of Trois-Rivières, then the commander-in-chief of the military forces, and then the eldest councillor. The eldest councillor was taken to mean the member with the longest tenure.[13] By 1767, four years later, the lieutenant governors of Montreal and Trois-Rivières were replaced with the chief justice, or in his absence the commander-in-chief of the military forces in the province.[14] The use of the chief justice of the colony or the commander-in-chief of the military forces in the colony (in locations where that role was not fused with the role of the governor) would follow in the second half of the eighteenth century as the number of colonial possessions grew and the complexity of administering them became more advanced. Employing a member of the bench for this purpose "was introduced in colonial times as a matter of expediency"[15] and as a byproduct of often having the chief justice serve on the governor's council. It also mirrored the establishment and growth in importance of the judiciary as the complexity of colonial societies grew.

When Governor General Robert Prescott was recalled to England in 1799,[16] the lieutenant governor of Lower Canada, Sir Robert Shore Miles, assumed the governor general's duties until 1805, when he too departed. At this point, the administration of the government devolved to Thomas Dunn, who was the senior executive councillor and presiding judge of the court of appeal. Dunn assumed government as "President and Commander-in-Chief" and would administer the Canadas from August 1805 until October 1807, when Governor Sir James Craig arrived. [17]

Lord Durham's appointment as captain-general and governor-in-chief of the provinces of Lower Canada, Upper Canada, Nova Scotia, New Brunswick, and Prince Edward Island in 1838 saw the introduction of the designation "administrator of the government" in British North America. In the event of Durham's absence or death his authority would devolve to "any such Lieutenant Governor" or "such Person as we may by Warrant under Our Sign Manual and Signet by Name appoint to be the Administrator of the Government of Our said Province ... and designate by his official Style and Title to be Administrator of the said Government."[18] There remained a provision for the senior military officer in the province to undertake the duties of the governor in the absence of the lieutenant governor or administrator.

## POST-CONFEDERATION

Following Confederation, the commission issued to Lord Monck upon his appointment as governor general of the Dominion of Canada included clause IX, "Temporary Administration of the Government," which was to be carried out by

Our Lieutenant Governor for the time being of Our said Dominion of Canada, or in the Absence of any such Lieutenant Governor ... such Person as we may by Warrant under Our Sign Manual and Signet appoint to be the Administrator of the Government of Our said Dominion of Canada, or in the Absence of any such Lieutenant Governor or Person as aforesaid to the Senior Military Officer for the time being in Command of Our Regular Forces in Our said Dominion.[19]

There never being a lieutenant governor of Canada or Dominion lieutenant governor appointed, and with no provision made for one of the provincial lieutenant governors to serve in this role, it was to the senior military officer in command, commonly referred to as the general officer in command of Canada (or GOC), that the role of the administrator was entrusted until 1901. It is not known why the senior provincial lieutenant governor was not made the default Dominion lieutenant governor. Perhaps it was because the provincial lieutenant governors were at the time seen as federal officers and potential agents of the federal cabinet. Elevating a humble provincial lieutenant governor, appointed on the advice of the prime minister of Canada, to the exalted imperial position as viceroy of the Dominion and agent for the British government in Canada would have been problematic on both the practical and the symbolic fronts. The distance required for one of the lieutenant governors to travel to Ottawa to take office could not be considered a valid concern, as the GOC was resident in Halifax and had to travel to the capital to execute the duties of the office. With the passage of time this distance would become an inconvenience.[20]

The administrator was seldom required during Monck's and Lisgar's tenures as governor general; however, as ocean travel became faster and safer, governors general began to return home more frequently. Lord Dufferin returned home for a total of 332 days over the course of his six years in office, on two occasions departing for more than 150 days at a time. This put some strain on the GOC, drawing him away from his full-time job defending the realm. The situation became more critical at the height of Canada's involvement in the South African War (1899–1902), when the country was experiencing a state of military activity not seen since the War of 1812. Naturally it became a topic of discussion between Governor General Lord Minto and Prime Minister Sir Wilfrid Laurier. It is worth recalling Minto's previous Canadian experience as military secretary to the governor general during the Northwest Rebellion of 1885 and his keen interest in Canadian military affairs.[21]

Laurier's experience with a number of senior British military officers during the South African War also added to his desire for a Canadian to fulfill the role of administrator, not a transient senior military officer who was not always attuned to the Canadian political landscape. They agreed that, as the GOC was based in Halifax, more than 1,200 kilometres away from the seat of executive government in Ottawa, the role of administrator should be vested in the chief justice of the Supreme Court of Canada. Laurier requested that Minto petition the Colonial Office to make this change on March 11, 1901, via an order-in-council.[22]

The Colonial Office in due course responded with an amendment to Minto's commission in relation to the succession of the government, allowing the King "to appoint for the time being the Chief Justice of the Supreme Court of the Dominion in the event of the death, incapacity, removal or absence of the Governor General, with all and singular the powers and authorities granted by the letters patent [1878]."[23] Although Minto's revised commission did not supersede the 1878 letters patent constituting the office of the governor general, it effectively brought to a conclusion the use of the GOC as the administrator. Thus, after 1901 only the chief justice of the Supreme Court or the senior puisne justice of the same court was appointed and sworn in as administrator. The first to serve in this role was Sir Samuel Strong, who was sworn in on June 9, 1902,[24] as Lord Minto departed for a month to visit to England. There was a nice quality to Strong's becoming the first Canadian to serve as administrator in the post-Confederation period, as he was an original member of the Supreme Court of Canada when it was established in 1875.

In 1905 the letters patent were updated to replace those which had been in operation since 1878. The first significant change was to "declare that there shall be a Governor-General and Commander-in-Chief in and over

Our Dominion of Canada."[25] This added to the governor general's style and authority the role of commander-in-chief, an authority delegated to the office by the sovereign.[26] It brought Canada into line with the newly constituted Commonwealth of Australia, where the sovereign's federal representative was both governor general and commander-in-chief.[27] The second change was to remove all reference to the GOC as the office-holder to serve in place of the governor general during absences, incapacity, or death. The 1901 amendment to Minto's commission was, in a legal sense, elevated to being part of the letters patent, which saw the GOC replaced with the chief justice of the Supreme Court or the senior judge of the Supreme Court who "shall act in the administration of the government." Strangely, the position of Dominion lieutenant governor was retained, even though none had ever been appointed. Although the style "Administrator" was not specifically referenced, the first chief justice to be sworn in under the new letters patent, Sir Henry E. Taschereau, was styled "Chief Justice of Canada and Administrator of the Government of Our said Dominion."[28]

During the lengthy absence of the Duke of Connaught, from May to October 1913, the longest post-Confederation absence of a Canadian governor general, lasting 217 days, the chief justice, Sir Charles Fitzpatrick, served the first two months, and then his commission as administrator was superseded by that of the senior puisne judge, Sir Louis Davies, who served for the remaining four months of Connaught's absence. There is little evidence that these administrators took on significant social duties; rather, they simply discharged the governor general's constitutional duties — approving orders-in-council, granting royal assent, and signing special warrants.

Amendments were made to the letters patent in 1931 because of provisions included in the *Statute of Westminster*; however, these changes did not touch on the role of the administrator. References to the Dominion lieutenant governor remained. When the letters patent were amended in 1935 to allow the governor general to travel to the United States, Newfoundland, and Bermuda without having to arrange for an administrator to be sworn in, the authority hitherto vested only in the administrator was transferred to the deputies of the governor general. This meant that the requirement for an administrator would be more infrequent, as the deputies of the governor general could act when he was travelling within North America. The person exercising the authority in the absence of the governor general remained the chief justice or the senior puisne judge. The amended letters patent noted that this would occur when the governor general was "temporarily absent from the Dominion, with Our permission, for the purpose of visiting some neighbouring State or territory for a period not exceeding one month."[29] Prior to this, even when a governor general wanted to travel to the United States for a few days, he was required to have an administrator sworn in. [30]

There appears to have been no connection between changes in the letters patent, the office that the role of the administrator was attached to, or the duties of the administrator and the length of absence of governors general. From 1867 to 1901, a period of thirty-four years, an administrator acted for a total of 793 days. Over the next period of thirty-four years, which covered the appointment of the chief justice as administrator and the 1935 changes to allow the governor general to leave Canada to visit neighbouring territories without having to arrange for an administrator, the administrator acted for 670 days.

New letters patent were issued by King George VI in 1947. The document combined elements of the 1931 and 1935 documents and further brought the document into line with Canada's constitutional position and the role of the governor general. Royal instructions were no longer issued, given how comprehensive the *Letters Patent, 1947* were with the significant expansion in the delegation of the King's powers to the governor general.[31] It was only with the adoption of these new letters patent that the stillborn office of Dominion lieutenant governor was finally abandoned and there was a return to the 1838 designation included in Lord Durham's various commissions of the "Administrator of the Government."

The most significant events to take place in relation to the administrator since 1947 relate to governors general suffering medical issues that have required the swearing-in of an administrator. Governor General Georges Vanier suffered a mild heart attack in May 1963, shortly before he was to deliver the speech from the throne, and Chief Justice Robert Taschereau was sworn in as administrator for all of six hours to allow for the opening of Parliament and delivery of the first speech from the throne of Pearson's premiership. Vanier's death in March 1967 required Taschereau to be called back into service, this time for forty-three days, allowing for a period of mourning and then time for the governor general designate, Roland Michener, to vacate his post as high commissioner to India and return to Ottawa to take up the viceregal office.

When Jules Léger suffered a serious stroke on June 8, 1974, while in Sherbrooke, Quebec, the immediate seriousness of the situation was not fully appreciated. Léger was released from hospital eleven days later and it was not until June 25 that Chief Justice Bora Laskin was sworn in as administrator. We do not know the reason for the delay, although Léger's condition was known to Prime Minister Pierre Trudeau, but we do know that Laskin's assuming the role as administrator was in large part linked to the 1974 royal tour of Queen Elizabeth the Queen Mother, who arrived only hours after Laskin was sworn in.[32] Laskin undertook a host of viceregal duties throughout Léger's convalescence, well beyond simply approving orders-in-council and granting royal assent. He aided in hosting the Queen Mother during the 1974 royal tour, routinely accepted letters of credence, presided over swearing-in ceremonies, investitures for various Canadian honours, and commissioning ceremonies for general officers in the Canadian Armed Forces, along with routine meetings with the prime minister. Laskin exercised a broad range of viceregal functions during his more than five months as administrator. He would help to set the pattern for his distant successor, Richard Wagner, who was sworn in as administrator in January 2021 following the resignation of Governor General Julie Payette, after an independent report revealed serious accusations of bullying and harassment of Rideau Hall staff and others. Payette's departure resulted in a record vacancy between governors general and it therefore became necessary to draw heavily upon the administrator to perform the role and function of the Queen's representative over a period of nearly six months. Despite the restrictions imposed upon in-person meetings and social events during the Covid-19 pandemic, the tenure of Richard Wagner as administrator enhanced Laskin's approach to the office; Wagner as administrator was even more publicly active than the governor general he was temporarily replacing. In addition to his duties as the administrator-in-council, signing orders-in-council, proclamations, commissions of appointment and other statutory and non-statutory instruments, Wagner undertook a host of other duties. He accepted letters of credence from ten ambassadors and welcomed two high commissioners, presided over seven virtual honours investitures, presented a grant of arms, and issued a message of condolence on the death of the Duke of Edinburgh and an official greeting to the Queen on her ninety-fifth birthday.

## SALUTES AND SALARY

Taking on the role of administrator requires the acceptance of duties additional to the officeholder's principal job as either the GOC, in the period from 1867 to 1901, or chief justice of the Supreme Court in the period since then. The assumption of the office has also come to be accompanied by certain symbolic privileges.

The somewhat peripheral issue of what additional salary, if any, the administrator should receive was a particular point of interest in the period immediately following Confederation when the GOC acted in the role. In this era, swearing in an administrator required them to relocate to Ottawa from Halifax, where the office of the GOC and British military forces in Canada were headquartered. Such occasions were unquestionably an inconvenience beyond the travel required. There was an old precedent that when a governor was absent, the senior councillor, acting in place of the governor "was usually allowed, in addition to his salary as councillor, £500 a year out of the governor's salary."[33] Until 1875, the Colonial Office had a policy that half the governor general's salary was to be paid to the administrator for the duration of the administrator's service and in a Colonial Office dispatch of April 8, 1875, it was proposed that this be changed.[34] The current administrator, being the GOC, was grandfathered: Cabinet agreed he should receive one-third of the governor general's salary while serving as administrator. Future administrators, however, would receive only one-quarter of the governor general's salary for the duration of the administrator's service.[35] In either case, the portion of the administrator's salary was deducted from the salary of the governor general, who was effectively financially punished for taking a holiday or travelling to the United States, the Caribbean, or Newfoundland on business. [36] Lord Minto, in perusing the files from the Dufferin and Lorne mandates, noted "the amount of pay concerned is very small but the principle involved is important."[37] Minto's interest was piqued by an impending trip to Alaska and also the knowledge that he would be summoned to attend the coronation of King Edward VII in 1902. By 1934, the issue of the administrator's compensation had been dealt with, it being noted in the manual for Government House, known as "The Green Book,"[38] that there were "no emoluments attached to the office; the Chief Justice, under the Judges Act earns $3,000 a year more than the other Judges of the Supreme Court in consideration of having these duties to perform."[39]

Occasionally there are principles which are more important than money, and this was certainly the case for Sir Henri E. Taschereau, who would serve as administrator on two occasions, totalling thirty-three days. The brevity of Taschereau's viceregal service did not prevent his firmly establishing that the administrator was entitled to all the ceremonial rights and privileges of the governor general, along with the authority to act in their place. Up until the time Taschereau was sworn in as administrator, administrators in Canada were not consistently afforded the style "Your Excellency" or granted the same salutes, escorts, or guards of honour that a governor general was entitled to. The under-secretary of state, Sir Joseph Pope, who had responsibility for royal tours, symbols, precedence, the installation of new governors general, and state funerals, among other duties, informed Taschereau that his role was purely constitutional and that

> an Administrator is appointed as a matter of necessity to do things that must be done, and he should do those things which are necessary as quietly and unostentatiously as possible. For these years on it is neither expected or desired that the Administrator should assume any social obligations in the way of entertainment, or do anything beyond what is imperatively required of him.[40]

For Pope, the administrator was a functionary and constitutional necessity, not the bona fide representative of the King-Emperor. Taschereau,
whom Lord Minto would describe as "a good lawyer, but very pompous,"[41]
was nonplussed by Pope's rigid interpretation of the role, so he cabled
the colonial secretary, Joseph Chamberlain, for clarification on the matter. The Colonial Office replied in the affirmative, that the administrator
was entitled to be styled as "Your Excellency" and to the other ceremonial honours associated with the office. Pope, who was nothing if not a
martinet when it came to protocol, would later note "the conduct of the
Administrator on this and subsequent occasions on which he was called
to act in that capacity struck me as childish in the extreme."[42] Since this
time, administrators have been accorded all the honours, salutes, guards of
honour, and ceremonial dignities that are given to governors general. The
first person born in Canada to exercise the full range of viceregal authority
of the administrator was Sir Lyman Duff, who over the course of several
periods in office dissolved government, swore in new ministries, delivered
the speech from the throne, prorogued Parliament, reviewed guards of
honour, and granted royal assent.[43] He even wore the civil uniform, it being
deemed inappropriate for him to wear judicial robes when acting as the
King's representative.

## CHALLENGES OF OFFICE

Having the most senior or second most senior member of the bench act
as administrator has certain undeniable advantages. The chief justice of
the Supreme Court comes to the administrator's role with a pre-existing
knowledge of the viceregal office and its function, having occasionally
acted as a deputy of the governor general. Granting royal assent, signing
orders-in-council, undertaking constitutional duties in Parliament, and
acting in a formal and dignified manner are familiar duties. The administrator also temporarily takes on the role as the sovereign's representative

with a firm understanding of how government operates and the legal/constitutional position of the office of the governor general. Lastly, and not insignificantly, they are known to the public nationally in a way few other unelected officeholders are. It should be no surprise that in Australia governors general and governors have routinely and successfully been plucked from the bench of the country's highest national and state courts. There is also a practical advantage of section VIII of the *Letters Patent, 1947,* providing for the role of administrator, after the chief justice, to default to the next senior justice of the Supreme Court. In the event of some colossal calamity such as natural disaster, terrorist attack,[44] invasion/war, or lethal pandemic, it provides for nine potential replacements for the governor general.

While the swearing-in of an administrator is not an extraordinary event, it has not been a routine occurrence in Canada since before the tenure of Georges Vanier as governor general. With the discontinuation of appointing a British peer as governor general, there was no longer the month or longer absence to visit "home," although both Vincent Massey and Vanier took lengthy holidays in Britain and France during their time in office. Until the ignominious resignation of Julie Payette in January 2021, the administrator had been sworn in very infrequently (see Table 1.1.), normally on occasions when the governor general was incapacitated for medical reasons. Nevertheless, there always remains the possibility of a disagreement arising between a prime minister and their governor general and the prime minister's advising the Queen to terminate the commission of a governor general. This would necessitate the administrator taking office if a successor governor general was not immediately recommended to the sovereign. If such an extraordinary, yet plausible, situation were to arise, whereby a constitutional crisis was precipitated by a governor general's being dismissed or forced to resign by the prime minister, the prime minister would, as noted by Anne Twomey, "face a Chief Justice who has an independent status and public standing in the field of constitutional law who will exercise the role and power of the viceregal office, before a more compliant appointee can be substituted … this knowledge alone might make a Prime Minister reluctant to advise the dismissal of a Governor-General."[45] So in this sense, having the chief justice serve as administrator may militate against a prime minister's circumventing viceregal authority by having a governor general ejected from office.

In the post-Charter era, where the independence of the judiciary has solidified even more, there are also distinct drawbacks to having the chief justice act as the Queen's representative for any period of time. Indeed, the potential for a conflict arising between the chief justice's role as head of the judiciary and also as head of the executive, albeit temporarily, resulted in the expansion of the role of the secretary to the governor general. Justices of the Supreme Court regularly complained about having to grant royal assent, out of a concern that their judicial independence would be jeopardized.[46] This very issue was argued before the Federal Court of Appeal in *Kassongo Tunda v. Canada (Minister of Citizenship and Immigration)*.[47] The case brought into question the independence of the judiciary, given that, under sections 14 and 55 of the *Constitution Act, 1867*, the governor general is authorized to appoint deputies, a role most frequently discharged by judges of the Supreme Court of Canada. The Court found that

> a distinction must be made on the one hand, the power, and on the other the desirability, for the Governor General to make such appointments, as Deputy Governor General, specifically with reference to the power conferred on Supreme Court judges to give Royal Assent to statutes which this Court, and the judges who approved them, may be required to consider for their constitutional validity. We can understand that this kind of delegation of the Governor General's powers may raise a question of desirability and may prompt doubts in the minds of certain people in a context of separation of powers ... but it is nonetheless legal. From this and a number of other Commonwealth examples, we see the potential for having the chief justice's perceived independence called into question because he or she is effectively double hatted while serving as administrator is one that has been argued before the courts in the past.[48]

Similar concerns have arisen in New Zealand about having the chief justice act as administrator. Is this an "arrangement consistent with the constitutional doctrine of the separation of powers?"[49]

The *Tunda* case played a role in the radical expansion of the role of the secretary to the governor general as a deputy of the governor general. The secretary had hitherto been granted a limited number of largely administrative authorities as a deputy, but in 2011 the commission of the secretary as a deputy of the governor general was broadened to "include all the powers authorities and functions vested in and of right exercisable by me as Governor General, saving and excepting the powers of dissolving, recalling and proroguing Parliament, or appointing members of the Ministry and of signifying Royal Assent in Parliament Assembled."[50] This change has resulted in the secretary to the governor general's being authorized to grant royal assent, albeit not in Parliament, thereby avoiding the awkward image of a civil servant who holds the courtesy rank of deputy minister parading before senators and MPs as the representative of the sovereign. It frees justices of the Supreme Court from having to grant royal assent and members of the judiciary from acting for the executive branch of government. This could potentially appear to pollute their judicial independence, even though they are acting in an executive capacity completely independent of their judicial office. Even the potential for a perceived conflict of interest is serious enough to be treated as a conflict when it comes to the rarefied world of judicial independence. Twomey acknowledges this disadvantage and the "potential to undermine the doctrine of the separation of powers. Where a chief justice acts upon executive advice in fulfilling a viceregal role, he or she may be seen as too close to the executive government, breaching the separations of powers and undermining the independence of the judiciary."[51]

There are additional impediments in relation to the administrator's dignified role as the temporary, ersatz representative of the sovereign. If the administrator is in office for any length of time, as was the case for Duff in 1940 following Lord Tweedsmuir's death — 129 days; Laskin following Jules Léger's stroke in 1974 — 157 days; or Wagner's 182-day tenure as administrator following the departure of Julie Payette, they must actually fulfill all aspects of the role, beyond simply executing legal and constitutional duties. There are investitures, dinners, receptions, diplomatic interactions, the role as stand-in for the commander-in-chief, and the special relationship that the Crown's representative has with members of the Canadian Armed Forces. Furthermore, the administrator generally does not know how long he or she will be in office, so it is impossible, and not advisable, for them to develop a set of themes for their mandate, which leaves a significant aspect of the viceregal role vacant.

The administrator, despite his or her esteemed status as chief justice — or as the senior puisne justice of the Supreme Court of Canada — also lacks the direct connection with the Queen, as an administrator is

The Right Honourable Richard Wagner, PC, Administrator of the Government of Canada, January 23, 2021, to July 26, 2021. First administrator to have his portrait displayed in public buildings.

simply the backup representative and not the tenured viceregal. A by-product of this is that the administrator lacks the moral voice of authority that a governor general can have during a crisis or a significant event of great national magnitude. This handicap was clearly demonstrated following the death of the Duke of Edinburgh in April 2021. While the administrator presided over the national commemoration of the Duke's life and service, it was former governor general David Johnston who offered a compelling and personal eulogy. Similarly, following the discovery of unmarked graves at the site of a former Indian residential school in Kamloops, British Columbia, there was unquestionably a moment when the governor general could have spoken to the nation and on behalf of the nation; yet there was no such non-partisan national voice — something that would have been all the more significant given the ancient Crown-Indigenous relationship and commitment of the previous two governors general to reconciliation.

Other less ethereal and symbolic difficulties arise in relation to having the role of the governor general as chancellor of the Order of Canada and the chief justice's role as chair of the advisory council of the Order fused in the person of the administrator. There is an instant contamination of the independence these two separate roles are supposed to have if the administrator attempts to exercise them together. How can the chair of the council write to himself or herself to advise the appointment of new members of the Order, and then sign the same instrument recommending the appointments on behalf of the Queen? It is one thing to preside over investitures and receive letters of credence and praise the good work of citizens; it is quite another to meld two distinct roles within the Canadian honours system into a single decision-maker. Fusing the roles is problematic in terms of the optics and appearance of a conflict of interest, and also the practical mechanics of such a role, which was designed to be bifurcated since the establishment of the Order of Canada as a non-partisan society of honour in 1967.

## CONCLUSION

The infrequency with which it has been necessary to swear in an administrator has played a part in the obscurity of the role and office of the ersatz governor general of Canada. This fact does not diminish the role and function of the position as being central to the continuity of government and the continuity of the Crown. Whether an administrator is required because of illness or death on the part of the incumbent governor general or an extraordinary event such as the protracted vacancy in the office of the governor general like that experienced following the termination of Payette's commission, it is a necessary part of our constitutional order. The very active approach taken by the most recent administrator, Richard Wagner, offers an avenue for additional study on how he robustly embraced the dignified (ceremonial and symbolic role) of the Queen's representative in Canada during the extended national emergency caused by the Covid-19 pandemic. While Duff and Laskin departed from Sir Joseph Pope's precept that the administrator "should do those things which are necessary as quietly and unostentatiously as possible,"[52] with the tools of social media and the internet during a time of social isolation for many Canadians, Wagner was able to enhance the reach of the role.

The last word on the role of the administrator is best left to the man who discharged the role with aplomb for nearly six months. Shortly after it was announced that the Queen had accepted the recommendation that Mary Simon be appointed thirtieth governor general of Canada, Richard Wagner issued a formal departure letter. Wagner, the first administrator to have his portrait hung in public buildings and who, despite the pandemic, was arguably the most active and publicly present administrator the country has ever had, reflected, "I have gained a deeper understanding of and appreciation for our institutions and have seen the strength of our constitutional monarchy up close and at work. It has been a reassuring realization, and confirmation, for me. We are fortunate to have these institutional mechanisms in place."[53]

## Table 1.1 Administrators of the Government of Canada, 1867–2021

| ADMINISTRATOR | DATES | GOVERNOR GENERAL | REASON |
|---|---|---|---|
| General Sir Charles Ash Windham | 14 November 1868 to 30 November 1868 (16 days) | Viscount Monck | Absence Departure for UK |
| Sir John Young (Lord Lisgar) | 1 December 1868 to 1 February 1869 (61 days) | | Absence Waiting to be sworn in as Governor General |
| Lieutenant-General Sir Charles Hastings Doyle[i] | 22 June 1872 to 24 July 1872 (31 days) | Lord Lisgar | Absence Departure for UK |
| Lieutenant-General William O'Grady Haly | 15 May 1875 to 21 October 1875 (159 days) | Lord Dufferin | Absence Visit to UK |
| | 12 October 1874 to 2 November 1874 (21 days) | | Absence |
| | 15 May 1875 to 21 October 1875 (158 days) | | Absence Visit to UK |
| | 21 January 1878 to 3 February 1878 (14 days) | | Absence Visit to USA; Washington DC and New York City |
| General Sir Patrick McDougall | 11 November 1881 to 20 January 1882 (69 days) | Lord Lorne | Absence Visit to UK |
| | 18 December 1882 to 30 January 1883 (42 days) | | Absence Visit to UK |
| General Lord Alexander Russell | 5 August 1886 to 7 November 1886 (94 days) | Lord Lansdowne | Absence Visit to UK |
| Lieutenant General Sir John Ross | 26 May 1888 to 10 June 1888 (14 days) | | Absence Departure for UK |
| General Sir Alexander Montgomery-Moore | 15 July 1893 to 17 September 1893 (64 days) | Lord Stanley | Absence Departure for UK |

| Administrator | Dates | Governor General | Reason |
|---|---|---|---|
| General Sir Alexander Montgomery-Moore | 13 October 1893 to 22 October 1893 (9 days) | Lord Aberdeen | Absence Visit to USA; Chicago World's Fair and Washington DC |
| | 28 November 1894 to 3 December 1894 (5 days) | | Absence Visit to USA; St. Andrew's Day dinner in New York City |
| | 12 February 1897 to 14 March 1897 (30 days) | | Absence Visit to USA; Chicago, Nashville, Cincinnati, Washington DC and New York City |
| | 20 October 1897 to 3 November 1897 (14 days) | | Absence Visit to USA; event at Princeton |
| General Lord William Seymour | 12 November 1898 on standby (0 days) | | Standby, not required[ii] |
| | 30 September 1899 to 4 October 1899 (5 days) | | Absence Visit to USA; Long Island, to see Gov. Roosevelt and Michigan |
| Sir Samuel H. Strong (Chief Justice) | 8 June 1902 to 26 July 1902 (50 days) | Lord Minto | Absence Visit to UK to attend Coronation of Edward VII |
| Sir Henri E. Taschereau (Chief Justice) | 20 November 1904 to 10 December 1904 (20 days) | | Absence Departure for UK |
| | 30 March 1906 to 12 April 1906 (13 days) | Lord Grey | Absence Visit to USA; New York City, Pilgrims Dinner and meeting with President Roosevelt |
| Sir Charles Fitzpatrick (Chief Justice) | 19 July 1907 to 8 August 1907 (20 days) | | Absence Visit to Newfoundland |

| Administrator | Dates | Governor General | Reason |
|---|---|---|---|
| Sir Charles Fitzpatrick (Chief Justice) | 26 March 1908 to 28 April 1908 (33 days) | Lord Grey | Absence Visit to Bermuda, USA; Washington DC to see British Ambassador, North Carolina to visit Vanderbilt's |
| Sir Charles Fitzpatrick (Chief Justice) | 18 March 1909 to 22 March 1909 (4 days) | | Absence Visit to USA; Albany, meet Governor of of New York and President Taft |
| | 28 June 1909 to 1 August 1909 (35 days) | | Absence Visit to UK |
| Désiré Girouard (Senior Puisne Justice) | 15 July 1910 to 18 August 1910 (34 days) | | Absence Visit to UK |
| Sir Charles Fitzpatrick (Chief Justice) | 9 January 1911 to 11 January 1911 (3 days) | | Absence |
| Sir Charles Fitzpatrick (Chief Justice) | 22 January 1912 to 28 January 1912 (6 days) | Duke of Connaught | Absence Visit to USA; New York City, Washington DC and President Taft |
| | 22 March 1913 to 11 May 1913 (see below) | | Absence Visit to UK Second commission issued 12 May 1913 |
| Sir Louis H. Davis (Senior Puisne Justice) | 12 May 1913 to 25 October 1913 (217 days total)[iii] | | Transfer of duties from Fitzpatrick |
| | 6 July 1914 to 20 July 1914 (14 days) | | Absent Visit to Newfoundland |
| Sir Charles Fitzpatrick (Chief Justice) | 13 October 1916 to 11 November 1916 (29 days) | | Absence Departure for UK |
| Sir Louis H. Davies (Chief Justice) | 15 March 1920 to 9 May 1920 (54 days) | Duke of Devonshire | Absence Visit to UK |

| ADMINISTRATOR | DATES | GOVERNOR GENERAL | REASON |
|---|---|---|---|
| Sir Louis H. Davies (Chief Justice) | 28 July 1921 to 11 August 1921 (14 days) | Duke of Devonshire | Absence Departure of UK |
| | 24 July 1925 to 30 July 1925 (6 days) | Lord Byng | Absence Visit to USA; Alaska |
| Francis A. Anglin (Chief Justice) | 30 September 1926 to 2 October 1926 (2 days) | | Absence Departure for UK |
| Francis A. Anglin (Chief Justice) | 5 December 1927 to 12 December 1927 (7 days) | Lord Willingdon | Absence Visit to USA, Washington DC |
| | 13 December 1929 to 13 January 1930 (31 days) | | Absence Visit to UK |
| Lyman Poore Duff (Senior Puisne Justice) | 16 January 1931 to 4 April 1931 (78 days) | | Absence Departure for UK |
| Sir Lyman Poore Duff (Chief Justice) | 12 February 1940 to 21 June 1940 (129 days) | Vacant | Vacancy Death of Lord Tweedsmuir |
| Thibaudeau Rinfret (Senior Puisne Justice) | 11 October 1945 to 20 November 1945 (40 days) | Lord Athlone | Absence Visit to London |
| Thibaudeau Rinfret (Chief Justice) | 16 March 1946 to 12 April 1946 (27 days) | | Absence Departure for UK |
| Patrick Kerwin (Senior Puisne Justice) | 11 June 1951 to 1 August 1951 (48 days) | Lord Alexander | Absence Visit to UK |
| Thibaudeau Rinfret (Chief Justice) | 28 January 1952 to 28 February 1952 (31 days) | Vacant | Termination of Lord Alexander's commission |
| Patrick Kerwin (Senior Puisne Justice) | 16 June 1953 to 22 July 1953 (36 days) | Vincent Massey | Absence Visit to UK |
| Patrick Kerwin (Chief Justice) | 16 June 1955 to 26 July 1955 (41 days) | | Absence Visit to UK |
| | 28 July 1956 to 30 July 1956 (2 days) | | Absence Medical procedure[iv] |

| Administrator | Dates | Governor General | Reason |
|---|---|---|---|
| Patrick Kerwin (Chief Justice) | 29 June 1957 to 2 September 1957 (65 days) | Vincent Massey | Absence Visit to UK |
| | 25 July 1960 to 30 August 1960 (~36 days) | | Absence Visit to UK |
| | 15 July 1961 to 31 August 1961 (46 days) | General Georges Vanier | Absence Visit to UK |
| Robert Taschereau (Chief Justice) | 16 May 1963 (6 hours) | General Georges Vanier | Incapacity Medical issue; heart attack |
| | 5 March 1967 to 17 April 1967 (43 days) | Vacant | Death of General Vanier |
| Bora Laskin (Chief Justice) | 25 June 1974 to 6 December 1974 (165 days) | Jules Léger | Incapacity Jules Léger suffered a stroke |
| | 21 May 1980 (1 day) | Ed Schreyer | Incapacity Medical issue |
| Beverly McLachlin (Chief Justice) | 8 July 2005 to 22 July 2005 (14 days) | Adrienne Clarkson | Incapacity Medical issue: heart surgery |
| John Major (Senior Puisne Justice) | 27 September (1 day) 2005 | | Swearing in of new governor general |
| Richard Wagner (Chief Justice) | 23 January 2001 to 26 July 2001 (182 days) | Vacant | Resignation of Julie Payette |

TABLE 1.1 was compiled using various references: *Journals of the Senate*; *Minutes of the Senate*; the *Canada Gazette*; N. Omer Coté, *Political Appointments, Parliaments and Judicial Bench in the Dominion of Canada, 1867–1893* (Ottawa: Thornburn and Company, 1896); the Diary of William Lyon Mackenzie King; and the biographies and diaries of a number of governors general. This list is not complete, as the absence of a governor general and swearing-in of an administrator was not consistently reported in the *Journals of the Senate* for periods when the Senate was not sitting. Although the custom has been for a proclamation to be issued and subsequently published in the *Canada Gazette*, this practice has not been followed invariably. The swearing-in of Chief Justice Richard Wagner

as Administrator on January 23, 2021, is the most recent occasion when a proclamation was not issued, and there are similar earlier examples.[54]

i   While serving as lieutenant governor of Nova Scotia.
ii  General Lord William Seymour arrived in Quebec City from Halifax in advance of Lord Minto's arrival from England, there being a concern that weather would delay the arrival of the governor general designate. Minto arrived on time and it was not necessary to swear in Seymour as administrator.
iii Medical treatment of the Duchess of Connaught and to attend the marriage of his daughter, Princess Patricia.
iv  *Canada Gazette* indicated Massey signed orders-in-council on July 26 and August 2; on July 31 the chief justice granted royal assent as "Deputy of His Excellency the Governor General." It is most likely that this brief incapacity was on account of a medical issue.

# Part Four

---

# Perspectives on the Crown in Canada

# 10

# A Right Honourable Journey: The Queen and Her Canadian Prime Ministers

*Arthur Milnes*

With the royal yacht *Britannia* docked in Toronto harbour, an elderly man refused offers of assistance as he walked assuredly, but slowly, up the gangway. He had been summoned by Her Majesty Queen Elizabeth II to a private audience. It was June 1959. Queen Elizabeth was the sixth monarch he had lived under in a remarkable life and career. Twice prime minister of Canada, and a force in the nation's politics through five decades, Arthur Meighen, in the twilight of his life, was largely forgotten by Canadians. But not by his sovereign.[1] His biographer, Roger Graham, describes the moment:

> The year 1959 brought [Arthur] Meighen one final honour to cherish. He … was received in audience by Queen Elizabeth. Meighen was now Her Majesty's senior Canadian privy councillor and the senior Canadian member of the Imperial Privy Council. He had served both her grandfather and her father in his various capacities and, although he was now past becoming

much excited by anything, even a royal audience, at the appointed hour proudly he went, Her Majesty's loyal and obedient servant, to pay his dutiful respects to the newest holder of the Crown which symbolized for him all the glory and the grandeur of the British peoples. After some very pleasant conversation and the presentation to the Meighens of signed photographs of the Queen and Prince Philip in a folding leather case, Her Majesty said, "Now I mustn't keep you," and her guests took their leave.[2]

Meighen would pass into history fourteen months after visiting Her Majesty.[3] And the Queen? She remains on the throne, sixty-three years after her audience with former prime minister Meighen on that day so long ago. That meeting with Meighen evinces the Queen's deep knowledge and understanding of our country and her prime ministers, one she has sustained since February 6, 1952, when she became Queen of Canada.

It is often said, and accurately, that Justin Trudeau is the twelfth Canadian prime minister to serve Her Majesty as her Canadian first minister. Yet the sovereign's experiences with Canadian leaders predate her accession to the throne in 1952: she met her first Canadian prime minister in the 1930s, while Mackenzie King held office.

Since 1867, Canada has had twenty-three prime ministers. Her Majesty has known fourteen of them.[4] It is safe to say that no Canadian can claim to have such personal knowledge of Canada's first ministers as can the Queen. Despite this amazing record, however, one is struck by the lack of available academic or journalistic studies of this unique aspect of both the Queen's reign and the Canadian premiership.

This chapter seeks to fill that gap in Canadian historiography. This overview is by no means a detailed examination of the policies various prime ministers have pursued regarding the Crown or Canada's constitutional monarchy. Rather, it offers a personal and anecdotal journey with the Queen through many decades of Canadian political history. Through interviews with Prime Minister Justin Trudeau and various living former prime ministers, and by examining the memoirs written by our heads of government past and present, a personal portrait of Her Majesty's relationship with her

Canadian first ministers is revealed. Wherever possible the author has allowed the prime ministers to speak in their own words.

———

The prime ministers of Canada the Queen has encountered, thirteen men and one woman, were and are all very different. They have been Conservative and Liberal, from varying walks of life, from differing parts of the country, and have each brought to their office very different personal attitudes about the place of the Queen and of the monarchy in Canadian life.

Today, for example, Prime Minister Justin Trudeau asserts that Her Majesty has proven — outside of his own family — the confidant and adviser he perhaps values most. Since taking office, he has eagerly drawn upon the Queen's vast knowledge and experience. His enthusiasm for his contacts with Her Majesty is palpable:

> I have taken every single opportunity I have had to have those personal moments and connections with her. Getting that personal connection is really, really important ... because I do so value her perspective and just enjoy chatting with her more than just about anyone else in the world.... Prime Ministers [of Canada] are in a very unique position ... It is a singular role that we play that nobody who wasn't a prime minister can properly understand what it is to be [one] ... And, it's not very often prime ministers find themselves in a position where they can sit down and talk to other PMs like a peer. With other leaders around the world, you have a contemporary relationship, but no one really knows what it is like to be Prime Minister of Canada.
>
> But the Queen, because she has seen it all, done it all, has been there for so many of my predecessors ... I made the instant decision that I could trust her entirely and talk to her about the things that were on my mind in a way that would be unbelievably helpful to me and invariably, she is: in her thoughtfulness, in her wisdom, in her perspective.

I've always taken it as she is our Queen, she is Queen of Canada. I am not visiting a foreign head of state; I am visiting with our own head of state and therefore will talk to her about anything and everything as candidly as she wants to try and get her best advice on a range of things. And that's always been the dynamic for me.[5]

Trudeau's first encounters with Her Majesty took place when he was a child, as he grew up at 24 Sussex Drive while his father served as prime minister. While world leaders coming by for visits and talks was nothing unusual, Justin Trudeau recalls that a visit by the Queen heightened the excitement in the household. "I remember everyone buzzing around because the Queen was coming ... We had important people come over but obviously this was a notch above in terms of importance ... I remember her asking me about school. She had a very nice interaction with me. I do remember that of all the various people I met in my dad's functions, she was the one who was very good at talking to kids. Some of those world leaders were not very good at talking to kids, [but] she was just lovely and had a real positive impact on me."[6,7]

Prime Minister Trudeau's early memories of Her Majesty and his duties as Canada's new first minister came together only days after he was sworn in as the nation's twenty-third prime minister in November 2015. With the Commonwealth Heads of Government gathered in Malta, it fell upon him to offer the toast to the Queen on behalf of all the assembled leaders. In doing so, Trudeau recalled Her Majesty's history with Canada and Canadians. His toast is worth quoting at length:

You were only nine years old when you carried out what was perhaps your first official duty on behalf of Canada — an appearance on a postage stamp ... That was 1935. From that moment to this, Your Majesty has been such a constant presence in the life of Canada that a modern history of our nation could be written entirely with vignettes from your life.

Here's one: In 1951, Princess Elizabeth attends her first hockey game, in Montreal, at the legendary Montreal Forum.

And another: in 1959, Queen Elizabeth opens the St. Lawrence Seaway. And another: in 1967, Queen Elizabeth cuts Canada's centennial cake on Parliament Hill as Canadians sing Happy Birthday. There are countless scenes like these to choose from. In a single tour in 1959, over 45 days, you visited 90 towns and cities. It is safe to say that you have seen more of Canada than almost any Canadian. And always, Canadians have watched and admired their indefatigable queen, forming cherished memories. Some of those memories are of formal state occasions. Some are more personal. And for a few, some are both. One that I personally remember well from my childhood and indeed, treasure is this: It is 1982, again on Parliament Hill. Queen Elizabeth signs the Constitution Act, thus empowering Canada's legal foundation, including our Charter of Rights and Freedoms. On that cool day in April, seated next to you, was my father. Pierre Elliott Trudeau was your fourth Canadian prime minister. I am your twelfth.

In 1947, you famously vowed that your whole life would be devoted to the service of the Commonwealth. You more than honoured your vow. And for that, on behalf of all Canadians and indeed, of all of us citizens of the Commonwealth, I thank you.[8]

As always, Her Majesty had the last word. And it made headlines around the world. "As Head of the Commonwealth, it is with great pleasure that I welcome you all here this evening," the Queen said. "Thank you, Mr. Prime Minister of Canada, for making me feel so old!"

Other vignettes, much older, yet illustrative of Her Majesty's long history with Canadian prime ministers, can be found in the private diaries of William Lyon Mackenzie King. As his descriptions of Princess Elizabeth and the accounts of the various discussions he had with her and her parents have received scant attention, they are worthy of lengthy mention here. In December of 1936, as the abdication crisis came to a close, King was already looking forward to the role Princess Elizabeth might play in restoring the Crown's reputation in the years ahead.

"In all probability with the Duke and Duchess of York as King and Queen, and with the little Princess Elizabeth in the picture, there will be a much happier situation in the New Year that there has been at any time since the time of George V," King wrote in his diary on December 8, 1936.[9]

Five years later, it is 1941 and Canada is at war. King, in the United Kingdom for discussions with Winston Churchill and others, is honoured with an invitation to visit King George VI and his family at Balmoral Castle. In the privacy of his diary, Canada's tenth prime minister paints an idyllic family scene:

> At luncheon I was seated to the Queen's right, with Princess Elizabeth to my right and Princess Margaret immediately opposite. The latter was quite entertaining in the way she laughed at different subjects that were discussed and particularly in making nicknames for [others]. She also made her eyes look crossed and tried to amuse others. The Queen told her to stop doing that for fear they might become fixed in that position and the King had also to tell her the same. When I talked to Princess Elizabeth about her [wartime radio] broadcast she was very sweet in the way she talked and was very natural in some further conversation we had together.[10]

With the Allied victory, Prime Minister King is in Britain again, this time in October of 1945. He is invited to Buckingham Palace for discussions with King George VI. Princess Elizabeth, age nineteen, joins her father and the Canadian prime minister. They are discussing Joseph Stalin of the USSR and Nazi leader Adolf Hitler when the future Queen makes a spirited intervention: "Some mention was made of Hitler," the Canadian visitor recorded. "When the King was speaking of not knowing whether Stalin was dead or alive, in addition to not knowing whether Hitler was dead or alive, the King said something about it being a pity that Hitler had not been shot. Princess Elizabeth said she would have been prepared to shoot him."[11]

A year later, Prime Minister King returned once again to London. At Buckingham Palace, on May 24, 1946, he attended another royal luncheon with Princess Elizabeth at his table. His diary entry for that day reveals a tantalizing detail that, once again, illustrates the deep knowledge of Canada and of our prime ministers she would later bring to the throne:

> I was seated to the King's right, and to the left of the Queen. Princess Elizabeth, next to the King and Princess Margaret Rose next to the Queen ... The King was especially interested in getting particulars of the Russian espionage matter. He had followed it pretty closely and seemed to be remarkably familiar with details. He told me that he thought what we had done might be a very helpful exposé in regard to similar situations in different countries. He spoke of feeling very greatly concerned about Russian attitude and behaviour. Their establishment of the 5th column and the like. Later in the afternoon, I sent H.M. a copy of Gouzenko's confession.[12]

It is doubtful any living person, aside from Her Majesty, can claim to have been involved in such a high-level discussion of the Gouzenko case with the Canadian prime minister of the day. King would retire from politics in 1948 and make way for Louis St-Laurent. It was on St-Laurent's watch that the people of Canada first saw their future Queen in person. Throughout the fall of 1951, Princess Elizabeth, accompanied by her husband Prince Philip, visited every single province in a gruelling five-week pan-Canadian tour — this a short four months before she would ascend the throne.

St-Laurent, who played the leading role in Canadianizing the Crown between 1948 and 1957, including nominating the first-ever Canadian to serve as governor general, Vincent Massey, was a prime minister greatly involved with all facets of the monarchy. Christopher McCreery writes,

> St. Laurent had a high opinion of the Crown, the parliamentary institutions that Canada had borrowed from Britain, and the various symbols and traditions that had come to be rooted in Canadian public and political life. He was a "devoted admirer of the Royal Family" and, in the summer of 1953, would tell

his cabinet that "the monarchy is more solidly established (in Canada) than ever." When it came to matters such as royal tours, the accession of the Sovereign, and changes to the Royal Style and Titles, he was intimately involved in the arrangements, discussions and final decisions: St. Laurent chaired the Canadian Coronation Executive Committee. These were issues in which St. Laurent had a personal interest, regardless of the detailed minutia.[13]

In June 1957, the St-Laurent Liberals were defeated, much to their surprise, by a Prairie firebrand named John Diefenbaker. Albeit the first-ever prime minister of neither French nor English origin, the thirteenth prime minister was very much a devoted monarchist. He combined this mindset with an intense belief in Canada's British traditions. As he would later demonstrate to Canadians during the flag debate of 1964, he was even willing to stake the very leadership of his party on defending Canada's British connection.

Surprisingly, however, Diefenbaker wrote relatively little of a personal nature about the Queen and his relations with her in his three-volume memoir, *One Canada*. This despite the fact that Her Majesty undertook her first official tours of Canada as Queen in 1957 and 1959. He did, however, describe his recollection of the Queen's opening a new session of Parliament in October 1957, when he was first prime minister.

"It began gloriously," Diefenbaker wrote, "when the Queen of Canada for the first time read the Speech from the Throne…. Through the medium of television, [it was] an opportunity for all Canadians to take part in this event. I had had the personal honour of being named Her Majesty's senior adviser during her [ensuing] visit to the United States, and had been made a member of Her Majesty's Imperial Privy Council."[14]

Diefenbaker then vigorously stated his reasons for supporting the Canadian Crown and Queen in the country's national life:

> I am a Canadian, first, last, and always, and to me the monarchy remains a vital force in the Canadian constitution. Not only is it the cornerstone of our institutional life, it remains a

highly functional and necessary office. The Queen, or in her absence, the Governor General, performs those many official and
social functions incumbent upon a head of state, thus relieving
the Prime Minister of many incredibly time-consuming duties.
More important are the prerogative powers of the Monarch to
be consulted, to advise, and to warn on all matters of state....
As prime minister I benefitted from [Her Majesty's] wisdom.[15]

In June 1962, Diefenbaker and his government were reduced to minority
status in the House of Commons. Some months later, in February 1963,
Diefenbaker was defeated on a non-confidence motion and a general election ensued. In April, Liberal leader Lester Pearson was elected as head of a
minority government.

Prime Minister Pearson would hold office for five years as the turbulent 1960s continued. Quebec was gripped by the changes wrought by the
Quiet Revolution, the FLQ began terror bombings in the province, and
youth everywhere questioned authority as never before. When it came to
the Crown in Canada, a prime minister — joined by Her Majesty — could
no longer count on an automatic acceptance of the monarchy from coast to
coast to coast. In Quebec, resistance to the Queen's role as the nation's head
of state climaxed during Her Majesty's visit to Quebec City in 1964.

The previous government had extended an invitation for the Queen
to visit Canada to help mark the hundredth anniversary of the Fathers of
Confederation gathering at Charlottetown and Quebec City in 1864. Upon
assuming office, it fell to Pearson to confirm the royal tour and his government to make the required preparations. Problems began immediately. As
Pearson wrote in his memoirs,

> The arrangements were found to be complicated; for Royal tours
> they always are. The problem was increased on this occasion,
> however, by the growing agitation of Quebec separatists against
> the visit as an insult to Quebec, an affront to their demand for
> freedom, a reminder of a colonial past and of an anglophone-
> dominated present. Threats against the Queen's safety and

threats to humiliate her were made and given wide publicity. Indeed, these threats were blown up by certain newspapers here and abroad to a point where Quebec was linked with Dallas [where John F. Kennedy had been assassinated], and such phrases as "awful risks," "flight into danger" were used to intimidate the government into advising cancellation of the visit.[16]

Such were the rising tensions and fears of officials that Pearson personally took part in four full meetings with the commissioner of the RCMP to go over Her Majesty's security arrangements. The British government even weighed in, asking Canada's prime minister if his government had in fact fully assessed the possible dangers to the Queen while in Canada.

The visit went ahead and Her Majesty arrived on Prince Edward Island on October 5, 1964. The Charlottetown Conference was duly celebrated the following day and the Queen also attended a gala performance in the provincial capital with the official opening of the Confederation Centre for the Arts. She then boarded HMY *Britannia* for the two-day journey to Quebec City. Her Majesty's program included her making public remarks at the Legislative Council Chamber of Quebec's Parliament and this event went off without a hitch. She also participated, at the Citadel, in ceremonies marking the fiftieth anniversary of the founding of the storied Royal 22nd Regiment. This, too, was a success. Then came the drive through the city, which had elicited much pre-visit concern. Riot police were everywhere. Students, many from Université Laval, protested by turning their backs as Her Majesty's motorcade drove by. One of the leaders of the youthful protest was a young law student who would, exactly twenty years later, almost to the day, become the Queen's seventh Canadian prime minister.

Brian Mulroney recalled the trouble he found himself in when his comments denouncing the royal visit, delivered in his role as spokesperson for the protesting students, were widely published in the Canadian press. "Then came the reaction"; he wrote:

"There seem to be too many bumptious, asinine people enrolled in universities," one angry monarchist from Toronto wrote to me at Laval. "Being an undergraduate seems to send a lot of them off the deep end. And we pay to keep the universities! Go and work your way through university the way I and countless others have done. Too many of your traitorous friends want all for nothing. People like you make universities 'stink.'" "I noticed your remarks concerning the tour of Her Majesty the Queen to this country," said another. "I think you ought to be ashamed of yourself for making such remarks. I would judge that you are a young, learned individual; you have a long way to go to improve yourself." Then came the kicker. "Many of us earn our way through university. Why the hell can't you? Of all the childish exhibitions, your publicity stunt takes the cake. Grow up!"[17]

It took almost a quarter-century for Her Majesty to visit Quebec City again. This time her host was Brian Mulroney, who in his memoirs reflected on the events of 1964, following an official dinner for the Queen. It was 1987:[18]

> I was honoured to host Her Majesty the Queen at a dinner at the Château Frontenac. It was the first time she had been there since her 1964 visit, and this trip had been tremendously successful. As I sat next to the Queen at dinner, I was proud to inform her that my father, an electrician, had wired the very room we were sitting in, decades earlier. Her Majesty was politely impressed. I did not get around to mentioning my inhospitable actions of 1964 to the Queen, and she never brought them up. Perhaps she wasn't aware of the role her future Canadian first minister had played. Perhaps not. But as anyone who has advised her knows full well, Her Majesty is always well briefed. Very well briefed.[19]

But Mulroney's reflections were still decades into the future. Prime Minister Pearson now had to deal with the aftermath of Her Majesty's controversial visit to Quebec City. The events caused him to consider serious questions about future royal visits to Canada: "We could no longer assume that the Monarch would receive a warm, popular welcome in all parts of Canada in all circumstances" he wrote in his memoirs. "In other words, a visit in the future to any part of Canada would have to be considered in the light of the political situation in every part of Canada."[20] Three years later, despite Her Majesty's successful visit to open Expo '67 in Montreal, Pearson began to question the very future of the monarchy in Canada. In London during the fall of 1967, he had extraordinary discussions with Her Majesty and with her veteran private secretary, Sir Michael Adeane. "I brought up with him the whole question of the monarchy in Canada and the changing attitude of Canadians, especially of younger Canadians to it," Pearson wrote.

> I emphasized that there was still a strong feeling of loyalty to the Crown in many quarters and, in all quarters, respect and admiration for the Queen ... But I thought that, apart from the general questioning of all established institutions by new generations, especially institutions that were old and seemed alien to a new and swiftly changing world, that was the anomaly that our very success in establishing the constitutional position as the Sovereign of Canada had backfired, in the sense that people would now argue that if she were really Queen of Canada, she should spend more time in Canada, should identify herself with the country in a more realistic way than by a visit every few years, or by being the object of a toast before every Rotary Club meeting or of an anthem before football games in Victoria or Halifax.[21]

Pearson then outlined a possible future for the monarchy's position in Canada:

> It might even be better to abandon these constitutional fictions and to consider the Queen as the sovereign of Britain, which she is, but also as Head of the Commonwealth, which she also is, rather than as an absentee monarch endeavouring, though with grace and dignity and charm, to live up to a designation which is theoretical rather than exact. This might mean that we would

theoretically become a republic, with a Canadian Head of State; there would be no formal relationship to the Crown, but an association with the Crown through ties of history and tradition and through the Commonwealth. These ties would ensure that, through the formal relationship would be with the Queen only as Head of the Commonwealth (as in India), in fact it would be closer than this and would encourage the same kinds of visits that now take place. But the reception of the Queen, which while as warm as ever in English-speaking Canada, would then be warmer in Quebec. I emphasized to Sir Michael that I was not proposing any such change and would do nothing to create discussion of it in Canada — which would undoubtedly be controversial, bitterly so in some areas. But I could see a trend towards this change, and believed we should be prepared for it. Adeane took all this very calmly and agreed that we should give thought to these matters. He knew that the Queen was knowledgeable about, and sensitive to, the currents of Canadian opinion.[22]

After this conversation with Adeane, Pearson then met privately with Her Majesty for thirty minutes. In his memoirs he doesn't tell us whether or not he planned to raise the issue of the future of the monarchy in Canada with the Queen. According to Pearson, however, she took matters into her own hands:

The Queen then asked me whether I would mind if she raised a rather delicate and difficult matter. I said that I would be flattered. So, on her own, she brought up the question of the monarchy in Canada as something that would, before long, have to be examined in depth. She was very anxious that the monarchy, or any controversy over it, should not become prejudicial to Canadian unity or a source of division. I was moved by her attitude and her sensitive understanding of the changing situation, and I talked with her for a time ... We left it at that, but it was very helpful to have had such an exchange of views.[23]

One cannot know if the Queen has ever raised this question privately with the prime ministers who followed Pearson.

Beginning in 1968, Her Majesty found herself with a new Canadian head of government, one who would serve her for sixteen years: Pierre Elliott Trudeau. A Quebec intellectual, Trudeau came to office with an attitude of pronounced indifference toward the Crown. But as he continued in office, his personal contacts with the Queen increased and so did his admiration for her.

In a confidential interview between Trudeau and author Ron Graham for use in his 1993 memoirs, published here for the first time, Trudeau discussed how impressive a figure Her Majesty was:

> As I got to meet the Queen, which we did at each Commonwealth meeting, she spent a short time, fifteen-twenty minutes, with each of us.... But when we'd come out of that meeting, each of us was amazed that she seemed to know a great deal about our respective countries and therefore, she certainly had the information and the ability to get it out of us by the kind of questions she asked. She obviously knew what she was, and the series would last, I suppose a day-and-a-half. So, it isn't as though she could spend a lot of time getting briefed on who's next coming in. She knew it well. And as I got to meet her on different occasions through my years in office, either through her visits here or my passages in Great Britain, or at other Commonwealth meetings, I had a feeling that she was pretty wise and I wondered if it was not more in her person than in the office itself. I mean, I'm not advocating that the monarchy should go on forever, but insofar as it was exercised by her, I thought that she was doing a pretty first-rate job.[24]

Prime Minister Justin Trudeau confirms his father's respect and admiration for Her Majesty: "I remember stories my father used to tell of conversations with her," he said. "I just grew up knowing that my father had a deep affection for and respect for the Queen and was happy whenever he got to see her."[25]

One of the most iconic photographs of the Pierre Trudeau era was taken on April 17, 1982, when the Queen signed the proclamation of the *Constitution Act* in a special ceremony on Parliament Hill. Trudeau's former principal secretary, Tom Axworthy, says Buckingham Palace, from the Queen on down, was an effective advocate for Canada when it came to securing approval from the British Parliament for passage of the act that attached the new Charter of Rights and Freedoms to Canada's Constitution.[26]

Almost a decade after leaving office, Pierre Trudeau still felt indebted to Her Majesty: "The Queen favoured my attempt to reform the constitution," he wrote. "I was always impressed not only by the grace she displayed in public at all times, but by the wisdom she showed in private conversation."[27]

Trudeau's successor, John Turner, during his short period as prime minister, famously flew to the United Kingdom to personally secure the Queen's permission to cancel her planned 1984 visit to Canada so the seventeenth prime minister could call an election. Although Her Majesty agreed, Turner and his party were defeated and Brian Mulroney took office.

Mulroney and the Queen developed a warm relationship over the ensuing nine years. On his watch, Her Majesty made four official tours of Canada. In addition, Canada's eighteenth prime minister held office during a period when the Commonwealth — and Canada — played an important role in the eventual end of South Africa's odious system of apartheid and the freeing of Nelson Mandela.

Mulroney says the Queen definitely sided with the wider Commonwealth, over Britain's Prime Minister Margaret Thatcher, on the issue: "She didn't say anything, but all you had to do was look at the body language. You wouldn't have to be too bright, I'll tell you, to read [Her Majesty's] body language [indicating her support for the battle against apartheid]."[28] These many years later, Mulroney still recalls the Queen's skill and knowledge: "She knew everything about everybody," he said. "I thought she was very smart and very well-informed and she had her own strong impressions about people."[29] Mulroney held office when international politics were dominated by larger-than-life figures such as U.S. President Ronald Reagan, Britain's Margaret Thatcher, the Soviet Union's Mikhail Gorbachev, and the newly freed Nelson Mandela. Canada's then prime minister says the Queen held a special place for him in that list of leaders: "She was right at the top," he said, "not for the power she wields, but for the person she was … Her institutional knowledge was formidable. This [her knowledge] was hard work, not something she could gain from a briefing note she read the night before a meeting. The Queen's knowledge was acquired over decades."[30]

During a private moment in 1991, Mulroney made a note to file confirming the mystery and majesty of the Canadian monarchy as personified by Queen Elizabeth: "Canada is a land of small contradictions and larger contrasts," he wrote. "A Roman Catholic prime minister swears allegiance to a sovereign who is also head of the Church of England and almost no one notices the irony. Few still would challenge it, and absolutely no one would consider changing it."[31] Mulroney was succeeded by Kim Campbell, who was then quickly followed by Jean Chrétien, a wily veteran who had served in the cabinets of both Lester Pearson and Pierre Trudeau. In those capacities he first met the Queen in 1967. Later, as Minister of Indian and Northern Affairs, he even accompanied Her Majesty, Prince Philip, Prince Charles, and Princess Anne on a multi-day tour through Canada's North: "Every day I travelled by plane for hours with the Queen and Prince Philip," Chrétien wrote, "and as the heir apparent never travels in the same plane as his mother, [my wife] Aline flew in another plane with Charles and Anne. The Queen preferred speaking French most of the time, which enabled her, she said, to practise her French."[32]

Chrétien's interactions with Her Majesty continued throughout his ministerial career under Pierre Trudeau. This was particularly the case during the debates concerning the project to repatriate Canada's Constitution. As he was prime minister for a decade (1993 to 2003), Chrétien's meetings with the Queen increased. It was he, for example, who welcomed Her Majesty to Canada when her Golden Jubilee was celebrated in 2002: "Canadians have been inspired by your abiding grace and dignity, by the dedication to ideals and duty that have so personified your life and by your never faltering commitment to others," he said movingly when she arrived in Nunavut that special year.[33]

After forty years of service to Canada, Chrétien left office in late 2003. Her Majesty publicly demonstrated her respect and affection for her ninth

Canadian prime minister in 2009 when she invested Chrétien with the Order of Merit, a personal honour only the monarch can bestow. He was only the third Canadian prime minister, after King and Pearson, to be so honoured. It was a fitting tribute.

Paul Martin then became the tenth prime minister to serve under the Queen. He had never met Her Majesty, but that changed in 2005 when the Queen visited Saskatchewan and Alberta to mark the hundredth anniversary of these provinces entering Confederation and Martin was granted a private audience. During their private discussion, held in Regina, Her Majesty raised a subject of great personal importance to Prime Minister Martin. Martin recalls,

> She said, "Tell me about the G20," and we got into a chat and we talked about why such international cooperation is so important. She was right on the money. It wasn't just a conversation with a Queen; it was a conversation with somebody who had a very strong view and, in my opinion, a correct view on foreign policy and how countries had to contribute … I pointed out that I thought that she was a real asset in that area and we then got into a long conversation about the need for [international] cooperation and she was right on top of it.[34]

In 2006, Martin was replaced by Stephen J. Harper. During his premiership, Canada, and the Commonwealth, marked Her Majesty's Diamond Jubilee in 2012. Harper, a serious student of Canadian history, recommended to the Queen that she appoint David Johnston as twenty-eighth governor general of Canada, after Harper directed the establishment of a detailed selection process. This would later be expanded to include all viceregal appointments with the creation of the Advisory Committee on Viceregal Appointments (abolished by his successor). These decisions have been widely celebrated across the political and academic spectrum.

Harper was gracious enough to grant a lengthy interview for this chapter and was asked to describe the "mechanics" of the relationship between a Canadian prime minister and the Queen: "I think it's important to say right off the bat what the big picture is," he said. "The big picture is that the monarchy in Canada, for all intents and purposes, is the governor general's office. In terms of the prime minister's dealing with the Crown on anything but occasions where the monarch is actually present, the governor general is the de facto Crown."[35] In fact, Harper noted that, in his experience, a prime minister designate receives no briefings from Privy Council officials and others in the public service with recommendations in this area. It is different, however, with regards to the governor general: "The governor general swears you in, so you get briefings certainly on that relationship and on the protocols around that relationship."[36] Harper went on to experience particularly warm encounters with Her Majesty. In fact, the Queen made what would become her final visit to Canada, in 2010, while Harper was prime minister. During his many audiences and private discussions with Her Majesty over his nine years in office, he found her a remarkable conversationalist and adviser, and someone he could trust implicitly.

"On the privy nature of the relationship, it really works two ways," Harper said. "You can consult her on anything, you can confess any weakness or misgiving [to] the Queen and never have any worry it is going to be communicated." When asked for specific examples, Harper, rightly, remains loyal and circumspect: "We had good conversations, that's all I'll say."[37] While not strictly in the Canadian context, Harper says that the Queen's Diamond Jubilee celebrations in London in June 2012, which he attended, were among the most personally rewarding aspects of his premiership:

> It was one of those rare times where I could be part of all those things, but the focus wasn't on me. I wasn't having to worry about holding press conferences. I could take part in everything at kind of the highest level, but actually enjoy just being part of the gallery. What was really moving, and I recall mentioning this to my cabinet afterwards, and I found it quite emotional, was the concert at Buckingham Palace. After performances by Sir Paul McCartney and others, they showed a film of the Queen's life as a young girl and becoming a princess, becoming Queen, and then her own family growing up. It really struck me; it was

really a demonstration of the power of monarchy, in the modern world, that properly constructed still and can very much matter. As you saw the Queen's life [played out on the large screens], particularly going from granddaughter to daughter, to Queen and to grandmother, they [the British audience in particular] were seeing their own life story in that. So, it really was a metaphor for everybody's family and for the nation's family, and there's a poetry to monarchy too that even the best constructed republics don't have. You could see how deeply woven that institution is in Britain, not just in the government, but in the very fabric of its society.[38]

Now, a decade later, as we celebrate the Queen's Platinum Jubilee, Her Majesty's service to Canada, as seen through the eyes of her Canadian prime ministers, remains one of the few constants over almost seven decades of Canadian political life. Though she is seen by many Canadians today as an absentee figurehead who lives an ocean away, the Queen's Canadian first ministers — from Louis St-Laurent to Justin Trudeau — tell a much different story. While some prime ministers might have come to office feeling the Queen's role was of little importance, each has left office profoundly respecting Her Majesty and valuing her counsel. Most importantly, our prime ministers have all learned first-hand of the Queen's profound commitment to Canadian unity and to Canada itself. Doubtless echoing the thoughts of all living past Canadian prime ministers, Justin Trudeau cannot imagine Canada without the Queen: "It's an impossible question. I can't go there in my mind. I won't go there in my mind. I can't think of that [Her Majesty's death] in any real substantive way. She just is. And she will be as long as possible, and I certainly hope she at least out-endures my entire tenure as prime minster, and I'm intending to stick around for many, many, more years."

# 11

# The Rise and Fall of French Canadian Loyalism

*Damien-Claude Bélanger*

It is easy to forget today that French Canadian thought once encompassed vigorous expressions of loyalty to Britain and to the Crown. Quebec historiography devotes little to no attention to French Canadian loyalism, and the doctrine's historical existence tends to raise eyebrows, even among historians. Certainly, loyalism has left little to no trace in contemporary debates.

To the extent that French Canadian loyalism has generated some scholarly discussion, debates have tended to centre specifically on the loyalty of the Roman Catholic Church. In the 1960s, some writers insisted that the Church had "collaborated" (a term that had acquired a very sinister connotation during the Second World War) with the British authorities in order to stifle Quebec's freedom.[1] In the context of the Quiet Revolution, these anticlerical charges found a ready audience. Scholars have since formulated a more nuanced vision of clerical loyalism. They tend to insist on its strategic dimension, arguing that the clergy cooperated with the British under duress, though some scholars also note that leading clerics often felt a strong affinity for monarchical government. Yvan Lamonde perhaps put it best when he wrote that the Roman Catholic Church followed a policy of loyalty "par conviction et par intérêt."[2]

Recent writing has pointed to the complexity of the loyalist phenomenon, which could be motivated as much by coercion as by sincere conviction. This chapter will develop this idea further by examining why loyalism emerged in French Canada, how its leading arguments became commonplace ideas, and why it eventually withered away. I also wish to examine the doctrine's various proponents, not merely those who wore a cassock.

In the context of French Canada, loyalty implies a faithfulness to the Crown. In the eighteenth and nineteenth centuries, it could be active, expressing itself through a willingness to uphold and defend British rule, or passive, which instead involved eschewing movements that sought to undermine British power. In this sense, both the *Canadiens* who fought against the invading Americans in 1775–1776 and those who merely refused to join or aid the rebels can equally be considered to have expressed their loyalty to the Crown.

Loyalism, by contrast, is a positive doctrine. It is the reasoned expression of the idea of loyalty and, in French Canada, it expressed a sincere devotion to the Crown, to British rule, and to British institutions. It rested first and foremost on the idea that the 1760 British Conquest of New France had been providential in nature, that it had been ordained by God, and that it had proven to be a fortunate event. Loyalists also reasoned that the British authorities acted with reasonable munificence, and that British political institutions were superior not only to the various republican systems that arose in continental Europe and the Americas, but also to those of pre-revolutionary France.

The nature and intensity of loyalism differed significantly in English- and French-speaking Canada. As Donal Lowry notes, French Canadians can be counted among the "ethnic outsiders" of the British Empire; their loyalism could not contain an ethnic and racial element, and its religious component could not be based on a shared faith.[3] French Canadians could participate in the British colonial project, but only in an ancillary sense, and they were ultimately far more likely to suffer than to perpetrate British colonialism. Yet expressions of loyalty to Britain were common in French

Canadian thought and writing for well over a century. Even Henri Bourassa, the consummate anti-imperialist, admired British institutions and regarded the British Conquest as ultimately beneficial for French Canada.

The Roman Catholic clergy were the first group in French Canada to formulate loyalist principles. They did this out of both conviction and pragmatism. Catholic doctrine advocates the submission to God's will and to legitimate authority. The Church interpreted the British Conquest as divinely ordained and, once it became apparent that London would not deport the Canadian population or outlaw Catholicism, the clergy began to preach submission to the British Crown. The clergy also viewed the power of the British authorities as divinely sanctioned. In Catholic doctrine, authority is sanctioned by God, and to refuse to submit to legitimate authority is to refuse submission to God.

Indeed, even before the formal cession of Canada, the higher clergy had called upon their flock to submit to British rule. In a *mandement* dated February 14, 1762, Jean-Olivier Briand, vicar-general and future bishop of Quebec, quoted from the Epistles of Peter and Paul, which would often be cited by the clergy to justify British rule. *"Le Dieu des armées qui dispose à son gré des couronnes,"* he wrote, had decided that Canada was to fall *"sous la domination de Sa Majesté Britannique."* He reminded his flock that Saint Peter, *"dans sa première Épître ordonne d'être soumis au Roi et à tous ceux qui participent à son autorité,"* and he noted that Saint Paul had called upon Christians to honour and respect their sovereigns. There was little doubt in Briand's mind that British rule was divinely ordained and thus legitimate, and he ordered that prayers for the king said during mass be amended to specifically refer to King George.[4]

But the clergy's loyalty also reflected the Catholic Church's vulnerability in the face of colonial power. After the Conquest, the institution's legal status was in limbo. The 1763 Treaty of Paris provided for the free exercise of the Roman Catholic faith in Canada, but only insofar as permitted by British law. The British governor interfered with clerical appointments, and various restrictions were placed on clerical recruitment and on relations with France and Rome. Moreover, the Church's title over its extensive property was not fully recognized by the colonial authorities. The clergy thus, in part, preached loyalty to Britain because it wished to ingratiate itself with the colonial authorities in the hope that London would eliminate or at least mitigate the various measures that constrained Catholicism in Quebec. Many clerics also reasoned that anything less than open loyalty would result in further constraints. They were aware that Catholics enjoyed greater religious freedom in the Province of Quebec than their co-religionists did in the United Kingdom, and they did not wish to see the full range of British anti-Catholic policies applied in Canada.

The clergy was quickly joined in its loyalist zeal by the seigneurial class. Some seigneurs opted to leave the colony after the Conquest, but those who chose to stay embraced British rule. *"Je suis destiné à vivre avec les Anglais,"* Michel-Gaspard Chartier de Lotbinière wrote to his father, *"mon bien-être est sous leur domination, je dépends entièrement d'eux, il est donc de ma politique de m'accommoder aux circonstances."*[5] Though his father had opted to return to France, the seigneur of Rigaud chose instead to stay in the colony and serve the British. He distinguished himself in the defence of Fort Saint-Jean during the American Revolution and would go on to become one of the leading political figures in Quebec.

Loyalism was integral to nascent French Canadian conservatism in the 1770s and would remain one of the hallmarks of conservative thought and writing in Quebec for over a century. It intensified after the 1774 *Quebec Act* expanded Catholic rights and granted legal recognition to the seigneurial system and would intensify further still during the American and French revolutions, when the advantages of British rule became more readily apparent to many conservative figures. It was assumed that British power protected Quebec from annexation and that the Conquest had spared the province the horrors of the French Revolution. Clerical loyalism in particular acquired a new dimension. It no longer simply reflected basic theological imperatives and strategic calculations; leading clerics increasingly regarded British power and institutions as a means to uphold a conservative and Catholic social order in Quebec.

The rise of Napoleon underscored the providential nature of the British Conquest to many observers. Clerics argued with increasing frequency that the Conquest was part of a divine plan to preserve Catholicism in Quebec.

The French, like the American rebels before them, were portrayed not only as the agents of political mayhem, but also as the agents of religious and social disorder. Increasingly, official clerical documents insisted on the protective nature of British rule.

However, as Jerry Bannister has noted, "loyalty to the Crown encompassed different political traditions" in British North America and it was not synonymous with reaction.[6] Indeed, by the turn of the nineteenth century, a liberal loyalism was fast developing among the French Canadian bourgeoisie and, for a time, a loyalist consensus characterized French Canada's middle and upper classes. The 1791 granting of representative government to Lower Canada helped to solidify this consensus. This reform, which was regarded as a fundamental British freedom, had been championed by leading French Canadian merchants and professionals for the better part of a decade. Liberal attachment to freedom and property, as well as to the rule of law and individual rights, was now partly expressed through the discourse of loyalty. Moreover, by this time, Quebec had become fully integrated into the British imperial economy. Defence spending and grain exports ensured that even Quebec's rural population experienced the economic benefits of British rule.

During the War of 1812, the protective nature of British rule was highlighted with great enthusiasm by various observers. British power was now regarded by leading clerics not only as integral to Lower Canadian order and stability but was also presented as a global force for order and righteousness, indeed as a bulwark against global radicalism. In an 1812 *mandement*, which was issued at the prompting of Governor General Prévost, Msgr. Joseph Octave Plessis of Quebec praised God for Lower Canada's status as a British possession:

> *Peut-être, Nos Très Chers Frères, qu'à nulle autre époque avant celle-ci, vous n'avez senti, comme vous le faites, combien la Divine Providence a été libérale envers vous, lorsqu'elle a permis que vous devinssiez sujets d'un gouvernement protecteur de votre sûreté, de votre religion, de vos fortunes; d'un gouvernement qui seul a su maintenir son honneur et sa gloire au milieu des débris de tous les*

*autres; d'un gouvernement auprès duquel les peuples opprimés, les souverains détrônés, les victimes sans nombre de l'ambition et de la perfidie d'un conquérant insatiable, viennent chercher un asile et des moyens de recouvrer leur liberté ravie ou de défendre le peu qu'il en reste.*[7]

French Canadian loyalty reached its high-water mark in the immediate aftermath of the War of 1812. The loyalist consensus formed in the previous generation held fast and embraced not only leading conservative figures but also reformers like Louis-Joseph Papineau. The young political leader eulogized George III in an 1820 speech to his voters. Since the advent of British rule, he exclaimed,

*Le règne des lois succède à celui de la violence: dès ce jour, les trésors, la marine et les armées de la Grande-Bretagne sont mis à contribution pour nous donner une protection invincible contre les dangers du dehors: dès ce jour, la meilleure partie de ses lois deviennent les nôtres, tandis que notre religion, nos biens, et les lois par lesquelles ils étoient gouvernés, restent intacts.*[8]

But the consensus could not hold. Papineau and his followers became increasingly disillusioned with Britain in the 1820s and 1830s. A bill introduced at Westminster in 1822 to unite Upper and Lower Canada into a single colony played a key role in radicalizing the reform movement. Papineau went to London in 1823 and successfully lobbied against the bill, but the experience shattered his illusions regarding Britain. In London, Papineau was exposed to the harsh realities of early nineteenth century British society, most notably to its gaping social inequalities, which shocked and appalled him. "*J'étais vraiment passablement bon sujet en Canada, sincère admirateur des Anglais et de leur gouvernement, mais j'y remarque tous les jours de si insupportables abus que j'y deviens assez mauvais sujet,*" he wrote to his wife Julie in July 1823. Papineau was also shocked to realize that the union bill garnered a great deal of support among British elites, whom he had hitherto assumed to be astute and liberally minded toward French Canada. On his return to Canada, he steadily abandoned the British political model in favour of that of the United States.[9] Papineau's abandonment of loyalism both presaged and fostered the radicalization of the Lower Canadian reform movement, which reached its summit in 1837 and 1838, when anticolonial rebellions occurred in the district of Montreal.

The Roman Catholic Church condemned the 1837–1838 rebels and refused them the sacraments. The Church had previously disapproved of the growing radicalism of the *patriotes*, who promoted the separation of church and state. Patriot radicalism brought the Church to collaborate ever more closely with the British, which, in turn, increasingly alienated the clergy from its flock. Loyalist sentiment in French Canada diminished significantly in the 1830s, as radicals depicted Britain as corrupt and oppressive, and it diminished further still after the British authorities suppressed the Lower Canada rebellions.

Even clerical loyalty diminished after the rebellions. This can be attributed, in part, to the 1840 *Act of Union*, which the clergy abhorred and lobbied against, but it was also a result of actions taken by the Special Council of Lower Canada, in the wake of the rebellions, that confirmed the title of the Church's extensive property. The intensity of loyalist sentiment diminished along with the Church's sense of vulnerability in the face of British power, but the sense of attachment to Britain did not disappear from clerical discourse until the twentieth century. The clergy continued to view British rule and, especially, British institutions, as bulwarks against radicalism and revolution.

The clergy was not isolated in its loyalism. Moderate reformers like Louis-Hippolyte Lafontaine and Étienne-Paschal Taché, who had refused to follow Papineau down the road to armed conflict, continued to praise British forms of government in the 1840s. They laid the groundwork for the emergence of the Conservative party in French Canada and found themselves called to cabinet once Britain granted responsible government to the Province of Canada.

The advent of responsible government in 1848 removed a significant inducement to loyalism — most offices no longer required official British patronage — but conservative figures could now boast that Canada enjoyed the full extent of British representative government. The colony also enjoyed the benefits of British preferential trade until the late 1840s, when the advent of free trade in Britain forced Canada to seek expanded commercial opportunities in the United States.

Clerical loyalism intensified during the turbulent 1860s, when annexation and the possibility of American aggression brought many clerics to acclaim Canada's imperial ties and to support Confederation. "*Des institutions républicaines ne nous iraient pas mieux qu'au grand peuple dont nous descendons, les Français!*" exclaimed Msgr. Charles Larocque, bishop of Saint-Hyacinthe and one of the most enthusiastic supporters of Confederation among the higher clergy, in an 1867 pastoral letter. As such, he continued,

> *Défions-nous de ces esprits inquiets, de ces journaux à principes plus qu'équivoques, qui font si bon marché de la religion et de la patrie, et qui prennent pour des réalités les rêves de liberté, de gloire et de bonheur qu'ils croiraient goûter en passant sous la bannière étoilée: comme si les droits, les immunités et les privilèges dont nous jouissons sous le drapeau britannique, nous laissaient quelque chose à envier aux peuples les plus libres de la terre, politiquement, civilement et même religieusement parlant!*[10]

Larocque's loyalism and support for Confederation reflected his fear of annexation, but they also expressed a fervent opposition to radicalism. In the Province of Canada, republicanism was expressed by the *Parti rouge*, which had been formed by radical elements of the reform movement in the late 1840s. The Roman Catholic Church condemned the *rouges* and regarded British institutions, and most notably the Crown, as bulwarks against radicalism.

Nevertheless, by creating a provincial state in which French Canadians controlled the major levers of political power, Confederation somewhat lessened the utility of loyalist discourse. Executive power in Quebec was vested in a lieutenant governor who was invariably French Canadian, and yet loyalism remained strong among French Canadian elites. It continued to play an important role in nurturing relations with English-speaking Canadians and it reflected the continued importance of British trade and investment to Quebec's economy.

The late nineteenth century also witnessed the re-emergence of liberal loyalism in French Canada, as Wilfrid Laurier sought to reorient the Liberal party toward British liberalism and to marginalize the party's republican wing, which was hostile to monarchy and clericalism. In his youth, Laurier had been sympathetic to *rougisme*, but by the late 1870s he actively sought to forge a moderate party that could accommodate itself to the political and religious status quo. In a landmark speech given in Montreal, Laurier insisted that he regarded Britain as "*la terre classique de la liberté*," that his "*libéralisme politique*" was essentially British in inspiration, and that a monarchical system of government was in no way incompatible with liberty.[11]

Laurier's efforts to marginalize his party's *rouge* wing bore fruit and by the early twentieth century most French Canadian Liberals embraced constitutional monarchy. Republicanism, which had once presented a major challenge to the Catholic Church and to British rule, was now more or less a spent force. The disappearance of a strong republican movement in early twentieth century Quebec played an important role in the decline of loyalism. Without a vigorous radical challenge, the clergy and conservative elites no longer sought a counter-revolutionary bulwark in British rule and in British political institutions. Debate surrounding the nature of political institutions diminished significantly in Quebec and loyalism lost much of its relevance.

The deathblow to loyalism occurred, however, because of rising imperialist sentiment in Canada and Great Britain in the late nineteenth and early twentieth centuries. The French Canadian press had generally praised British imperialism before the 1890s. Nevertheless, Britain's repeated calls for military assistance, which began during the South African War and were loudly echoed in English-speaking Canada, were regarded by many French Canadians as disruptive of the imperial status quo. Britain's standing as a benevolent protector increasingly waned among French Canadian elites. Quebec's modern nationalist movement was born during the debate surrounding Canada's participation in the South African War, 1899 to 1902.

The rise in imperialist sentiment was accompanied, moreover, by a move-ment outside Quebec to suppress French and Catholic education. Sectarian and language tensions increased significantly at the turn of the twentieth century and French Canadian appeals for British "fair play" were often re-buffed with calls for Canada to fully embrace its British destiny. Aggressive and exclusionary notions of Britishness had undermined loyalist assertions in French Canada since the late eighteenth century, but their sheer intensity now threatened loyalism's political sustainability.

Increasingly, leading French Canadians began to focus their loyalty on the Crown at the expense of the Empire.[12] Henri Bourassa, for instance, praised British forms of government, but denounced imperialism as a betray-al of British notions of liberty. In 1914, he tentatively supported Canada's participation in the First World War, though he soon reversed his stance. Bourassa's tentative support for participation was partly motivated by a pastoral letter issued by the French Canadian bishops and archbishops in September 1914. In this letter, the clergy lamented the outbreak of war, but noted that it was Canada's duty to come to Britain's aid:

> *Nous ne saurions nous le dissimuler: ce conflit, l'un des plus terribles que le monde ait encore vu, ne peut manquer d'avoir sa répercussion sur notre pays. L'Angleterre y est engagée, et qui ne voit que le sort de toutes les parties de l'Empire se trouve lié au sort de ses armes? Elle compte à bon droit sur notre concours, et ce concours, Nous sommes heureux de le dire, lui a été généreusement offert en hommes et en argent.*[13]

The government of Sir Robert Borden had lobbied the clergy to make a statement in support of participation, and the ensuing document marked one of the last major milestones in the history of French Canadian loyalism. The subsequent crisis surrounding conscription frayed Anglo-French rela-tions in Canada and battered loyalist assumptions. Loyalism never recovered from the events of the Great War, and the subsequent decline of British trade and investment further diminished the doctrine's relevance, as did the advent of Canadian independence.

French Canadian loyalism did not disappear in the 1920s, however. Senator Thomas Chapais published his monumental *Cours d'histoire du Canada*, which updated the idea of a providential conquest, during the interwar years. But Chapais's thesis regarding British rule, which would have been generally accepted at the turn of the century, now generated a great deal of criticism, most notably from a rising nationalist movement led by Abbé Lionel Groulx.

French Canadian political leaders occasionally trotted out loyalist platitudes during royal visits in the 1950s, but even that had ceased by the Quiet Revolution. In the meantime, loyalism's role as a doctrine favourable to the political status quo had been assumed by federalism. Loyalism did not transform itself into federalism, but the two doctrines rested upon similar reasoning and drew support from similar sources: the business community, the military, Laval University, French-language minority groups, etc.

For over a century, French Canadian loyalists articulated a vision of Britishness that was essentially civic in character. Henri Bourassa, for instance, was fond of referring to Canada as a "British community," by which he meant that the Dominion was an (Anglo-French) state whose fundamental institutions and liberties were British in nature. He believed, moreover, that "the very basis of our British institutions" rested not on racial or religious precepts, but rather on the idea "that there shall be perfect equality before the law for all nationalities and for all religions."[14] This conception of Britishness was not widely shared among English-speaking Canadians, who tended to regard Canada's status as a "British community" as implying that the Dominion was to be a Protestant and English-speaking nation whose leading citizens should be of British birth or ancestry. This logic was deployed relentlessly during the Jesuit Estates controversy, and also during the schools crises in Manitoba and Ontario, so that by the end of the First World War it had become painfully evident in Quebec that civic notions of Britishness were not likely to prevail in Canada. Loyalist sentiment withered accordingly.

Loyalism was a complex phenomenon. It responded to numerous factors, including the importance of British trade and investment to Quebec's economy. It was primarily a doctrine of the middle and upper classes, though royal visits and celebrations could certainly generate enthusiasm among the general population. Even among Catholic clerics, loyalism appears to have been more intense among the upper clergy than among ordinary parish priests. Loyalist sentiment also appears to have been stronger in the Quebec City region than in the Montreal area, likely for reasons related to Quebec City's stronger economic ties to Britain, but also because of its more moderate political and intellectual culture.

Loyalism and nationalism could go hand in hand. Quebec's Catholic Church, for instance, issued loyalist *mandements* while simultaneously resisting British attempts to assimilate the local population. In some loyalist texts, praise for Britain was sometimes followed by scorn for British colonists. Indeed, some of the greatest threats to loyalist sentiment in French Canada resided in the actions of Canada's Protestant and English-speaking population.

As C.A. Bayly noted, "the creation of colonies was never simply a question of domination. It involved a long process of political dialogue, of challenge and response, and of accommodation."[15] Loyalism played a key role in fostering the wider adaptation of French Canadians to British rule and, especially, to British institutions. British power and institutions were accepted, indeed often embraced, because they served the interests of various groups within French Canadian society. For the Roman Catholic Church, loyalism was strategic, reflecting the institution's vulnerability in the face of British power, but it also proceeded from genuine belief. Many ultra-loyalist *mandements* were issued at the prompting of the British authorities, to be sure, but the available evidence generally indicates that these requests were acceded to with enthusiasm and that their content was sincere. And the depth of this sincerity becomes more evident after the Special Council of Lower Canada solidified the legal status of Church property and again when responsible government significantly diminished the power of the British authorities over Canadian affairs. The bishops of Quebec were not compelled to issue calls for loyalty in the 1860s; they did so because they genuinely believed that British power and institutions had become integral to the preservation of Quebec's Catholic social order.

If loyalism emerged because British power was found to serve the interests of various groups within French Canada, the doctrine correspondingly declined when Britain threatened or became irrelevant to those same groups. The reformists of the *Parti canadien* championed British rule in the wake of the 1791 granting of representative government, but their radical heirs, the *patriotes* of the 1830s, denounced Great Britain when the colonial authorities refused to move forward on further reform. Likewise, the Roman Catholic Church celebrated the British Conquest in the eighteenth and nineteenth centuries when radicals posed a real threat to established order, but once the republican menace faded away in the early twentieth century, the need to praise monarchical government diminished accordingly.

Loyalism died a very slow death, which speaks to its longstanding relevance within French Canadian thought. It did eventually disappear, however, because it had become politically, economically, and socially irrelevant. It also disappeared because it had become symbolically irrelevant. Loyalism expressed a desire among French Canadian elites for Quebec to find a place within the British Empire. In this effort, however, loyalists advocated a vision of Britishness that was doomed to fail — not because it did not appeal to ordinary French Canadians, which it did, but because their English-speaking fellow citizens did not embrace it.

# 12

# Royal Tours of Canada in the Reign of Queen Elizabeth II

*Carolyn Harris*

Over the course of her seventy-year reign, Queen Elizabeth II has visited Canada more than any other country outside the United Kingdom. From the opening of Parliament in 1957 to the celebration of Canada Day on Parliament Hill in 2010, the Queen has undertaken twenty-two official visits to Canada. The Queen was accompanied on her official visits by her consort Prince Philip, Duke of Edinburgh (1921–2021), who also carried out official and working visits on his own, travelling to Canada more than seventy times from the opening of the British Empire and Commonwealth Games in Vancouver in 1954 to the presentation of new colours to the 3rd Battalion of the Royal Canadian Regiment in 2013. Queen Elizabeth the Queen Mother visited Canada on fourteen occasions during her daughter's reign, building on the popular goodwill that she received during the 1939 royal tour with King George VI, the most successful Canadian royal tour in history. The Prince of Wales has visited Canada eighteen times over the past fifty-two years and founded the Prince's Charities Canada (now the Prince's Trust Canada) in 2011. The Queen's children, grandchildren, great-grandchildren, and extended family have also spent time in Canada in both official and personal capacities, strengthening the relationship between the Crown and Canadian institutions, charities, and the Canadian Armed Forces.[1]

The length, structure, press coverage, and popular responses to royal tours have changed significantly over the past seventy years, reflecting innovations in travel and transport, the changing composition of the royal family over successive generations, new developments in Canadian politics, culture, and society, and increased debate concerning the future of the monarchy in Canada during the late twentieth and early twenty-first centuries. Through all these changes, however, royalty on tour in Canada during Queen Elizabeth II's reign continued to follow precedents set by royal tours in previous reigns, including principal appointments in the Canadian Armed Forces as colonel-in-chief and similar positions, patronage of philanthropic institutions, engagement with Indigenous Peoples, meeting Canadians from a wide variety of backgrounds, and engaging with Canadian landscapes, sports, and pastimes. Royal tours in subsequent reigns will probably take place less frequently because there will be fewer members of the royal family undertaking public engagements, but future tours will continue to build on the changes and continuities from the current reign.

## HISTORICAL PRECEDENTS

Royal tours in the reign of Queen Elizabeth II have followed certain precedents set by royalty who visited Canada in previous reigns. As early as the reign of Queen Victoria, royalty were expected by the Canadian press and public alike to behave differently in Canada than they did in the United Kingdom, embracing a greater degree of informality in their engagement with the public and joining in Canadian outdoor sports and pastimes.[2] When Queen Elizabeth II dropped the puck at a National Hockey League game in Vancouver in 2002, as a gold royal cypher, *E II R*, appeared on the

Jumbotron above the "I am Canadian" Molson Canadian beer logo, the event was "dubbed in advance the most imaginative moment of the 12-day Golden Jubilee tour across Canada."[3] There were clear historical precedents, however, for the Queen's engagement with an ice hockey game, including the tobogganing and curling parties hosted by Queen Victoria's daughter Princess Louise and her husband the Marquis of Lorne during Lorne's term as governor general of Canada from 1878 to 1883, and the future King George V's watching a lacrosse game and participating in a duck hunt during the 1901 royal tour. These events allowed the public to view the royal family in a Canadian context and place their activities in the context of Canadian culture.

There are also elements of continuity in the itineraries of royal tours from the first royal visits to Canada to the present day. The earliest royal tours of what is now Canada were late-eighteenth-century periods of naval or military service by King George III's sons, the future King William IV and Prince Edward, Duke of Kent and Strathearn, who eventually became the father of Queen Victoria.[4] Military parades and commemorations of key military engagements have remained central to the itineraries of royal tours during the present Queen's reign. In 2014 alone, the Princess Royal (Princess Anne) made an official visit to Ottawa with her husband, Vice Admiral Sir Timothy Laurence, to rededicate the National War Memorial, and the Prince of Wales and the Duchess of Cornwall toured Canada to commemorate the hundredth anniversary of the First World War.

The Queen, Prince Philip, and their children have all served as colonels-in-chief of Canadian military units over the course of the Queen's reign. Principal appointments in the Canadian Armed Forces also involve the Queen's extended family, including cousins and more distant relatives who were not full-time working members of the royal family in the United Kingdom at the time of their Canadian tours. In September 1964, Queen Victoria's granddaughter Lady Patricia Ramsay, formerly Princess Patricia of Connaught, who had resided in Canada while her father, Prince Arthur, Duke of Connaught, served as governor general from 1911 to 1916, made an official visit to Edmonton for the fiftieth anniversary of Princess Patricia's Canadian Light Infantry Regiment.[5] This tour was notable because Patricia had relinquished her royal title and stepped back from royal duties after her marriage to Captain Alexander Ramsay in 1919. Her Canadian regiment was one of the few royal patronages she retained after this retirement from public life.

Engagement with Canadians from a wide variety of backgrounds has been a constant feature of royal tours for more than two hundred years. King George III's sons and Queen Victoria's eldest son, the future King Edward VII, toured British North America as unmarried princes, which limited the number of events that included women. Subsequent Canadian tours by Princess Louise and Lord Lorne, the future King George V and Queen Mary, and King George VI and Queen Elizabeth allowed for more addresses from women and opportunities for charities benefiting women to receive visits and patronage from female members of the royal family.[6]

The introduction of cross-country royal train tours provided more opportunities for members of the royal family to meet with Canadians from a variety of social backgrounds, as whole communities gathered at train stations to welcome the royal visitors. Canadian artist C.W. Jeffries, who created newspaper illustrations during the 1901 royal tour, later recalled the future King George V and Queen Mary visiting a lumber camp outside Ottawa and enjoying a meal of pork and beans with French Canadian lumberjacks.[7] These opportunities to converse with working Canadians in 1901 anticipated the royal couple's visits to British working-class neighbourhoods after King George V's accession in 1910.[8] King George VI and Queen Elizabeth (the Queen Mother) began the tradition of royal walkabouts when they joined a crowd of First World War veterans at the National War Memorial in Ottawa during the 1939 royal tour.[9] Queen Elizabeth II's revival of this tradition during her reign has allowed members of the royal family to meet Canadians from all social backgrounds.

Despite the British Imperial context for early royal tours, there were opportunities for members of the royal family to meet with people from a variety of cultural backgrounds, setting precedents for modern royal tours. Princess Louise and Lord Lorne met with Indigenous people and Chinese Canadians during the first-ever royal tour of British Columbia in 1882.[10] The future King George V and Queen Mary also met with Indigenous leaders as they travelled westward by train, and received an address from the descendants of Black Loyalists in Halifax in 1901.[11] Queen Elizabeth II's Canadian tours have included opportunities to engage with Canadians from diverse cultural backgrounds. For example, the Queen marked the 150th anniversary of the incorporation of the City of Toronto in 1984 by visiting a variety of neighbourhoods, including a walkabout in Little Italy.[12] In a 1973 speech delivered at an official dinner at Toronto's Royal York Hotel, the Queen emphasized the role of the monarch as a unifying figure in multicultural Canada, stating, "It is as Queen of Canada that I am here — Queen of Canada and of all Canadians, not just of one or two ancestral strains. I would like the Crown to be seen as a symbol of national sovereignty, a link between Canadian citizens of every national origin and ancestry."[13] The Queen reinforced this sentiment at Canada Day celebrations in Ottawa in 1977, stating, "The diversity of the country and people never fails to amaze me. In that diversity there lies much strength."[14]

The younger generations of the royal family have built upon this theme of engaging with Canadians from diverse backgrounds and their concerns. During the Prince of Wales's 1998 Canadian tour, he marked the International Day for the Elimination of Racial Discrimination.[15] Royalty have also played a role in welcoming newcomers to British North America and then Canada from the late eighteenth century to the present. The first royal tour of Upper Canada, in what is now Ontario, by Prince Edward, Duke of Kent and Strathearn, in 1792 included visits to newly founded Loyalist communities. In 2011, the Duke and Duchess of Cambridge became the first royal couple to attend a citizenship ceremony, presenting twenty-five new Canadians with Canadian flags.[16] The comparative informality of royal tours of Canada has allowed royalty to engage with a diverse cross-section of society for centuries. Royalty on tour in Canada during Queen Elizabeth II's reign have built upon these historical precedents to emphasize the importance of a Canadian Crown that represents all Canadians.

PERSPECTIVES ON THE CROWN IN CANADA

## ROYAL TOURS AT KEY MOMENTS IN CANADIAN HISTORY

While comparatively informal interactions with the public, distinctive elements of Canadian culture, military parades, and engagement with Canadians from all backgrounds and walks of life have remained key aspects of royal tours of Canada from previous reigns to the present, the circumstances of planning of a royal tour changed with the accession of Queen Elizabeth II in 1952. Prior to the Queen's reign, royal tours of Canada were shaped by conditions in the wider British Empire and Dominions or unfolded within the context of a royal couple's extended residence in Canada through a viceregal appointment. Queen Victoria was invited by the Province of Canada to open the Victoria Bridge in Montreal,[17] but the eventual tour by her eldest son, the future King Edward VII, on her behalf in 1860 also reflected the British government's acknowledgement of Canadian contributions to the Crimean War (1853–1856).[18] The future King George V requested the addition of Canada to his round-the-world tour in 1901 in the aftermath of the Boer War, writing to British Prime Minister Lord Salisbury, "Please ask the Queen [Victoria] whether we can visit Canada on our way home from Australia. She is averse to it owing to our long absence from England. But we think it would cause great disappointment and perhaps jealousy."[19] The 1939 royal tour was planned following the *Statute of Westminster, 1931* as the first visit to Canada by a reigning sovereign and consort; but the timing of the tour just before the outbreak of the Second World War gave it additional diplomatic significance, strengthening Anglo-Canadian relations just before the outbreak of hostilities.

In contrast, royal tours during the reign of Queen Elizabeth II have reflected distinctly Canadian concerns. In his analysis of the 1959 royal tour, Philip Buckner noted, "Neither the brief 1957 visit (which was tacked on to a visit to the United States) nor the lengthy 1959 tour had any particular imperial significance, or for that matter served any specific need of British foreign policy ... It was the Canadian government — not the British government — that wanted the [1959] tour."[20] The Queen has been present for key events in Canadian history over the past seventy years, including the opening of the St. Lawrence Seaway in 1959, the centennial of Canadian Confederation in 1967, the Montreal Olympic Games in 1976, and the patriation of the Constitution in 1982. Royal tours in the reign of Queen Elizabeth II have also commemorated anniversaries of historic milestones, such as the 1970 tour by the Queen, Prince Philip, Prince Charles, and Princess Anne to mark the one hundredth anniversary of the Province of Manitoba and the 1983 tour by the Prince and Princess of Wales to mark the two hundredth anniversary of the arrival of the United Empire Loyalists to British North America in the aftermath of the American Revolution. The Queen's reign has also seen royal milestones celebrated in a Canadian context, with tours by the Queen and Prince Philip to mark the Silver Jubilee in 1977 and the Golden Jubilee in 2002 and a tour by the Prince of Wales and the Duchess of Cornwall to mark the Diamond Jubilee in 2012. Since the Queen's official birthday in Canada coincides with the Victoria Day holiday, Victoria Day weekend has become a popular time for royal tours, especially those that mark royal milestones.

In her roles as Queen of Canada and Head of the Commonwealth, the Queen has exerted subtle influence during her time in Canada. In addition to her support of Canadian multiculturalism, she has delivered several speeches in support of Canadian federalism that attracted extensive press coverage. In 1964, during a controversial tour where the monarch's presence was protested by supporters of Quebec sovereignty, she delivered a speech in French to the provincial legislature in Quebec City, emphasizing Quebec's proud history and place within Canada. During her Silver Jubilee tour, the Queen delivered a speech broadcast on television where she stated that "The Confederation itself was not a French idea or a British idea." The *New York Times* interpreted this broadcast as the Queen lending "her immense prestige to the effort of Prime Minister Pierre Elliott Trudeau's Government to keep the country united in the face of a separatist threat by the largely French-speaking province of Quebec."[21]

Canada was crucial to the development of the Queen's role as Head of the Commonwealth, a position that she inherited from King George VI upon her accession in 1952. A formal invitation from Prime Minister Pierre Trudeau allowed the Queen to attend the 1973 Commonwealth Heads of

Government Meeting (CHOGM) in Ottawa without the necessity of consulting the British Government, which had discouraged the Queen from attending the inaugural CHOGM in Singapore two years previously.[22] The Queen's presence set a precedent for her prominent role in future CHOGMs, where she was able to foster a rapport between Commonwealth leaders and work with them to address a variety of issues, including sanctions against the apartheid regime in South Africa.[23] The Queen continued to lend her "immense prestige" to the support of Canadian unity and multiculturalism even as royal tours became shorter and more focused on individual regions of Canada.

## THE EVOLUTION OF THE CANADIAN ROYAL TOUR

Queen Elizabeth II's reign witnessed a major change in the format of royal tours from rail travel to air travel, which allowed for more frequent royal tours and the inclusion of remote communities in Canada's north in royal tour itineraries. After the Duke and Duchess of Connaught travelled across Canada by train in 1890, train travel was a central aspect of Canadian royal tours, and a royal visit also served as opportunity to showcase the Canadian Pacific Railway and the wide scope of Canadian landscapes and communities from the Atlantic to the Pacific oceans. The future King George V and Queen Mary in 1901 and King George VI and Queen Elizabeth in 1939 crossed Canada twice by train during their respective tours and the royal train became a key symbol of royal tours of Canada.[24]

During the 1950s, royal tours of Canada combined train travel and air travel. The future Queen Elizabeth II and Prince Philip were the first royal couple to arrive in Canada by air, on their first official tour of Canada, in 1951, representing King George VI. Photographs of the royal couple at the airport cemented their image as representatives of a modern monarchy, an image reinforced by comparatively informal moments on the tour, such as Princess Elizabeth and Prince Philip square dancing at Rideau Hall (an image that became a popular Canadian Christmas card design) and Prince Philip wearing a white stetson hat to the Calgary Stampede. The forty-five day 1959 royal tour, the longest Canadian royal tour of the Queen's reign, was the last to include a train journey across the country. By 1959, flights and automobile journeys, as well as the royal yacht *Britannia* (decommissioned in 1997), were already central to Commonwealth tours and it was clear that the long train journeys of the first half of the twentieth century would not be repeated. Prince Philip commented at a press reception on *Britannia* that "the Palace was wondering whether big royal tours really had outlived their usefulness and ought to be replaced by shorter, more focused regional events," comments that were widely reported in the press and heralded a significant change in the length and scope of Canadian royal tours.[25]

The modern royal tour is far shorter than the cross-country train journeys of 1901, 1939, and 1959, usually lasting less than two weeks, in the case of a major tour such as the Golden Jubilee tour by the Queen and Prince Philip in 2002 or the Duke and Duchess of Cambridge's first overseas tour as a married couple in 2011, or even just a few days, as in the case of the Prince of Wales and the Duchess of Cornwall's Diamond Jubilee tour in 2012 and celebration of the 150th anniversary of Canadian confederation in 2017. These changes to the structure of Canadian royal tours have resulted in significant innovations unique to the reign of Queen Elizabeth II. Over the course of the past seventy years, there have been royal visits to Yukon, the Northwest Territories, and Nunavut that would have been unimaginable in previous reigns, when the itinerary was shaped by the railway. Short-haul flights to the territories have allowed the royal family to expand their engagement with Indigenous people and include events showcasing Inuit culture. Prince Philip travelled extensively in Yukon and the Northwest Territories in 1954.[26] In 1970 the Queen and Prince Philip and their two eldest children, Prince Charles and Princess Anne, undertook a historic tour of communities in the Northwest Territories and what is now Nunavut, which had never before received a royal visit. The Queen visited the new territory of Nunavut on her Golden Jubilee tour, where Inuit children sang "God Save the Queen" in Inuktitut,[27] and the Prince of Wales and Duchess of Cornwall began their 2017 tour for Canada's sesquicentennial in Iqaluit.

The Queen's reign has also seen the emergence of clear distinctions between official visits by the monarch, the heir to the throne, and the second in line to the throne, and private and working visits by members of the Queen's extended family with connections to Canadian regiments, philanthropic organizations, or cultural institutions. Private visits to Canada by members of the royal family have taken place since the nineteenth century. Princess Louise and Lord Lorne, Duke and Duchess of Connaught, and the Earl and Countess of Athlone all received visits from other members of the royal extended family during their periods of residence at Rideau Hall. Queen Elizabeth II's grandchildren continue to make private visits to Canada. Princesses Beatrice and Eugenie attended the Toronto Film Festival with their mother in 2008, attending a screening of *The Young Victoria*, a film co-produced by the Duchess of York, in which Princess Beatrice has a cameo role. Prince Harry also made private visits to Toronto to visit his future wife, the actress Meghan Markle, who lived in Canada while filming the television series *Suits*.

A distinction between official visits and working visits emerged early in Queen Elizabeth II's reign, shaped by Prince Philip's diverse array of military appointments and philanthropic patronages in Canada. While Prince Philip almost always accompanied the Queen on her official visits to Canada, he also undertook numerous working visits in his capacity as colonel-in-chief of Canadian regiments and patron of the World Wildlife Fund and the Duke of Edinburgh's Award program. Commonwealth study conferences were another impetus for his solo working visits to Canada. Since the 1990s, the Queen, the Prince of Wales, and the Duke of Cambridge have undertaken official visits organized at the federal level, while other members of the royal family mostly undertake working visits organized at the provincial level in conjunction with their patronages. While working visits receive limited press coverage, with occasional high-profile exceptions such as Prince Harry's and Meghan Markle's first public appearance together, at the Invictus Games in Toronto in 2017, official visits to Canada by senior members of the royal family often prompt discussion and debate concerning the future of the monarchy in a Canadian context.

## DEBATING THE MONARCHY

Throughout the Queen's reign, the presence of members of the royal family in Canada has prompted discussion and debate concerning the popularity of the monarchy in Canada and the future of the Canadian Crown. Prior to the current reign, critical press coverage of Canadian involvement in British imperial objectives was usually careful to exempt the Crown and members of the royal family from censure. Instead, Canadians were encouraged to engage with visiting royalty on their own terms. In 1939, *La Presse* criticized the displays of British flags and decorations in Quebec as "imperialistic propaganda" and instead placed the royal tour by King George VI and Queen Elizabeth in a French Canadian context, stating, "Why don't we, French Canadians, profit from the occasion to manifest our loyalty and attachment to our sovereigns, certainly, but also to our language, our nationality, our rights, our ethnic character. If we must have inscriptions, let them be worded in French, if we cheer, cheer in French."[28] King George VI and Queen Elizabeth were well received in Quebec, as the 1939 royal tour had the support of key French Canadian political and religious leaders and the Crown was perceived as a guarantor of the French language, the Roman Catholic Church, and Quebec Civil Law, dating back to the *Quebec Act* of 1774 during the reign of King George III. This positive attitude toward royal tours declined during the reign of Queen Elizabeth II, which witnessed periods of hostility and comparative indifference to the presence of royalty in Quebec.

The nature of debates concerning the monarchy changed during Queen Elizabeth II's reign, as questions were raised in press coverage of royal tours concerning the degree of Canadian support for the monarchy and the future of the institution beyond the present reign. Canadian debates concerning the royal image and the future of the monarchy over the course of the Queen's reign fall into three broad categories: responses to existing critiques in the United Kingdom, press coverage of critical comments by prominent Canadians, and analysis of polling data in the aftermath of Canadian tours. An early example of British criticism of the royal image appearing in

Canadian media coverage of one of the Queen's tours occurred in 1957, when the Queen visited Ottawa for the first time as sovereign, to open Parliament and read the speech from the throne. This tour also included a televised address to the Canadian people. *Maclean's Magazine* reported, "When Elizabeth II faces Canadian television cameras in Ottawa on October 13 the object of millions in her audience will be to determine whether Lord Altrincham was right when he said last August that her speeches give the listener 'a pain in the neck.'"[29] British criticism of members of the royal family also shaped Canadian press coverage of royal tours during the 1990s, when the breakdowns of the marriages of three of the Queen's four children prompted newspaper columns to predict that the Queen would be Canada's last monarch. A 1994 editorial in the *Globe and Mail* concluded, "Long Live the Queen; may the next head of state be a Canadian Governor-General,"[30] the same year that the Queen and Prince Philip toured Canada, opening the Commonwealth Games in Victoria.

Popular debates concerning the importance and future of the monarchy in Canada have also been prompted by prominent Canadian journalists and political figures commenting on Canadian royal tours. In 1959, CBC journalist Joyce Davidson remarked on an American television program, NBC's *Today*, that she was "pretty indifferent" to the royal tour and that these sentiments were typical of "the average Canadian."[31] Her remarks were condemned by prominent Canadians at the time. Toronto Mayor Nathan Phillips stated that Davidson "doesn't represent Canadians or the people of Toronto."[32] A similar controversy occurred during Queen Elizabeth II's Golden Jubilee tour in 2002, when Deputy Prime Minister John Manley remarked just before the arrival of the Queen and Prince Philip in Canada that "I continue to think that for Canada after Queen Elizabeth, it should be time to consider a different institution for us, and personally I would prefer a wholly Canadian institution."[33] Although critical attitudes toward the monarchy in Canada were more widespread in 2002 than 1959, Manley's comments were criticized by the press and public in Canada because he was the official escort for the tour. Despite the controversy surrounding the comments of Davidson in 1959 and Manley in 2002, royal tours of Canada continue to prompt critical commentary in the press concerning the future of popular support for the royal family in subsequent reigns.

In the aftermath of Canadian royal tours, there are often polls intended to measure popular support for the monarchy. The responses to these polls vary by province and by the wording of the question. For example, polling data shows lower support for the monarchy in Quebec and when the question focuses on royal finances. The polling data shows higher support for the monarchy, however, in the Maritime provinces, and when the question focuses on personal respect for the Queen's decades of public service. The evidence of popular interest in the monarchy resulting from this polling data is sometimes contradictory because of widespread misconceptions concerning Canada's system of government. For example, during the Golden Jubilee year in 2002, responses to an EKOS Research Associates poll indicated that 55 percent of Canadians agreed with the statement, "The monarchy is one of those important things that provide Canadians with a unique identity separate from the U.S." But when asked to name Canada's head of state, only 5 percent of respondents correctly identified the Queen, with others assuming the answer was the prime minister or the governor general.[34] A successful royal tour often results in subsequent polls showing evidence of increased support for the monarchy as an institution. Recent polling data suggesting growing indifference to the monarchy in Canada may be a response to the absence of Canadian royal tours in recent years because of the circumstances of the Covid-19 pandemic.[35]

## THE FUTURE OF ROYAL TOURS OF CANADA

The Covid-19 pandemic beginning in March 2020 resulted in a hiatus in Commonwealth tours by members of the royal family. The most recent working visit to Canada by a member of the royal family was undertaken by the Queen's daughter-in-law, Sophie, Countess of Wessex, who spent two days in Toronto in November 2019 visiting Toronto General and Toronto

Western hospitals, of which she is patron. Prince Harry and Meghan, Duke and Duchess of Sussex, spent Christmas 2019 on a private visit to Canada with their infant son Archie and then lived on Vancouver Island from January to March 2020 after announcing their plans to step back from their roles as senior members of the royal family. Although their time in Canada attracted intense media interest and prompted comparisons to past royalty who had made their home in Canada for extended periods of time, they relocated to California just before the Canadian-American border closure in response to the Covid-19 pandemic in March 2020 and have remained there to the present day. Extended periods of residence in Canada by senior members of the royal family are unlikely to occur in the future. Private time in Canada, such as Harry's visits to Meghan in Toronto prior to their engagement, and their later residence on Vancouver Island, prompts public scrutiny of the cost of security for royalty in Canada.[36]

During the pandemic, the Queen embraced virtual engagements through videoconferencing platforms, which allowed her to engage with the United Kingdom and Commonwealth realms through periods of social distancing. In July 2021, the Queen met with Canadian Governor General designate Mary Simon for the first time through a videoconference.[37]

Virtual engagements are likely to continue beyond the pandemic as the Queen gradually reduces her schedule of public engagements. The smaller number of working members of the royal family in the 2020s compared to previous decades will also necessitate virtual engagements in addition to traditional royal tours in Canada and the other Commonwealth realms. There are currently eight adult working members of the royal family: the Queen, the Prince of Wales and the Duchess of Cornwall, the Duke and Duchess of Cambridge, the Princess Royal, and the Earl and Countess of Wessex. The Queen has not travelled outside of Europe for more than a decade and the younger working members of the royal family have increased responsibilities representing the Queen and assuming additional patronages in the United Kingdom. As a result, opportunities for Canadians to connect with the royal family in a Canadian context will probably be less frequent as the twenty-first century continues. There will continue to be in-person royal tours for key moments in Canadian history and royal patronage of

Canadian institutions as well as of philanthropic endeavours in Canada, but a smaller royal family will need to make use of new technologies and innovations to build on the precedents set during Canadian royal tours over the past seventy years of Queen Elizabeth II's reign.

# 13

# Queen Elizabeth II: A Personal Tribute

*David Johnston*

Personal lessons I have learned from Queen Elizabeth II are captured in three words: graciousness, duty, and faith.

## GRACIOUSNESS
### "Never miss an opportunity to be gracious"

In June 2010 my wife, Sharon, and I met Her Majesty at a reception at the Royal York Hotel in Toronto. After a brief greeting in the reception line Her Majesty said very quietly with a warm smile, "I look forward to seeing you both soon." The Queen and Prince Philip were the only ones in that gathering who, apart from Sharon and me, were aware of a closely held secret.

Several weeks prior, Sharon and I had met Prime Minister Stephen Harper and his wife Laureen for dinner at 24 Sussex Drive. He asked me to become Canada's twenty-eighth governor general. Only he and the advisory committee for the selection, and the Queen, who had agreed to his recommendation, and Her Majesty's private secretary, knew of this. But the Queen's gracious smile was a touching signal of welcome.

We were lucky in our timing. The custom is for a new governor general to meet the Queen for tea or lunch at Buckingham Palace to receive the commission of appointment, or letters patent constituting the appointment as governor general and commander-in-chief of Canada, and the insignia of Canada's national orders. The Queen and Prince Philip customarily spent August at Balmoral Castle in the Scottish highlands, a large estate of fifty thousand or so acres with the perimeter secured, but with a totally relaxed atmosphere at the Castle, which is rather more like a comfortable country manor house. We were there for the weekend.

The Queen and Prince Philip were on the doorsteps to meet us with the friendliest of greetings. We had come with a wardrobe of formal clothes, not expecting recreation. At dinner that evening the Queen began making plans. Sharon ran a thirty-six-horse training stable at our farm in Waterloo, Ontario, before we came to Ottawa, and she loved horses. The Queen, whose interest in horses is legendary, advised Sharon the two of them would spend the Saturday morning in the stables. Sharon looked delighted but then grimaced as she looked down at her feet and stammered, "but I don't have proper shoes." The Duke, without missing a beat, looked under the table at Sharon's feet and then his wife's and said, "same size, I think." The Queen promptly left the table, went upstairs and returned with a well-worn pair of her brogues, which Sharon immediately put on, and wore for the weekend!

Saturday evening involved a journey on the estate over a narrow, stony, one-car-width highland road, towering a half-kilometre or so above a river. The Queen was driving her Land Rover with me in the passenger seat. Prince Philip was driving his Land Rover with Sharon beside him. We arrived at a distant shepherd's hut. The Duke began to barbecue the venison he had shot on the estate a week before. It was clear that was his job and he needed no help from me. I proceeded into the kitchen. There was the Queen setting the table herself. I immediately began arranging plates, knives, and forks. She paused from her labours and remarked, "you do that very well. Your mother would be proud!" In my mind's eye I was hoping Her Majesty was also thinking, *and you'll be just fine as GG*.

Midway through our dinner, after the sun had set, we heard bagpipes. Descending from the hill was a piper, accompanied by two plaid-clad young women. They greeted us with a highland dance and introduced themselves as Canadians on exchange with the Palace as part of an internship. They were scintillating, and we had a wonderfully animated discussion about what they had learned. How enlightening that was for Sharon and me and how characteristic of Her Majesty to bring a Canadian flavour to our visit.

On the return home from a remarkable evening, the Queen and I were in her Land Rover, which Her Majesty always drives herself. Sharon was driving with the Duke, with whom she had established a special rapport — fully engaged with his iconic wit. It was pitch-black, with only a sliver of a moon. The Duke's Land Rover was bouncing over the narrow roads with Sharon's laughter erupting from the open windows of their vehicle. The Queen looked at me with a broad smile that said, *I think they have found common ground.*

We left on the Sunday, with this most gracious couple seeing us off as if we were long-standing friends. As we drove out the long driveway we agreed that we had experienced the most surprising — and delightful — weekend we could ever imagine. I should add that as we parted the Queen said to me, "I do read letters, you know." This was unexpected but I managed to reply, "I shall comply with pleasure, and when they become dull and boring, please advise me and I shall cease and desist." I followed the routine of penning a letter every quarter or so during our seven years at Rideau Hall. This is one of my peculiar continuing habits of earlier times — sending handwritten letters. Shortly after the Balmoral visit, and inspired by the Canadian dancers, we arranged for one of our senior staff to go on an exchange with the Palace to give our Rideau Hall team an opportunity to get to know their counterparts in London. As she was finishing her week, the Queen invited her for a farewell tea and said to her, "Please tell the Governor General how much I enjoy his personal letters. But would you please give special thanks to his assistant who takes the trouble to type the letters so they are legible!"

After I had written these personal reflections on the unforgettable Balmoral visit, I had a concern that I might be taking too much liberty with the convention that communications with Her Majesty are confidential.

WINDSOR CASTLE

The Rt. Hon. David Johnston.

On the occasion of your 80th birthday,
I am pleased to send you my congratulations
together with my warmest good wishes for
your continued health and happiness. I have
happy memories of our meetings over a
number of years, especially your visit to
Balmoral in 2010.

*Elizabeth R*

28th June, 2021.

Letter from Queen Elizabeth II to former governor general David Johnston
on the occasion of his eightieth birthday in 2021.

And then I received a surprise. It was my eightieth birthday, and, unbeknown to me, my friends at the Rideau Hall Foundation had solicited letters of congratulations and printed them in a book titled *Letters from a Nation*, a play on the title of the first book I wrote after becoming governor general, titled *The Idea of Canada: Letters to a Nation*, following my practice of letter-writing. I set out above the opening letter in the book *Letters from a Nation*, which you will see eased my mind totally about revealing these personal reflections.

In 2017, during the Queen's Diamond Jubilee, her sixtieth anniversary as monarch, Her Majesty attended a reception at Canada House in Trafalgar Square. She was proceeding down the outdoor staircase on a red carpet. I was about a foot behind Her Majesty. I noticed there was a significant wrinkle/overlap on the carpet's last step. As the Queen placed her foot on the wrinkle, I thought I saw her ankle turn and I had a nightmare flash of a tumble. By instinct, I quickly took Her Majesty's elbow.

The next day the British tabloids, as is their custom, reported in large type my breach of protocol in touching the Queen's arm. We shortly received a brief message from the Queen's private secretary simply observing that the Queen appreciated that chivalry is alive and well.

I am lucky to be able to recount a few of these events to shed light on the Queen as a person whom few of us in Canada have had the chance to know. If all of us had that chance, we would be overwhelmed and touched by Her Majesty's graciousness, empathy, common sense, and good humour.

## DUTY
### "Do your duty, no matter how humble the task"

Upon the death of Her Majesty's father when she was just twenty-five, the new Queen said, "So long as I live it shall be my duty to serve my people to the best of my ability." What is stirring is that Her Majesty had not expected to become Queen. It was only on the abdication of her uncle Edward, when Her Majesty was ten, that these royal duties were thrust upon her. She now has served for seven decades, and is the longest-reigning British monarch in history. If there were two words to describe that tenure they would be "steadfast duty." She epitomizes the servant-leader. This concept is as old as the Bible and the ancient writings of Lao Tzu, Plutarch, and Xenophon, but in 1970 Robert Greenleaf modernized the term thus: "A servant leader focuses primarily on the growth and well-being of people and the communities to which they belong. While traditional leadership generally involves the accumulation and exercise of power by one at the 'top of the pyramid,' servant leadership is different. The servant leader shares power, puts the needs of others first, and helps people develop and perform as highly as possible."

Servant-leadership traits illustrated from Greenleaf's writings are: listening, empathy, stewardship, foresight, persuasion, conceptualization, awareness, healing, commitment to the growth and development of people, and building community. How well the Queen personifies each of these ten characteristics.

At age twenty-one, when it was clear she would become Queen, Her Majesty said in a Christmas broadcast, "I declare before you all that my whole life whether it be long or short shall be devoted to your service and the service of our great imperial family to which we all belong."

One of the most touching tales of this early sense of duty and place comes from a story that the late Stuart McLean of CBC's *Vinyl Café* told at a ceremony for a Diamond Jubilee reception in Toronto. It concerned a couple who had moved to Montreal just before the 1980 referendum on sovereignty for Quebec. They were anxious to learn French. They quickly befriended the building manager of the apartment in which they lived. He had his open office at the entrance and was always willing to help them with their pronunciation.

One day he invited them in for coffee. They saw on his wall a large and beautiful portrait of the young Queen Elizabeth. They said, *"Monsieur Tremblay, cette photo est une surprise, vous aimez la Reine?"* He replied, *"J'adore la Reine."* He then explained that in the Second World War he was a sergeant in the Royal 22nd Regiment — the "Van Doos" — stationed in England. On a motorized training exercise he came upon a military ambulance at the side of the road with a flat tire. Three young women in uniform were tenaciously trying to change the tire with relatively feeble results. He stopped and said, "I can help. We have better tools to do that." They agreed. He continued, "Why don't you sit here in the shade of our vehicle and my corporal will make you tea?" One of the women replied, "No sir, you are my superior officer. I will stand here till the job is done." As he began repairing the tire, he thought the woman looked familiar. Only on leaving the scene of the successful repair did he realize this was the young Princess Elizabeth.

One could write so much about the Queen's steadfast sense of duty. But the record speaks for itself. Seventy years on the throne has been dramatic not simply in the length of tenure but above all in the lasting legacy of leadership by example and the roots of that are revealed in the next section on faith. But before turning to that, let me cite two other examples of how the Queen has lent her influence to encouraging servant-leadership in Canadian honours.

In 1996, Governor General Roméo LeBlanc created the Caring Canadian Award to celebrate volunteerism, in particular to recognize those unsung heroes who as volunteers made their communities better. He was mindful of his modest upbringing in a small Acadian village where volunteerism was the lifeblood of the community. In fact, I would extrapolate to say that if you wish to judge the "health" of any community in Canada, calculate the number of volunteers per capita in that community. If that number is up, so is that community. If it is down, so is the community. Governor General LeBlanc was sensitive to the fact that when we initiated the Order of Canada we missed out on the unsung heroes who quietly run the myriad of volunteer works at the community level. He began with fifty or so Caring Canadian Awards per year during his tenure, but the award was gradually phased out in the subsequent years because of budget cuts at Rideau Hall.

When we created the Rideau Hall Foundation in 2012 to amplify the reach of the office of the governor general, one of our first projects was to raise $5 million as an endowment to restore this volunteers' award and bulletproof it from future budget cuts. It became a grand success. When we briefed Her Majesty through her private secretary about it, we proposed that it become a Queen's honour — like the Order of Canada — and that we call it the Queen Elizabeth Medal for Volunteerism. Her Majesty enthusiastically accepted. But the Queen preferred that it be called the "Sovereign's Medal for Volunteers" so that it would be sustained through the generations. In my last year as governor general, 2017, over a thousand of these awards were conferred on Canada's unsung heroes. And we should do many more!

A second example is the "Queen Elizabeth Scholars" program. It began with the Queen Elizabeth II Diamond Jubilee. Former prime minister Jean Chrétien was asked by Prime Minister Harper to match a $10 million initial grant from the federal government with contributions from the provinces, corporations, foundations, and individuals across the country. Mr. Chrétien, with the collaboration of the Department of Global Affairs, partnered with the Rideau Hall Foundation and Universities Canada to enhance young Canadians' sense of service to the world through a program sending them abroad for educational or research exchanges or volunteer assignments and for international students to come to Canada for advanced study. This was the Queen's vision of young people broadening their world perspective and learning to help "the other." To date it has invested about $100 million and supported over three thousand students. All of them see themselves as global citizens, meeting the needs of the entire planet. One more leader-as-servant life-changing experience.

# FAITH
## "Connect with your faith to see beyond the darkness"

My own Christian faith was challenged, reaffirmed, and reinvigorated during the privileged years Sharon and I spent at Rideau Hall, particularly through our understanding of the Queen's faith and the circumstances and weight of her responsibilities. Her Christian faith has been at the core of her leadership as servant. I am a lay reader in the Anglican Church. As such, I have spoken at a number of mayor's prayer breakfast gatherings in cities across Canada. I occasionally employ the Queen's own Christian message in these testimonials. I refer to some of them here.

I spoke of the Queen's faith and how it grounded Her Majesty's sense of service and message of love. In my own case the Christian faith has been my rock. I grew up in northern Ontario in the Anglican tradition. While at university in Boston, I took a short course at the Episcopal Theological College to become a lay reader. Among other things, it opened a whole new window in my life. For several summers I filled in on Sundays for the Anglican clergy serving the three First Nations reserves and other rural parishes near my hometown of Sault Ste. Marie. It was my first in-depth encounter with First Nations people both on and off reserve.

In the foreword to a little book about Her Majesty's faith that was published in honour of the Queen's ninetieth birthday, titled *The Servant Queen — and The King She Serves*, Her Majesty indicated that her trust in faith began early in her life. She referred to a poem quoted by her father King George VI in his Christmas broadcast in 1939. Europe again found itself at war. The invasion of Britain was an imminent peril. The King, who had to work to overcome a debilitating stammer, had been thrust onto the Throne only two years earlier, surprised and unprepared after the abdication of Edward VIII. This is the poem, which he read without a stammer:

> And I said to the man who stood at the gate of the year:
> "Give me a light that I may tread safely into the unknown."
> And he replied:
> "Go out into the darkness and put your hand into the
>     Hand of God.
> That shall be to you better than light and safer than a
>     known way."
> So I went forth, and finding the Hand of God, trod gladly
>     into the night.
> And He led me towards the hills and the breaking of day in
>     the lone East.

What is less known is who gave that poem to King George. It was the future Queen, Princess Elizabeth, his thirteen-year-old daughter. Typical of Her Majesty's lifelong tendency to understate and depersonalize, that information is not contained in Her Majesty's foreword. It is only disclosed later in the book, by others.

The Queen's faith is robustly rooted and ever-present. In her annual Christmas broadcasts Her Majesty always refers to Jesus Christ and his teachings. In 1984, Her Majesty said, "For me, the life of Jesus Christ, the Prince of Peace whose birth we celebrate today is an inspiration and an anchor in my life. A role-model of reconciliation and forgiveness, He stretched out His hands in love, acceptance and healing. Christ's example has taught me to seek respect and value all people of whatever faith or none."

The Queen's strong Christian faith does not lead Her Majesty to exclude other faiths or minorities but rather to embrace them, to accord them the same respect and dignities she does to those who share Her Majesty's beliefs. The late Chief Rabbi Lord Jonathan Sacks of the United Kingdom in 2012 said,

> We do not always appreciate the role the Queen has played in one of the most significant changes in the past sixty years: the transformation of Britain into a multi-ethnic, multi-faith society. No one does interfaith better than the Royal Family, and it starts with the Queen herself. Her presence and her family role as the human face of national identity is one of the great unifying forces in Britain, a unity we need all the more, the more diverse religiously and culturally we become.

Rabbi Sacks's observations apply equally well to Canada. Service springs from The Queen's faith.

After she pledged a lifetime of service on her twenty-first birthday, sixty-one years later, in her 2008 Christmas broadcast, Her Majesty said,

> I hope that, like me, you will be comforted by the example of Jesus of Nazareth who, often in circumstances of great adversity, managed to live an outgoing, unselfish and sacrificial life. Countless millions of people around the world continue to celebrate his birthday at Christmas, inspired by his teaching. He makes it clear that genuine human happiness and satisfaction lie more in giving than receiving; more in serving than in being served. We can surely be grateful that, two thousand years after the birth of Jesus, so many of us are able to draw inspiration from His life and message, and to find in Him a source of strength and courage.

What is the secret of the Queen's remarkable consistency of service? In her Christmas broadcast in 2002 she said, "I know just how much I rely on my faith to guide me through the good times and the bad. Each day is a new beginning. I know that the only way to live my life is to try to do what is right, to take the long view, to give of my best in all that the day brings, and to put my trust in God ... I draw strength from the message of hope in the Christian gospel."

The Queen sees, as my wife reminds me, that service is love made real. It is interesting to me — but not surprising — that love, especially the commandment to "love thy neighbour," is at the core not only of the Christian religion but of so many other great faiths around the world.

In another Christmas broadcast, the Queen showed her understanding of the practicality of this commandment. She said, "Many will have been inspired by Jesus' simple but powerful teaching: love God and love thy neighbour as thyself — in other words, treat others as you would like them to treat you. His great emphasis was to give spirituality a practical purpose."

And which parable of Jesus does Her Majesty most often quote? It is the story of the Good Samaritan, which tells of a Hebrew man beaten by robbers and left wounded by the roadside. He was bypassed by his well-placed kinsmen, first a priest and then a Levite. Then along came the Samaritan, who was from a different tribe — not friend or kin — who took him up and restored him as a simple act of compassion.

For Her Majesty, another of the essential guideposts of love is forgiveness. In the Queen's 2013 Christmas broadcast, Her Majesty said,

> Although we are capable of great acts of kindness, history teaches us that we sometimes need saving from ourselves — from our recklessness or our greed. God sent into the world a unique person — neither a philosopher nor a general (important though they are) — but a Saviour with the power to forgive. Forgiveness lies at the heart of the Christian faith. It can heal broken families, it can restore friendships, and it can reconcile divided communities. It is in forgiveness that we feel the power of God's love.

Perhaps the most powerful of Her Majesty's lessons for me is the one from the Queen's 1975 Christmas broadcast, which speaks of this fundamental truth of love and its impact throughout our society. She said,

Christ's simple message of love has been turning the world upside down ever since [his birth]. He showed that what people are and what they do, does matter and does make all the difference. He commanded us to love our neighbours as we love ourselves, but what exactly is meant by "loving ourselves"? I believe it means trying to make the most of the abilities we have been given, it means caring for our talents. It is a matter of making the best of ourselves, not just doing the best for ourselves.

I want to end this brief journey through the Queen's inspiring dedication to faith, service and love by appraising the impact of Her Majesty's observations and Her Majesty's life. The title of my installation address delivered in 2010 when I began the job of governor general was "A Smart and Caring Nation — a Call to Service." This was about the good society, about calling on our better angels. And so much of what I have tried to do since has been influenced by Christian faith as illuminated by the Queen's messages. So let me end with a final quote from the 1975 Christmas broadcast, where Her Majesty spoke of the impact and the legacy of love:

We are all different, but each of us has his own best to offer. The responsibility for the way we live life with all its challenges, sadness and joy is ours alone. If we do this well, it will also be good for our neighbours.

If you throw a stone into a pool, the ripples go on spreading outwards. A big stone can cause waves, but even the smallest pebble changes the whole pattern of the water. Our daily actions are like those ripples, each one makes a difference, even the smallest. It does matter therefore what each individual does each day. Kindness, sympathy, resolution, and courteous behaviour are infectious. Acts of courage and self-sacrifice, like those of the people who refuse to be terrorised by kidnappers or hijackers, or who defuse bombs, are an inspiration to others.

And the combined effect can be enormous. If enough grains of sand are dropped into one side of a pair of scales they will, in

the end, tip it against a lump of lead. We may feel powerless alone
but the joint efforts of individuals can defeat the evils of our time.
Together they can create a stable, free and considerate society.

The infectiousness of this message gives me great inspiration and opti-
mism about how this applies to us as individuals. Some years ago I attended
a mayor's prayer breakfast in Montreal where Mother Teresa was the guest.
A group of our neighbours had the opportunity to meet with her before
the breakfast began. One of them, moved by her work with the poor in
Calcutta, asked Mother Teresa how she, a single individual, could help.
Mother Teresa replied, "Just look around you. In your own neighbourhood
there is a family who needs your care and love."

Shortly afterward, I read a newspaper criticism of Mother Teresa's
work. It minimized her work, saying her shelter in Calcutta gave succour
to perhaps two hundred people in a city where millions lived in abject
poverty. Her work was described as one small drop in an ocean. In other
words, it did not count for much in the "sea of things." Some years later
I realized the shortcomings of this criticism. It was looking at her work
from the point of view of physics, rather than chemistry. I came to this
realization in an unusual way. At that time, my children were aged two
to nine and they were unsatisfied with the entertainment I was providing
at their birthday parties. They would ask me, "Why can't you do a magic
show like Dean MacFarlane instead of telling us ghost stories that no one
believes?"

In those days, Andy MacFarlane was the dean of journalism at the
University of Western Ontario, where I was the dean of law. Being quite
competitive, I attended the next birthday party at the MacFarlane home,
where Andy was dressed as a magician, with a long cape and flowing sleeves
and doing card tricks that mesmerized the children. Then he began his special magic trick, "turning water into wine." He took a glass of clear water,
raised it in the air and uttered that magic phrase, *Abracadabra!* He then
swept the glass into his sleeves while whirling 360 degrees, surreptitiously
adding a few drops of red vegetable dye into the glass, and emerged with a
glass of a lovely rose-hued liquid.

At that moment, I realized that the work Mother Teresa was doing was changing the culture of Calcutta, and indeed that of the world. It was the transformation of the water — not the addition to it — that was improving the lives of so many families. I had been responding to the criticism in terms of mathematics or physics and not chemistry! Queen Elizabeth has been casting little stones and big ones into ponds for seven decades, changing the culture of the waters and challenging us to draw out inspiration from the ripples. And so we celebrate Her Majesty's lessons.

# Notes

## Introduction

1   *The Invisible Crown: The First Principle of Canadian Government* (University of Toronto Press, 1995, reprinted with a new preface, 2013).
2   In Australia, Anne Twomey, *The Chameleon Crown: The Queen and Her Australian Governors* (Sydney: The Federation Press, 2006). In New Zealand, Cris Shore and David V. Williams, ed., *The Shapeshifting Crown: Locating the State in Postcolonial New Zealand, Australia, Canada and the United Kingdom* (Cambridge University Press, 2019).

## Chapter 1
### The Crown, the Queen, and the Structure of the Constitution

1   *Reference re Secession of Quebec*, [1998] 2 S.C.R. 217, para. 49.
2   *Constitution Act, 1867*, preamble; first and third recitals.
3   *Imperial Conference 1926; Inter-Imperial Relations Committee* (London: HMSO, 1926), 3.
4   *Statute of Westminster, 1931*, preamble; second recital. "Dominion" was defined in s. 1 of the statute as meaning the Dominion of Canada, the Commonwealth of Australia, the Dominion of New Zealand, the Union of South Africa, the Irish Free State, and Newfoundland.
5   See for example, the *Constitution Act, 1867*, sections 107 to 119, and 125 dealing with public debt, public property, and taxation of lands or property after the union.
6   Ibid.
7   See David E. Smith, *The Invisible Crown: The First Principle of Canadian Government* (Toronto: University of Toronto Press, 1995, 2013), 28–30: "The imperial Crown became divisible because the Empire evolved into a Commonwealth of autonomous member states. The Canadian Crown divided within the confines of a nation state, and for this reason the fission could not be so complete."

8   See, notably, David E. Smith, Christopher McCreery, and Jonathan Shanks, "Yet Symbols Still Matter," chapter 6 in their *Canada's Deep Crown: Beyond Elizabeth II, the Crown's Continuing Canadian Complexion* (Toronto: University of Toronto Press, 2022), 106–25.

9   Section 3, *Constitution Act, 1867* (Declaration of Union); the Royal Proclamation of May 22, 1867, fixed the date of union as July 1st of that year.

10  Section 128 of the *Constitution Act, 1867* and the fifth schedule to the Act setting out the form and terms of the oath.

11  Section 2 of the *Constitution Act, 1867* (subsequently repealed and replaced by a rule of interpretation identical in substance) and the fifth schedule thereto.

12  See *Motard c. Procureur général du Canada*, Court of Appeal of Quebec, judgment rendered on October 28, 2019, upholding (as did the Quebec Superior Court), the constitutional validity of Canada's *Succession to the Throne Act, 2013*. Leave to appeal that judgment to the Supreme Court of Canada was denied by the Supreme Court on April 23, 2020.

13  See Warren J. Newman, "The Succession to the Throne in Canada," in *Royal Progress: Canada's Monarchy in the Age of Disruption*, ed. D. Michael Jackson (Toronto: Dundurn, 2020). 127–52.

14  The command-in-chief of the armed forces is also declared to be vested in the Queen, by s. 15 of the *Constitution Act, 1867*. This has been delegated by the *Letters Patent* of 1947 to the Governor General of Canada.

15  Section 11, *Constitution Act, 1867*.

16  *Liquidators of the Maritime Bank of Canada v. Receiver-General of New Brunswick*, [1892] A.C. 437 at p. 441 (J.C.P.C., *per* Lord Watson).

17  For a recent and thorough treatment of aspects of the question, see Patrick F. Baud, "The Crown's Prerogatives and the Constitution of Canada," *Journal of Commonwealth Law* 3 (2021), 219–71.

18  For a useful analysis as well as an incisive critique of other recent academic writings on the royal prerogative, see chapter 3, "The Dispersal of Power," and particularly "The Royal Prerogative in Historical Perspective," "Defining the Prerogative," and "Limits on the Royal Prerogative," in Smith, McCreery, and Shanks, *Canada's Deep Crown*, op. cit., 48–70.

19  Section 58 of the *Constitution Act, 1867*.

20  Section 60 of the Act.

21  *Liquidators of the Maritime Bank of Canada v. Receiver-General of New Brunswick*, [1892] A.C. 437 at p. 443.

22  See sections 58 and 60 of the *Constitution Act, 1867*. See notably Andrew Heard, "The Provincial Crown and Lieutenant Governors," in *Royal Progress*, op. cit., 43–77.

23  Section 17 provides: "There shall be One Parliament for Canada, consisting of the Queen, an Upper House styled the Senate, and the House of Commons."

24   Section 55 of the *Constitution Act, 1867.*

25   *In re Initiative and Referendum Act,* [1919] A.C. 935, at p. 943 (J.C.P.C, per Viscount Haldane). See also s. 90 of the *Constitution Act, 1867,* which extends, *inter alia,* the power of royal assent to the lieutenant governor.

26   *Imperial Conference 1926; Inter-Imperial Relations Committee* (London: HMSO, 1926).

27   Letter from Prime Minister Pierre Trudeau tabled in the House of Commons on July 21, 1975, Sessional Papers, No. 301-5/185.

28   See W.J. Newman, "The Rule of Law, the Separation of Powers and Judicial Independence in Canada," in *The Oxford Handbook of the Canadian Constitution,* ed. Peter Oliver, Patrick Macklem, and Nathalie Des Rosiers (New York: Oxford University Press, 2017), 1031–49.

29   See, notably, *Girouard* v. *Attorney General of Canada,* 2020 FCA 129; leave to appeal to the Supreme Court of Canada refused, February 25, 2021.

30   *Reference re Supreme Court Act, ss. 5 and 6,* [2014] 1 S.C.R. 433; see also W.J. Newman, "The Constitutional Status of the Supreme Court of Canada," *Supreme Court Law Review* 47 (2009): 429–43.

31   *In re Initiative and Referendum Act,* [1919] A.C. 935, at 943.

32   Ibid., and see s. 55 and s. 90 of the *Constitution Act, 1867,* read together.

33   *Ontario (Attorney General) v. OPSEU,* [1987] 2 S.C.R. 2, at 46.

34   Ibid., 47.

35   *Reference re Senate Reform,* [2014] 1 S.C.R. 704, at para. 48 (*per curiam*).

36   *An Act respecting royal assent to bills passed by the Houses of Parliament,* S.C. 2002, c. 15.

37   *An Act respecting the Governor General,* R.S.C. 1985, c. G-9, and para. (1)(n) of the *Income Tax Act,* R.S.C. 1985, c. 1 (5th Supp.), both as amended by the *Jobs, Growth and Long-term Prosperity Act,* S.C. 2012, c. 19, s. 16.

38   W.J. Newman, "Constitutional Amendment by Legislation," in *Constitutional Amendment in Canada,* ed. Emmett Macfarlane (Toronto: University of Toronto Press, 2016), 105–25.

39   *Canada Act 1982* (U.K.), s. 2.

40   *Reference re Secession of Quebec,* [1998] 2 S.C.R. 217, para. 46: "Canada's evolution from colony to fully independent state was gradual ... Canada's independence from Britain was achieved through legal and political evolution with an adherence to the rule of law and stability."

41   *Royal Style and Titles Act,* now found in R.S.C. 1985, c. R-12; preamble. The style and titles Her Majesty was authorized by the statute to proclaim read as follows (s. 2): "Elizabeth the Second, by the Grace of God of the United Kingdom, Canada and Her other Realms and Territories Queen, Head of the Commonwealth, Defender of the Faith." And in French: « Elizabeth Deux, par la grâce de Dieu Reine du Royaume-Uni, du Canada et de ses autres royaumes et territoires, Chef du Commonwealth, Défenseur de la Foi. »

42  See W.J. Newman, "Some Observations on the Queen, the Crown, the Constitution, and the Courts," *Review of Constitutional Studies* 22, no. 1 (2017): 55–79, especially 69–73; Mark D. Walters, "Succession to the Throne and the Architecture of the Constitution of Canada," in *La Couronne et le Parlement / The Crown and Parliament*, ed. Michel Bédard and Philippe Lagassé (Montreal: Editions Yvon Blais, 2015), 287, 291.

43  *Secretary of State for Foreign and Commonwealth Affairs, ex parte: The Indian Association of Canada*, Court of Appeal of United Kingdom, 28 January 1982, [1982] Q.B. 892 (C.A.), Lord Denning at paras. 73-78, 88; Lord Kerr at paras. 104, 108-109; Lord May at paras. 147–48, 150.

44  Proclamation Designating July 28 of Every Year as "A Day of Commemoration of the Great Upheaval," commencing on July 28, 2005, made on December 10, 2003; registration 2003-12-31; SI/2003-188.

45  Ibid.

46  *St. Catherine's Milling Lumber Co. v. The Queen*, [1886] 13 S.C.R. 577; per Gwynne J., 652 (and cited in *Calder, infra*).

47  *Calder et al. v. Attorney-General of British Columbia*, [1973] S.C.R. 313, *per* Hall J., dissenting, with Spence and Laskin JJ., 395.

48  *Province of Ontario v. Dominion of Canada*, [1909] 42 S.C.R. 1, *per* Idington J., 103-104 (and also cited in *Calder*).

49  *Taku River Tlingit First Nation v. British Columbia*, [2004] 3 S.C.R. 550, para. 24.

50  *Haida Nation v. British Columbia (Minister of Forests)*, [2004] 3 S.C.R. 511, para. 16.

51  *Taku River, supra*, para. 24.

52  *Manitoba Métis Federation v. Canada (Attorney General)*, [2013] 1 S.C.R. 623, per McLachlin C.J. and Karakatsanis J., para . 71. 69

53  The reference to "Indians" (or First Nations) in this federal head of legislative power is now read coextensively with the definition of the "aboriginal peoples of Canada" in section 35 of the *Constitution Act, 1982*; in other words, Parliament's legislative authority in relation to "Indians" extends to "the Indian, Inuit, and Métis peoples of Canada."

54  *R. v. Sparrow*, [1990] 1 S.C.R. 1075, *per* Lamer C.J., 1109.

55  See *Mikisew Cree First Nation v. Canada (Governor General in Council)*, [2018] 2 S.C.R. 76, and the broad range of reasons for judgment therein, by Karakasanis J. (Wagner C.J. and Gascon J., concurring); Abella J. (Martin J. concurring); Brown J., and Rowe J. (Moldaver and Côté JJ. concurring). On the duty to consult, the Crown, and regulatory agencies, see *Clyde River (Hamlet) v. Petroleum Geo Services Inc.*, [2017] 1.S.C.R. 1069.

56  *Toronto (City) v. Ontario (Attorney General)*, [2021] SCC 34, reasons *per* Wagner C.J. and Brown J., with Moldaver, Côté, and Rowe JJ., paras 62, 63.

## Chapter 2
## The Crown's Contemporary Constitutional Legitimacy

1    *The Economist*, "How monarchies survive modernity" (April 27, 2019).
2    This chapter is especially reliant on Robert Macgregor Dawson. The second edition of *The Government of Canada* was published in 1954 and provides a snapshot of the role of the Crown in relation to Canada immediately following the Queen's accession. The next six editions, three of which were written by Norman Ward, illustrate developments in relation to the Crown during the reign of Elizabeth II.
3    R. Macgregor Dawson, *The Government of Canada* (Toronto: University of Toronto Press, 1947), 169.
4    Ibid.
5    John Van Der Kiste, *Crowns in a Changing World: The British and European Monarchies 1901–36* (London: Grange Books, 1993). Since then, the Greek monarchy has been abolished, restored, and again abolished, while the other continental monarchs have survived as constitutional heads of state with parliamentary systems of government.
6    *Constitution Act, 1867*, s. 17; *Interpretation Act*, s. 35(1).
7    *Constitution Act, 1867*, s. 9.
8    *Canada Gazette*, Part I, February 9, 1952, 323.
9    S.A. de Smith, "The Royal Style and Titles," *International and Comparative Law Quarterly* 2, no. 2 (Apr., 1953): 263–74, 265.
10    *Liquidators of the Maritime Bank of Canada v. Receiver General of New Brunswick*, 1892 A.C. 437.
11    *Constitution Act, 1867*, ss. 10, 11.
12    *Constitution Act, 1867*, ss. 58, 62, 66.
13    *Constitution Act, 1867*, ss. 102–26.
14    Bora Laskin, *The British Tradition in Canadian Law* (London: Stevens & Sons, 1969), 118.
15    W.P.M. Kennedy, "The Royal Style and Titles," *University of Toronto Law Journal* 10, no. 1, (1953): 83–87.
16    House of Commons, *Journals*, no. 18 (December 15, 1952).
17    *Canada Gazette*, May 29, 1953, no. 6 EXTRA.
18    This alteration to the letters patent was not intended to change existing practices and there was an understanding that matters that traditionally had been submitted to the King "would not be transferred to the Governor General without the consent of the Palace." J.R. Mallory, *The Structure of Canadian Government* (Toronto: Gage Publishing, 1984), 37.
19    Conrad Swan, *Canada: Symbols of Sovereignty* (Toronto: University of Toronto Press, 1976), 74–75. J.R. Mallory, "Seals and Symbols: From Substance to Form in Commonwealth Equality," *Canadian Journal of Economics and Political Science* 22, no. 3 (August 1956).

20  Christopher McCreery, "Myth and Misunderstanding: The Origins and Meaning of the Letters Patent Constituting the Office of the Governor General," in *The Evolving Canadian Crown*, ed. Jennifer Smith and D. Michael Jackson (Montreal and Kingston: McGill-Queen's University Press, 2012).

21  Ibid., 52.

22  *Re: Resolution to amend the Constitution*, [1981] 1 SCR 753 at 882.

23  Justin McElroy and Richard Zussman, "Showdown at Government House: The Meeting That Ended 16 Years of B.C. Liberal Rule," CBC News, June 30, 2017, cbc.ca/news/canada/british-columbia/government-house-stakeout-clark-horgan-guichon-1.4185404.

24  R. Macgregor Dawson, *The Government of Canada* (Toronto: University of Toronto Press, 1947), 196.

25  Philip Murphy, *Monarchy & the End of Empire* (Oxford: Oxford University Press, 2013), 7.

26  Since then, Barbados has become a republic.

27  *Succession to the Crown Act, 2013*.

28  "Proceedings of the Standing Senate Committee on Legal and Constitutional Affairs Issue 32 – Evidence for March 21, 2013," sencanada.ca/en/Content/Sen/Committee/411/LCJC/32ev-50040-e.

29  Peter W. Hogg, "Succession to the Throne," *National Journal of Constitutional Law* 33 (2014): 83–94; Mark D. Walters, "Succession to the Throne and the Architecture of the Constitution of Canada," in *The Crown and Parliament*, ed. Philippe Lagassé and Michel Bédard (Montreal: Éditions Yvon Blais, 2015), 263–92.

30  Anne Twomey, "Regency in the Realms," *Public Law Review* 27, no. 3 (2016).

31  Warren J. Newman, "The Succession to the Throne in Canada," in *Royal Progress: Canada's Monarchy in the Age of Disruption*, ed. D. Michael Jackson (Toronto: Dundurn, 2020), 127–52.

32  *Motard c Procureur général du Canada*, 2019 QCCA 1826, application for leave to appeal to the Supreme Court dismissed with costs to the attorney general. The plaintiffs in this litigation were not motivated by the same structural constitutional arguments as Anne Twomey; rather, they were candid in admitting that they were not interested in the monarchy, but were seeking to force the federal government to negotiate other constitutional amendments with the provinces, in particular with the province of Quebec. Stéphanie Marin, "La Loi sur la succession du trône sera contestée en Cour lundi," *La Presse*, May 31, 2015, lapresse.ca/actualites/politique/politique-canadienne/201505/31/01-4874043-la-loi-sur-la-succession-du-trone-sera-contestee-en-cour-lundi.php: "Car si le gouvernement refuse d'ouvrir la Constitution pour les demandes du Québec et des Autochtones, il n'aura peut-être pas le choix cette fois face au respect de la monarchie et de ses obligations envers le Commonwealth."

33  Philippe Lagassé, "The First and Last 'Queen of Canada'?," *Policy Options*, September 9, 2015, policyoptions.irpp.org/magazines/september-2015/

the-first-and-last-queen-of-canada/; "The Queen of Canada is Dead; Long Live the British Queen: Why the Conservatives Must Rethink Their Approach to Succession," *Maclean's*, February 3, 2013; Ottawa *Citizen*, "Canada's Independence Is at Stake," July 6, 2016; "Citizenship and the Hollowed Canadian Crown," policyoptions.irpp.org/2015/03/02/citizenship-and-the-hollowed-canadian-crown/.

34 Philippe Lagassé and James W.J. Bowden, "Royal Succession and the Canadian Crown as a Corporation Sole: A Critique of Canada's Succession to the Throne Act, 2013," *Constitutional Forum* 23, no. 1 (2014): 17–26.

35 F.W. Maitland, "The Crown as Corporation" (1901) 18 L.Q.R. 131.

36 See, e.g., J.W.F. Allison, *The English Historical Constitution: Continuity, Change and European Effects* (Cambridge: Cambridge University Press, 2007), 58, "the "English conception of the Crown" is an "ambivalent institutional outcome — a corporation arguably both aggregate and sole." See also Edmund Bayly Seymour Jr., "The Historical Development of the Common-Law Conception of a Corporation," *American Law Register (1898-1907)* 51, n.s. 42, no. 9 (September, 1903): 529–51: "The corporation sole seems to have been an ingenious adaptation of theory on the part of the princes of the Church. ... It is curious to observe that this *hocus-pocus* operation has given rise to the maxim "the king never dies." As happened so often the courts, reasoning by strained analogies, decided that for purposes of various sorts the king was a corporation sole."

37 Nelson Goodman, *Fact, Fiction, and Forecast*, 4th ed. (Cambridge, Mass.: Harvard University Press, 1979), 34.

38 Arthur Berriedale Keith, *Responsible Government in the Dominions*, 2nd ed. (Oxford: Clarendon, 1928), xiii.

39 S.A. de Smith, "The Royal Style and Titles," *International and Comparative Law Quarterly* 2, no. 2 (April, 1953): 263–74.

40 Ibid.

41 W.P.M. Kennedy, "The Royal Style and Titles," *University of Toronto Law Journal* 10, no. 1 (1953): 83–87.

42 Timothy Endicott and Peter Oliver, "The Role of Theory in Canadian Constitutional Law," in *The Oxford Handbook of the Canadian Constitution*, ed. Peter Oliver, Patrick Macklem, and Nathalie Des Rosiers (Oxford: Oxford University Press, 2017), 940.

## Chapter 3

### Canada's Entrenched Monarchy: The "Offices" of the Queen and Her Representatives

1 See the preamble and s.9 of the *Constitution Act, 1867.*

2 Andrew Heard, "The Crown in Canada: Is There a Canadian Monarchy?"

in *The Canadian Kingdom: 150 Years of Constitutional Monarchy*, ed. D. Michael Jackson (Toronto: Dundurn, 2018), 113–32.

3   *Liquidators of the Maritime Bank of Canada v. The Receiver General of New Brunswick*, [1892] AC 437; *In re The Initiative and Referendum Act*, [1919] AC 935 at 942; *Bonanza Creek Gold Mining Co. v The King*, [1916] 1 AC 566; *Reference re The Power of the Governor General in Council to Disallow Provincial Legislation and the Power of Reservation of a Lieutenant-Governor of a Province*, [1938] SCR 71; *The King v Carroll*, [1948] SCR 126.

4   Parliament of Canada, "Minutes of Proceedings and Evidence of the Special Joint Committee of the Senate and of the House of Commons on the Constitution of Canada," no. 53, February 4, (1981): 59, primarydocuments.ca/53-special-joint-committee-1980-81/.

5   "An Act to Provide for the Amendment in Canada of the Constitution of Canada," solon.org/Constitutions/Canada/English/Proposals/Fulton-Favreau.html.

6   J. Peter Meekison, "The Amending Formula," *Queen's Law Journal* 8 (1982/1983): 99–122, 113. See also: Kenneth Munro, "The Constitution Act, 1982 and the Crown: Twenty-Five Years Later," *Constitutional Forum* 49, no. 2 (2008): 49–57, 51–52; Roy Romanow, John Whyte and Howard Leeson, *Canada … Notwithstanding: The Making of the Constitution 1976–1982*, Anniversary Edition (Toronto: Carswell, 2007), 50–51.

7   Noel Cox, *The Royal Prerogative and Constitutional Law* (Abingdon: Routledge, 2021), 166–67; Guy Régimbald and Dwight Newman, *The Law of the Canadian Constitution* (Toronto: LexisNexis, 2013), 46.

8   See: Noel Cox, above, n.7; Craig Forcese, "The Executive, The Royal Prerogative, and the Constitution," in *The Oxford Handbook of the Canadian Constitution*, ed. Peter Oliver, Patrick Macklem, and Nathalie Des Rosiers (New York: Oxford University Press, 2017), 151–69; Tom D. McKinlay, *Halsbury's Laws of Canada: The Crown* (Toronto: LexisNexis, 2021), 333–73; Sebastien Payne, "The Royal Prerogative," in *The Nature of the Crown — A Legal and Political Analysis*, ed. Maurice Sunkin and Sebastien Payne (Oxford: Oxford University Press, 1999), 77–110; David E. Smith, Christopher McCreery, and Jonathan Shanks, *Canada's Deep Crown: Beyond Elizabeth II, The Crown's Continuing Canadian Complexion* (Toronto: University of Toronto Press, 2021), 48–70.

9   There is some controversy whether certain British statutes are part of Canada's constitutional law, or if those statutes are simply British laws that have practical consequences in Canada. The Quebec Court of Appeal, for example, ruled that the United Kingdom's *Succession to the Crown Act, 2013* is not a part of Canada's constitutional law: *Motard v AG Canada*, 2019 QCCA 1826. There is also ongoing debate as to whether a regent appointed under United Kingdom law would have authority to exercise the Queen's powers with respect to Canada.

10 An example of acceptable provincial legislation permits granting royal assent in the lieutenant governor's office rather than in the legislative assembly.

11 For discussion of the provincial legislatures' powers with respect to their lieutenant governors, see: Ian MacIsaac, "Provincial Constitutions and the Lieutenant-Governor: The Constitutional Amending Process and Legal Responses to the 2012 Ontario Prorogation," *Journal of Parliamentary and Political Law* 9 (2015): 345. The question whether provincial legislation may amend documents in the formal Constitution became a live issue in 2021 with the debate over Quebec's Bill 96, which would amend the *Constitution Act, 1867* by adding two new sections. The House of Commons eventually approved a motion related to the issue proposed by the Bloc Québécois leader, Yves-François Blanchet: "That the House agree that section 45 of the *Constitution Act, 1982* grants Quebec and the provinces exclusive jurisdiction to amend their respective constitutions and acknowledge the will of Quebec to enshrine in its constitution that Quebeckers form a nation, that French is the only official language of Quebec and that it is also the common language of the Quebec nation." House of Commons, *Journals,* June 16, 2021, 43rd Parliament, 2nd Session, no.119; ourcommons.ca/DocumentViewer/en/43-2/house/sitting-119/journals.

12 In practice there is little to distinguish powers assigned in law to a governor personally or to the governor in council. Apart from exceptional circumstances, the first minister and cabinet make the decisions about how all those powers are exercised. The Queen and governors may only act on their personal discretion with respect to certain "reserve powers" in rare situations; see: Andrew Heard, *Canadian Constitutional Conventions: The Marriage of Law and Politics,* 2nd ed. (Toronto: Oxford University Press, 2014), 34–83.

13 See sections 56 and 90 of the *Constitution Act, 1867.*

14 *Reference re Supreme Court Act, ss. 5 and 6,* 2014 SCC 21. For a broader discussion, see: Warren J. Newman, "Grand Entrance Hall, Back Door or Foundation Stone? The Role of Constitutional Principles in Construing and Applying the Constitution of Canada," *Supreme Court Law Review* 14 (2001): 197; Mark D. Walters, "The Common Law Constitution in Canada: Return of *lex non scripta* as Fundamental Law," *University of Toronto Law Journal* 51, no. 2 (2001): 91.

15 *Reference re Secession of Quebec,* [1998] 2 SCR 217, para. 50; *OPSEU v. Ontario (Attorney General),* [1987] 2 S.C.R. 2, at p. 57; *Supreme Court Act Reference,* above, n.14, para. 82, and *Senate Reform Reference,* 2014 SCC 32, para 26.

16 See: *New Brunswick Broadcasting Co. v. Nova Scotia (Speaker of the House of Assembly),* [1993] 1 SCR 319.

17 *Reference re Remuneration of Judges of the Provincial Court (P.E.I.),* [1997] 3 SCR 3 para 109.

18 *Beauregard v. The Queen,* [1986] 2 SCR 56; *Reference re Remuneration of Judges,* above, n.17.

19  *Reference re Manitoba Language Rights*, [1985] 1 S.C.R. 721; *Trial Lawyers Association of British Columbia v. British Columbia (Attorney General)*, 2014 SCC 59.

20  *New Brunswick Broadcasting*, above, n.16; *Canada (House of Commons) v. Vaid*, 2005 SCC 30; *Chagnon v. Syndicat de la fonction publique et parapublique du Québec*, 2018 SCC 39.

21  Both federalism and democracy featured in *Reference re Secession of Quebec*, [1998] 2 SCR 217.

22  *Toronto v. Ontario*, 2021 SCC 34.

23  Ibid.

24  *Motard v. AG Canada*, 2019 QCCA 1826 para 92.

25  Warren J. Newman, "Some Observations on the Queen, the Crown, the Constitution, and the Courts," *Review of Constitutional Studies* 22 (2017): 55–79, 65.

26  Philippe Lagassé and Patrick Baud, "The Crown and Constitutional Amendment after the Senate Reform and Supreme Court References," in *Constitutional Amendment in Canada*, ed. Emmett Macfarlane (Toronto: University of Toronto Press, 2016), 253.

27  Heard, *Canadian Constitutional Conventions*, above, n.12, 64–76.

28  *Toronto v. Ontario*, 2021 SCC 34.

29  See: Richard Albert, "The Expressive Function of Constitutional Amendment Rules," *McGill Law Review* 59, No.2 (2013): 225–81, para 41.

30  *Motard v. AG Canada*, 2019 QCCA 1826, para 92.

31  *In re The Initiative and Referendum Act*, [1919] AC 935.

32  Doug Stolz, "Dissolution of the Legislatures: Constitutional Change, Institutional Continuity,"*Journal of Parliamentary and Political Law* 5 (2011): 357–59.

33  Quebec preserves the Lieutenant Governor's power of "commuting and remitting sentences": *Executive Power Act*, SQ E-18, s.2.

34  The designation of individual ministerial appointments is a governor-in-council power in British Columbia, Alberta, Manitoba, and New Brunswick; Saskatchewan, Quebec, Nova Scotia and Prince Edward Island retain the formal personal power of the lieutenant governors to appoint members of the executive council and specific ministers under the great seal of the province (which would involve cabinet collaboration in its use). Newfoundland and Labrador alone stipulates in law that the executive council appointments are made on the advice of the premier: *Executive Council Act*, RSNL 1990 E-16.1, s.4(1). Ontario legislation provides the lieutenant governor with the power to appoint members of the executive council and to designate ministers but gives the governor in council the power to stipulate responsibilities of ministers and ministries. *Executive Council Act*, RSO 1990, c. E-20, sections 1 & 2.

35  British Columbia Ministry of Forests, Lands, and Natural Resource Operations, *Crown Lands: Indicators and Statistics Report*, 2010, 5–6. gov.bc.ca/

assets/gov/farming-natural-resources-and-industry/natural-resource-use/
land-water-use/crown-land/crown_land_indicators__statistics_report.pdf.

36 Patrick J. Monahan, Byron Shaw, and Padraig Ryan, *Constitutional Law*, 5th
ed. (Toronto: Irwin, 2017), 209.

37 Sébastien Grammond, "The Protective Function of the Constitutional
Amending Formula," *Review of Constitutional Studies* 22, No. 2 (2017):
171–209, 171.

38 *Supreme Court Act Reference*, above, n.14.

39 See the discussion above, n.11.


## Chapter 4
## The Promise of the Crown in Indigenous-Settler Relations

1 *Taku River Tlingit First Nation v. British Columbia* (Project Assessment
Director), 2004 SCC 74 (CanLII), [2004] 3 SCR 550, canlii.ca/t/1j4tr, retrieved on November 4, 2021.

2 See for example Brian Slattery's discussion of this contradiction in "The
Aboriginal Constitution," *Supreme Court Law Review* 67 (2014) 319, 2014:
CanLIIDocs 33324, canlii.ca/t/ss8x, retrieved on November 4, 2021.

3 *Mitchell v. M.N.R.*, 2001 SCC 33 (CanLII), [2001] 1 SCR 911, canlii.ca/
t/521d, retrieved on November 4, 2021.

4 Technically, Canada was not an independent nation state after 1867 but
rather a self-governing dominion within the British Empire. Full autonomy
was acquired incrementally. Canada and the other Commonwealth dominions achieved legislative equality with Britain through the 1931 *Statute of
Westminster*, except in those areas the dominions chose not to request. In
practical terms the *Statute of Westminster* gave Canada autonomy over foreign policy. The British Judicial Committee of the Privy Council remained
Canada's final court of appeal until 1949, and Canada did not acquire the
right to modify its own constitution until 1982. Even after the passing of the
1947 *Canadian Citizenship Act* Canadians simultaneously remained British
citizens. Only after the passage of the *Citizen Act of 1977* did Canadians
cease to be British subjects and become Canadian citizens alone.

5 Section 141 of the 1927 *Indian Act* stated that anyone who accepted money
to pursue claims against the Crown on behalf of First Nations people "shall
be guilty of an offence and liable upon summary conviction for each such
offence to a penalty not exceeding two hundred dollars and not less than
fifty dollars or to imprisonment for any term not exceeding two months."

6 King George III, "By the King, A Proclamation, Given at Our Court at St.
James, the 7th Day of October, 1763, in the Third Year of our Reign."

7 The *Declaration of Independence*. archives.gov/founding-docs/
declaration-transcript.

8   Sir Edward Bulwer-Lytton to James Douglas, no. 6, July 31, 1858, CO 410/1, 147–57.

9   Ibid.

10  Speech of Sir Edward Bulwer-Lytton, Government of New Caledonia Bill, 2nd Reading, July 8, 1858, in Hansard's *Parliamentary Debates: Third Series*, CLI (London: Cornelius Buck, 1858), 1100–1102.

11  See, for example, Treaty 7 Tribal Council, Walter Hildebrandt, Sarah Carter, and Dorothy First Rider, *The True Spirit and Original Intent of Treaty 7* (Montreal: McGill-Queen's University Press, 1996).

12  Keith Thor Carlson, "Rethinking Dialogue and History: The King's Promise and the 1906 Aboriginal Delegation to London," *Native Studies Review* 16, no. 2 (2005), 1–38.

13  See *Victoria Daily Colonist*, July 6, 1906.

14  Charlie Isipaymilt, testimony before the Royal Commission on Indian Affairs in the Province of British Columbia, May 27, 1913.

15  See, for example, coded telegram from Governor General Earl Grey to High Commissioner Lord Strathcona, PRO, C.O. 42/907; Governor General Earl Grey to High Commissioner Lord Strathcona, August 4, 1906, PRO, C.O. 42/907; "Great White King," *Daily Chronicle*, August 14, 1906; "Chiefs Go to Buckingham Palace Today," *Daily Express*, August 13, 1906.

16  "Redskins to See The King — Chiefs Go to Buckingham Palace Today," *Daily Express*, August 13, 1906.

17  See Rachel Gugielmo, "'Three Nations Warring in the Bosom of a Single State': An Exploration of Identity and Self-Determination in Quebec," *The Fletcher Forum of World Affairs* 21, no. 1 (Winter/Spring 1997).

18  See Lisa Blee, *Framing Chief Leschi: Narratives and Politics of Historical Justice* (Chapel Hill: University of North Carolina Press, 2014).

19  For a recent discussion of the genocide of Indigenous people in California, see Benjamin Madley, *An American Genocide: The United States and the California Indian Catastrophe, 1846–1873* (New Haven: Yale University Press, 2017).

20  James Douglas to the Duke of Newcastle, Victoria, October 25, 1860, BCA, C.O. 60/8, 232–55. Hereafter cited C.O. 60/8, 232–55; Governor Douglas, C.B., to His Grace The Duke of Newcastle, Victoria, October 25, 1860, in *Papers Relating to British Columbia*, Part IV, 27–28.

21  I discuss Douglas' anticipatory reserve system in greater detail in Keith Thor Carlson, "'The Last Potlatch' and James Douglas' Vision of an Alternative Settler Colonialism," in *To Share, Not Surrender: Indigenous and Settler Visions of Treaty Making in the Colonies of Vancouver Island and British Columbia*, ed. Peter Cook, Neil Vallance, John Lutz, Graham Brazier, and Hamar Foster (Vancouver: UBC Press, 2021).

22  James Douglas to the Duke of Newcastle, Victoria, October 9, 1860, BCA, C.O. 60/80 B-1427, 196–226.

23 *Royal Commission on Indian Affairs for the Province of B. C.* "Evidence from Hearings: Meeting with Harrison River Band or Tribe of Indians at Chehalis I.R. #4, on Monday, January 10th, 1915." gsdl.ubcic.bc.ca/cgi-bin/library.cgi?e=q-00000-00---off-0newwestm--00-2----0-10-0 ---0---0direct-10---4-------0-1l--10-en-50---20-about-sir+james--00-3-1 -00-0--4--0--0-0-01-10-0utfZz-8-00&a=d&c=newwestm&srp=0& srn=0&cl=search&d=HASH41eb0adc8523cf1b27dfdc.26.3 (accessed July 1, 2019).

24 Carlson, "'The Last Potlatch.'"

25 I discuss these matters in detail in my *The Power of Place, the Problem of Time: Aboriginal Identity and Historical Consciousness in the Cauldron of Colonialism* (Toronto: University of Toronto Press, 2010). See especially 157–231.

26 Carlson, *Power of Place*, 247–55.

27 See J.R. Miller, *Compact, Contract, Covenant: Aboriginal Treaty-Making in Canada* (Toronto: University of Toronto Press, 2009).

28 Chiefs of Douglas Portage, the Lower Fraser and other Tribes on the Seashore, "Petition to Supt. of Indian Affairs I.W. Wood Powell," July 14, 1874; reproduced in *A Stó:lō Coast Salish Historical Atlas*, ed. Keith Thor Carlson (Vancouver: Douglas and McIntyre, 2001), 173; James Lenihan to Provincial Secretary May 26, 1875.

29 James Lenihan, RG 10, Ref/Vol.: *Sessional Papers 1876*; Page: 54. Source: "Annual Report on Indian Affairs for the year ending June 30, 1875."

30 Governor Douglas promised Coast Salish people that they would continue to have the right to hunt and gather and do other things on open and unclaimed lands in British Columbia, and that the developed lands would be like a fruit tree producing benefits for Indigenous and settler society alike.

31 *Royal Commission on Indian Affairs for the Province of B.C.* "Evidence from Hearings: Meeting with the Matsqui Band or Tribe of Indians on Monday, January 11th, 1915." Complete transcript available through the Union of BC Indian Chiefs website, gsdl.ubcic.bc.ca/cgi-bin/library .cgi?site=localhost&a=p&p=about&c=royalcom&l=en&w=utf-8.

32 This is not to imply that the Canadian government has not engaged in coercive activities to penalized and marginalized particular segments of the population. The RCMP deemed a wide range of activists "deviants" and conducted extensive surveillance campaigns on the members of groups like the Voice of Women, the New Feminists, the League for Socialist Action/Ligue socialiste ouvriére, the Montreal Women's Liberation (Anglophone), the Ligue des femmes du Québec, the Front de libération des femmes, Women Against Soaring Prices, and the Canadian Union of Students. Similarly, the Canadian military and public service both regarded communists and members of the LGBTQ+ community as threats and undesirables well into the 1970s.

Chapter 5

## Overturning Royal Monuments: Confronting History, Reconciliation, and the Honour of the Crown

1   CBC, Manitoba. "2 Statues of Queens Toppled at Manitoba Legislature," July 1, 2021, cbc.ca/news/canada/manitoba/queen-victoria-statue-winnipeg -1.6087684; BBC, "Statues of Queen Victoria and Queen Elizabeth II Torn Down in Canada," July 2, 2021, bbc.com/news/world-us-canada -57693683.

2   There were 139 residential schools across the country, according to the Truth and Reconciliation Commission, from 1831 to 1996.

3   The severed head of the King was found in an old public well in 1834 and is now in the collection of the McCord Museum in Montreal.

4   Alex von Tunzelmann, *Fallen Idols: Twelve Statues That Made History* (New York: HarperCollins, 2021), 89.

5   The monument of Queen Victoria was erected in a park in 1897 to mark the Diamond Jubilee of the Queen. The remaining head of the Queen is presented in the permanent exhibition of the Musée de la civilisation in Quebec City.

6   Daniel Girardin and Christian Pirker. *Controversies: A Legal and Ethical History of Photography* (Paris: Actes Sud, 2012).

7   Ibid., note 4, 27 & ff.

8   Gary Laplante, "Unkept Promises and the Great Mother," *Toronto Star*, May 22, 2021.

9   See, for example, the monument of Paul Chomedey de Maisonneuve (1893), founder of Montreal, in front of Notre Dame church in Old Montreal.

10  Britain had colonies on the five continents. In Africa, Rhodesia became in-dependent in 1964, but its apartheid system ended only in 1980. In Europe, Cyprus became independent in 1960. In Oceania, many islands after 1970. In Asia, the UK finally left Hong Kong in 1997.

11  Motto printed on a commemorative mug under the two sides of a globe, widely distributed among the public on the occasion of the Diamond Jubilee of Queen Victoria, 1897.

12  Bill S-3, 2016, *An Act to amend the Indian Act in response to the Superior Court of Quebec decision in Descheneaux v. Canada*, 2015. Sean Fine, "Ottawa Files Notice of Appeal on Indigenous Child Welfare Ruling, but Plans to Hold Settlement Talks," *Globe and Mail*, October 29, 2021. Those negotiations were supposed to be concluded by the end of 2021. This litiga-tion was initiated in 2007; it will have taken fifteen years of court proceed-ings before achieving a settlement.

13  *Guerin v. R.*, [1984] 2 SCR 335.

14  David Arnot, "The Honour of First Nations — The Honour of the Crown: The Unique Relationship of First Nations with the Crown," queensu.ca/iigr/sites/webpublish.queensu.ca.iigrwww/files/files/conf/Arch/2010/

ConferenceOnTheCrown/CrownConferencePapers/The_Crown_and_the_
First_Nations.pdf, 4.

15  Ibid., 8.

16  J.R. Miller, "'I Will Accept the Queen's Hand': First Nations Leaders and
the Image of the Crown in the Prairie Treaties," in *Reflections and Native-
Newcomers Relations*, ed. James Rodger Miller (Toronto: University of
Toronto Press, 2002), 242–66.

17  Perry Bellegarde, "Crown–First Nations Treaty Relationships," in *Royal
Progress: Canada's Monarchy in the Age of Disruption*, ed. D. Michael Jackson
(Toronto: Dundurn Press, 2020), 20.

18  "We call upon the Government of Canada, on behalf of all Canadians,
to jointly develop with Aboriginal peoples a Royal Proclamation of
Reconciliation to be issued by the Crown […]."

19  J.R. Miller, "I Will Accept the Queen's Hand …"

20  Article 9, *Constitutional Act of 1867*: "The Executive Government and
Authority of and over Canada is hereby declared to continue and be vested
in the Queen."

21  We have not been able to identify royal monuments in the Atlantic provinces.
See Appendix 1 for a list of royal monuments.

22  Alberta: Ralph Steinhauer, 1974–1979; Manitoba, Yvon Dumont, 1993–
1999; Ontario: James Bartleman, 2002–2007; New Brunswick: Graydon
Nicholas, 2009–2014; British Columbia: Steven Point, 2007–2012;
Saskatchewan: Russell Mirasty, 2019–). Many Indigenous persons have
also occupied the function of territorial commissioner in Yukon, Northwest
Territories, and Nunavut.

23  The original bust was brought back to France at the cession of New France in
1763. The present bust was cast after the Coysevox original that ornamented
Place Royale in the Lower Town of Quebec during the French regime.

## Chapter 6

### Treaty Spaces: The Chapels Royal in Canada

1  H. Walton, ed., *Speeches and Addresses of Lord Dufferin* (London: John
Murray, 1882), 209.

2  Freda F. Wilson, "Queen Anne and 'The Four Kings of Canada': A
Bibliography of Contemporary Sources," *Canadian Historical Review* 16,
no. 3 (1935): 266–75.

3  Perry Bellegarde, "Address at Historic Gathering of the Queen's
Representatives in Canada and First Nations Leaders," June 12, 2019.

4  Chief R. Stacey Laforme, letter to Chapel Royal Committee, September 6, 2016.

5  Massey College, "The Chapel Royal," masseycollege.ca/the-chapel-royal/.
Accessed January 8, 2022.

6   Nathan Tidridge, *The Queen at the Council Fire: The Treaty of Niagara, Reconciliation, and the Dignified Crown in Canada* (Toronto: Dundurn, 2015).

7   The members of the original Chapel Royal steering committee were John Fraser, Elder Carolyn King, Sandra Shaul, Clara Fraser, Audrey Rochette, Benjamin Gillard, Junior Fellow Owen Kane, and Nathan Tidridge. Elder Garry Sault and Chief Stacey Laforme acted as advisors.

8   There were exceptions, including Manitoba's second lieutenant governor, Alexander Morris (1872–1877), whose advocacy of Indigenous rights during treaty negotiations for Treaties 3, 4, 5, and 6 often brought him into conflict with John A. Macdonald's government in Ottawa. See Robert Talbot, *Negotiating the Numbered Treaties: An Intellectual and Political History of Alexander Morris* (Saskatoon: Purich Publishing, 2009).

9   Mississaugas of the Credit First Nation, "Chapel Royal Tobacco," October 6, 2020.

10  Mary Simon, installation speech as Governor General of Canada, July 26, 2021.

## Chapter 7

## The Enduring Crown in Canada: Reflections on the Office of Governor General at the Platinum Jubilee

1   Quintet Consulting, "Final Review Report into Workplace Conditions at Rideau Hall," redacted version, January 12, 2021, theglobeandmail.com/files/editorial/News/GG/Report-into-workplace-conditions-at-Rideau-Hall.pdf.

2   "Maryland Court Releases Payette Divorce Documents," CBC News, August 29, 2017, cbc.ca/news/politics/payette-divorce-documents-1.4258921.

3   Ashley Burke and Kristen Everson, "PMO Failed to Check with Key Former Employers Before Payette's Appointment as Governor General: sources," CBC News, September 21, 2020, cbc.ca/news/politics/governor-general-julie-payette-hr-issues-past-employers-1.5732109.

4   Lee Berthiaume, "Trudeau Calls Payette 'Excellent' Governor General, Says No Plans to Replace Her," CTV News, September 2, 2020, ctvnews.ca/politics/trudeau-calls-payette-excellent-governor-general-says-no-plans-to-replace-her-1.5089645.

5   *The Sun*, Transcript of Oprah Winfrey interview with the Duke and Duchess of Sussex, March 8, 2021, thesun.co.uk/news/14277841/meghan-markle-oprah-interview-full-transcript/, accessed October 4, 2021.

6   William Shakespeare, *Henry V*, 4.1.243–45.

7   For more detail, see Barbara J. Messamore, "George VI's 1939 Royal Tour of Canada: Context and the Constitution," *Royal Studies Journal* 5, no. 1 (2018): 126–46.

8   Campbell Clark, "A Hot Debate About Head of State," *Globe and Mail*, October 10, 2009, theglobeandmail.com/news/politics/a-hot-debate-about-head-of-state/article4290596/, accessed October 6, 2021.

9 Walter Bagehot, *The English Constitution* (London: Chapman & Hall, 1867; (Oxford University Press, 2001), 7. Citation refers to the Oxford edition.

10 Andrew Gailey, *The Lost Imperialist: Lord Dufferin, Memory and Mythmaking in an Age of Celebrity* (London: John Murray, 2015), 132; Barbara J. Messamore, *Canada's Governors General, 1847–1878: Biography and Constitutional Evolution* (Toronto: University of Toronto Press, 2006), chapter 8; and, for example, Dufferin to Kimberley, October 26, 1873, Dufferin MS, A 406, Library and Archives Canada (LAC).

11 Dufferin to Kimberley, private, August 5, 1873, Dufferin MS, A 407, LAC.

12 Lorne to Hicks Beach, private, April 6, 1879, Lorne MS, A 717, LAC.

13 Hicks Beach to Lorne, private, June 13, 1879, Lorne MS, A 717, LAC.

14 Lorne to Hicks-Beach, Dec. 3, 1878; Hicks Beach to Lorne, February 11, 1879, Lorne MS, A 717 LAC.

15 C.P. Stacey, "Britain's Withdrawal from North America, 1864–1871," *Canadian Historical Review* 36, no. 3 (September 1955), 187; Richard Preston, *The Defence of the Undefended Border: Planning for War in North America, 1867–1939* (Montreal and Kingston: McGill-Queen's University Press, 1977), 1; Lorne to Lansdowne, June 17, 1883, Lorne MS, A 716, LAC.

16 Stanley to John A. Macdonald, July 20, 1890, Stanley MS, A 446, LAC.

17 As quoted by John Buchan in *Lord Minto: A Memoir* (London: Thomas Nelson, 1924), 148. Minto's difficult negotiations of the question of Canadian military aid during the South African War are treated in depth in Carman Miller, *The Canadian Career of the Fourth Earl of Minto: The Education of a Viceroy* (Waterloo: Wilfrid Laurier University Press, 1980).

18 R.H. Hubbard, *Rideau Hall: An Illustrated History of Government House, Ottawa, from Victorian Times to the Present Day* (Montreal: McGill-Queen's University Press, 1977), 137.

19 Jeffery Williams, *Byng of Vimy: General and Governor General* (Toronto: University of Toronto Press, 1992), 267.

20 Hubbard, *Rideau Hall*, 195, 199.

21 *Statute of Westminster*, 1931, 22 Geo. V, c. 4 (U.K.), justice.gc.ca/eng/rp-pr/csj-sjc/constitution/lawreg-loireg/p1t171.html, accessed October 6, 2021.

22 Mackenzie King, as quoted by Peter Marshall in "The Balfour Formula and the Evolution of the Commonwealth," *The Round Table* 90, no. 361 (September 2001), 546.

23 Claude Bissell, *The Imperial Canadian: Vincent Massey in Office* (Toronto: University of Toronto Press, 1986), 239.

24 See Jeffery Williams, *Byng of Vimy*, 268, 316, 318-19; Anne Twomey, *The Veiled Sceptre: Reserve Powers of Heads of State in Westminster Systems* (Cambridge University Press, 2018), 388–402.

25 Hubbard, *Rideau Hall*, 161, 170.

26 Bissell, *The Imperial Canadian*, 239.

27  As quoted by David E. Smith in *The Invisible Crown: The First Principle of Canadian Government* (Toronto: University of Toronto Press, 1995), 123.

28  Memorandum by A. Shuldham Redfern, 1945, as quoted by David E. Smith in *The Invisible Crown*, 123.

29  John Buchan, *Memory Hold-the-Door* (Toronto: Musson, 1940), 241.

30  John Buchan, *The King's Grace, 1910–1935* (London: Hodder and Stoughton, 1935), gutenberg.net.au/ebooks/n00005.html.

31  John Buchan, *Memory Hold-the-Door*, 243.

32  J. William Galbraith, *John Buchan: Model Governor General* (Toronto: Dundurn, 2013), 32, 108–09.

33  Galbraith, *John Buchan*, 32, 108–13, 432 n. 91.

34  Galbraith, *John Buchan*, 148–49.

35  Tony McCulloch, "Roosevelt, Mackenzie King and the British Royal Visit to the USA in 1939," *London Journal of Canadian Studies* 23 (2007–08), 86. Galbraith, *John Buchan*, 151; as quoted by Arthur Bousfield and Garry Toffoli in *Royal Spring: The Royal Tour of 1939 and the Queen Mother in Canada* (Toronto: Dundurn, 1989), 23.

36  Lord Tweedsmuir, as quoted by William Buchan in *John Buchan: A Memoir* (Toronto: Griffin House, 1982), 235; Galbraith, *John Buchan*,151–53.

37  Galbraith, *John Buchan*, 101–04, 204–05.

38  Messamore, "George VI's 1939 Royal Tour of Canada," 137–40.

39  Carolyn Harris, "Alexander Cambridge, Earl of Athlone," *The Canadian Encyclopedia*, thecanadianencyclopedia.ca/en/article/alexander-cambridge -earl-of-athlone.

40  *The London Gazette*, March 13, 1936, p. 1657, thegazette.co.uk/London/ issue/34264/page/1657

41  *The Memoirs of Field-Marshal Earl Alexander of Tunis, 1940-1945* (London: Cassell, 1962), 129–30.

42  *Letters Patent Constituting the Office of Governor General of Canada*, 1947, solon.org/Constitutions/Canada/English/LettersPatent.html, accessed October 12, 2021.

43  Peter W. Hogg, *Constitutional Law of Canada*. 5th ed., supplemented vol. 1 (Toronto: Thomson Canada, 2007), chapter 11.3, chapter 11.2.

44  Bissell, *The Imperial Canadian*, 53, 237–39.

45  The Oxford University Ice Hockey Club is a virtual who's who of Canada's elite. See Trent Taylor and Alan Keeso, "Oxford University Ice Hockey Club," *Canadian Encyclopedia*, April 8, 2016, thecanadianencyclopedia.ca/ en/article/canadians-at-oxford-university.

46  Robert Speaight, *Vanier: Soldier, Diplomat & Governor General* (Toronto: Collins, 1970), 93.

47  Some short films available online provide useful surveys of Vanier's distin-guished career. See Historica Canada, "The Canadians: Georges Vanier" (2002), youtube.com/watch?v=yjxte83LscA; and National Film Board of

Canada, "George P. Vanier: Soldier, Diplomat, Governor General," (1960), youtube.com/watch?v=5gNz5ZRdCX0.

48  Speaight, *Vanier*, 114–15, 399.
49  George Vanier, 1959 Installation speech, in *Only to Serve: Selections from Addresses of Governor General George P. Vanier*, ed. George Cowley and Michel Vanier (Toronto: University of Toronto Press, 1970), 3-4; see also Mary Frances Coady, *Georges and Pauline Vanier: Portrait of a Couple* (Montreal and Kingston: McGill-Queen's University Press, 2011), chapter 16.
50  Greg Hudson, "The GGGG: Welcome to the Governor General Guessing Game," *Toronto Life*, April 6, 2010, torontolife.com/city/the-gggg-welcome-to-the-governor-general-guessing-game/. See also Chris Windeyer, "Sources tout Mary Simon as next Governor General," *Nunatsiaq News*, February 21, 2010, nunatsiaq.com/stories/article/89768_sources_tout_mary_simon_as_next_governor_general/.
51  Catharine Tunney and Darren Major, "Mary Simon Officially Becomes Canada's First Inuk Governor General," July 26, 2021, CBC News, cbc.ca/news/politics/mary-simon-installed-as-governor-general-1.6114622.

## Chapter 8

## The Lieutenant Governors — Second Fiddles or Coordinate Viceregals?

1  *The Liquidators of the Maritime Bank of Canada v. The Receiver-General of New Brunswick*, [1892] AC 437.
2  *The King v. Caroll*, [1948] S.C.R. 126.
3  David E. Smith, *The Invisible Crown: The First Principle of Canadian Government* (Toronto: University of Toronto Press, 1995, 2013). See also D. Michael Jackson, *The Crown and Canadian Federalism* (Toronto: Dundurn, 2013).
4  Andrew Heard, "The Provincial Crown and Lieutenant Governors," in *Royal Progress: Canada's Monarchy in the Age of Disruption*, ed. D. Michael Jackson (Toronto: Dundurn, 2020), 54, 58.
5  In Australia, the governors of the states are appointed by the Queen on the advice of the state premiers, a practice entrenched by the *Australia Acts* of 1986.
6  In 2015 the Harper government amended the table to give status to the lieutenant governors immediately after the prime minister at events held in their province. Note 1.1 in canada.ca/en/canadian-heritage/services/protocol-guidelines-special-event/table-precedence-canada.html.
7  "The Provincial Crown and Lieutenant Governors," 61.
8  Christopher McCreery, "The Provincial Crown: The Lieutenant Governor's Expanding Role," in *Canada and the Crown: Essays on Constitutional Monarchy*, ed. D. Michael Jackson and Philippe Lagassé (Montreal & Kingston: McGill-Queen's University Press, 2013).
9  Christopher McCreery, "The Vulnerability of Vice-Regal Offices in

Canada," in *The Canadian Kingdom: 150 Years of Constitutional Monarchy*, ed. D. Michael Jackson (Toronto: Dundurn, 2018).

10  "The Provincial Crown: The Lieutenant Governor's Expanding Role," 157.

11  Office of the Prime Minister of Canada, "PM announces new Advisory Committee on Vice-Regal Appointments." web.archive.org/web/20121106084858/http:/pm.gc.ca/eng/media.asp?category=1&featureId=6&pageId=26&id=5139. Queen's Printer for Canada. Archived from the original on November 6, 2012. Retrieved November 4, 2012. See also Christopher McCreery, "Subtle Yet Significant Innovations: The Vice-Regal Appointments Committee and the Secretary's new Role" in *The Crown and Parliament*, ed. Michael Bédard and Philippe Lagassé (Toronto: Thompson Reuters, 2015).

12  "The Provincial Crown and Lieutenant Governors," 63–64.

13  Ibid., 61.

14  "The Vulnerability of Vice-Regal Offices in Canada," 156.

15  For the history of the provincial Government Houses, see R.H. Hubbard, *Ample Mansions: The Viceregal Residences of the Canadian Provinces* (Ottawa: University of Ottawa Press, 1989).

16  "The Vulnerability of Vice-Regal Offices in Canada," 161.

17  See Christopher McCreery, *Government House Halifax: A Place of History and Gathering* (Fredericton: Goose Lane Editions, 2020).

18  See D. Michael Jackson, *The Crown and Canadian Federalism*, 143–48.

19  For a discussion of this role, see David E. Smith, *The Invisible Crown*; D. Michael Jackson, *The Crown and Canadian Federalism*; and Andrew Heard, "The Provincial Crown and Lieutenant Governors."

20  See D. Michael Jackson, *The Crown and Canadian Federalism*, 115–25.

21  See Andrew Heard, "British Columbia's 2017 Extraordinary Contribution to Constitutional Conventions," *Journal of Parliamentary and Political Law* 11 (2017): 563–69.

22  See in this volume Damien-Claude Bélanger, "The Rise and Fall of French Canadian Loyalism."

23  *Les Cahiers de Droit* 58, no 4 (2017), abstract, 626. We thank Andrew Heard for drawing this article to our attention.

24  Ibid., 627, 644.

25  "Amendments to the Constitution in relation to the 'office of the Queen, the Governor General and the Lieutenant Governor of a province' are subject to the strictest amending procedure under paragraph 41(a) [of the Constitution Act, 1982], which requires the unanimous consent of the Houses of Parliament and the provincial legislative assemblies … it was evidently meant to provide Canada's constitutional monarchy with the highest degree of constitutional protection." Philippe Lagassé and Patrick Baud, "The Crown and Constitutional Amendment after the *Senate Reform* and *Supreme Court References*" in *Constitutional Amendment in Canada*, ed. Emmett Macfarlane (University of Toronto Press, 2016), 248.

26 *Journal des Débats de l'Assemblée nationale*, February 10, 2021. assnat
.qc.ca/fr/travaux-parlementaires/assemblee-nationale/42-1/journal-debats
/20210210/289491.html#_Toc64361725.

27 "Lieutenant-Gouverneur: Moderniser sans révolutionner," *La Presse*, March
12, 2021 (our translation).

28 J. Michael Doyon taught history at the CEGEP level and at Laurentian
University in Sudbury. He holds a degree in Law and a PhD in History from
Université Laval and a PhD in Philosophy from Laval.

29 See note 23.

30 Caroline Plante, "La Covid-19 dangereuse pour la démocratie, dit le lieutenant-gouverneur," *La Presse*, April 22, 2020 (translation).

31 "The Provincial Crown: The Lieutenant Governor's Expanding Role," 147.

32 See Christopher McCreery, *The Canadian Honours System*, 2nd ed. (Toronto:
Dundurn, 2015), 344–63 and 573–88; and D. Michael Jackson, *The Crown
and Canadian Federalism*, 173–81.

33 Attempts by some governors general to be involved in these deliberations have
led to controversy, most notably in the case of Julie Payette (2017 to 2021).

34 Christopher McCreery, *The Order of Canada: Genesis of an Honours System*
(Toronto: University of Toronto Press, 2018), 210.

35 See David Johnston's chapter in this volume, "Queen Elizabeth II: A Personal
Tribute."

36 Until the establishment of the national honours system in 1967, Canada
had shared in commemorative medals of the British Empire or the
Commonwealth for jubilees and coronations of reigning monarchs, the last
being the coronation of Elizabeth II in 1953. In addition to creating the
Order of Canada in 1967, the federal government issued a commemorative
medal for the Centennial of Confederation. This was followed by medals for
the Silver (1977), Golden (2002), and Diamond (2012) Jubilees of Queen
Elizabeth II and for the 125th anniversary of Confederation in 1992. The
administration of Prime Minister Justin Trudeau broke with this pattern
when it failed to create commemorative medals for the 150th anniversary of
Confederation in 2017 and the Queen's Platinum Jubilee in 2022.

37 The federal government's lacklustre Platinum Jubilee program — a far
cry from the extensive Diamond Jubilee celebration in 2012 — was limited to an emblem created by the Canadian Heraldic Authority; a lapel pin
issued by the Department of Canadian Heritage but distributed for them
by the Monarchist League of Canada; a coin and a postage stamp; a brief,
three-day tour in May by the Prince of Wales and Duchess of Cornwall
to Newfoundland and Labrador, the National Capital Region, and the
Northwest Territories; a small grant program; and a display in Ottawa.

Provinces undertook a number of initiatives in addition to the commemorative medals and the Jubilee Gardens. Other organizations marked the
Jubilee with specific projects; for example, the Royal Canadian Geographical

Society created website material and "GeoMinutes" about the Queen's reign and devoted a special issue of its magazine Canadian Geographic to the Jubilee; the Institute for the Study of the Crown in Canada posted a series of "Backgrounders" on the Crown on its website, published the present volume with Dundurn Press, and planned a Jubilee conference on the Crown in St. John's, Newfoundland and Labrador.

38  For further discussion of this topic, see Nathan Tidridge, *The Queen at the Council Fire: The Treaty of Niagara, Reconciliation and the Dignified Crown in Canada* (Toronto: Dundurn, 2015); D. Michael Jackson, *The Crown and Canadian Federalism*, 185–87 and 241–45; David Arnot, "The Honour of the First Nations — The Honour of the Crown: The Unique Relationship of First Nations with the Crown," in *The Evolving Canadian Crown*, ed. Jennifer Smith and D. Michael Jackson (Montreal & Kingston: McGill-Queen's University Press, 2012), 165–66.

39  Perry Bellegarde, "Crown–First Nations Treaty Relationships," in *Royal Progress: Canada's Monarchy in the Age of Disruption*, ed. D. Michael Jackson (Toronto: Dundurn, 2020), 21.

40  *Grassy Narrows First Nations v. Ontario (Natural Resources)*, [2014] 2 S.C.R. 447.

41  "L'indivisibilité de la Couronne a servi d'assise à la reconnaissance du statut des gouvernements provinciaux comme interlocuteurs des Premières Nations dans les champs de compétence provinciaux." Julien Fournier and Amélie Binette, "La Couronne: vecteur du fédéralisme canadien," *Les Cahiers de droit* 58, no. 4 (December 2017), 647.

42  *Activity Report*, The Honourable Elizabeth Dowdeswell, April 2020–March 2021 (Toronto: Queen's Printer of Ontario, 2021), 21–23. lgontario.ca/custom/uploads/2021/05/2020-2021-LG-AR-English-Full-V.4ACC2-2.pdf, 21–23.

43  See in this volume John Fraser, Carolyn King, and Nathan Tidridge, "Treaty Spaces: The Chapels Royal in Canada."

44  Honourable Janet Austin, Lieutenant Governor of British Columbia Blog, "Reconciliation," April 20, 2022, ltgov.bc.ca/category/blog/reconciliation/.

45  "Recommendations for the Office of the Governor General," January 11, 2019.

46  "An Empowered GG Could Restore the Crown's Role as Treaty Partner," *Policy Options*, May 15, 2020. policyoptions.irpp.org/fr/magazines/may-2020/an-empowered-gg-could-restore-crowns-role-as-treaty-partner/.

47  Information provided by the Office of the Lieutenant Governor of Saskatchewan, January 2022.

48  Frank MacKinnon, *The Crown in Canada* (Calgary: McClelland & Stewart West, 1976).

49  See Andrew Heard, "The Provincial Crown and Lieutenant Governors," 61–66; D. Michael Jackson, *The Crown and Canadian Federalism*, 187–96; Christopher McCreery, "The Provincial Crown: The Lieutenant Governor's Expanding Role" and "The Vulnerability of Vice-Regal Offices in Canada."

50   See Andrew Heard, "The Provincial Crown and Lieutenant Governors," 61, and *Journal des débats de l'Assemblée nationale — Assemblée nationale du Québec* (assnat.qc.ca/fr/travaux-parlementaires/assemblee-nationale/42-1/ journal-debats/20210210/289491.html#_Toc64361725).

## Chapter 9
## The Spare Fire Extinguisher: The Administrator of the Government of Canada

1   *Canada Gazette*, Part 1, April 10, 2021.

2   Although the Duke of Connaught was absent from his post as governor general for 217 days, from March 22 to October 25, 1913, the appointment of an administrator was split between Chief Justice Sir Charles Fitzpatrick and the senior puisne judge, Sir Louis H. Davies, over the period. See Table 1.1.

3   Frank MacKinnon, *The Crown in Canada* (Calgary: McClelland and Stewart West, 1976), 124.

4   Christopher McCreery, "Myth and Misunderstanding: The Origins and Meaning of the Letters Patent Constituting the Office of the Governor General" in *The Evolving Canadian Crown*, ed. *Jennifer Smith and Michael Jackson* (Montreal and Kingston: McGill-Queen's University Press, 2012), 32.

5   *Letters Patent Constituting the Office of the Governor General*, 1947, clause VIII.

6   In 2019, the practice for appointing administrators in the provinces was changed, whereby the previous protocol, which required a separate order in council to be issued on every occasion on which an administrator took office, was replaced by a list system that appointed (in most jurisdictions) the chief justice of the province and the four senior justices of the provincial court of appeal to serve as administrators in the case of the absence or incapacity of the lieutenant governor. In essence, this new system leaves in place a dormant commission that is activated whenever required at the direction of the lieutenant governor via communication with the chief justice in his capacity as administrator.

7   Christopher McCreery, "The Provincial Crown: The Lieutenant Governor's Expanding Role," in *The Evolving Canadian Crown*, 154.

8   There is one contemporary example of a living lieutenant governor vacating office before a successor was sworn in; this occurred in 1968 in New Brunswick, when John B. McNair resigned after three and a half years in office. McNair's resignation was implemented by order in council and there was a one-day vacancy in the office prior to his successor, Wallace Bird, being sworn into office. Bird's death in 1971 while serving resulted in a six-day vacancy prior to Hédard Robichaud being sworn in and assuming the viceregal office.

9   The death of Saskatchewan's 22nd lieutenant governor, Thomas Molloy, in May 2019, and the death of New Brunswick's 31st lieutenant governor, Jocelyne Roy-Vienneau, in August 2019.

10  Previously in Virginia, if the council could not select a person to act for the governor the role devolved to the lieutenant governor and then to other members of the council, depending on what other offices they held.

11  Leonard W. Labaree, *Royal Government in America; A Study of the British Colonial System Before 1783* (New York: F. Ungar Publishing Company, 1958), 127.

12  Percy Scott Flippin, *The Royal Government in Virginia*, vol. 84, no. 1 of *Studies in History, Economics and Public Law* (New York: Columbia University Press, 1919), x.

13  Royal Instructions to Governor James Murray, Quebec, December 7, 1763.

14  Leonard Woods Labaree, ed., *Royal Instructions to British Colonial Governors, 1670–1776* (New York: D. Appleton-Century Co, 1935), 28–29.

15  Alison Quentin-Baxter and Janet McLean, *This Realm of New Zealand: The Sovereign, the Governor-General, the Crown* (Auckland: Auckland University Press, 2017), 140.

16  Although he would remain nominally in office until 1807, Prescott never returned to Canada.

17  Pierre Tousignant and Jean-Pierre Wallot, *Dictionary of Canadian Biography* entry for Thomas Dunn, biographi.ca/en/bio/dunn_thomas_5E.html.

18  Lord Durham's Commissions: Lower Canada, Upper Canada, and New Brunswick, March 30, 1838; Nova Scotia, February 6, 1838; Prince Edward Island, February 6, 1838.

19  Commission appointing Lord Monck as governor general of Canada, July 1, 1867.

20  Anne Twomey, *The Veiled Sceptre: Reserve Powers of Heads of State in Westminster Systems* (Cambridge: Cambridge University Press, 2018), 847.

21  John Buchan, *Lord Minto: A Memoir* (London: Thomas Nelson and Sons, 1924), 76.

22  Order-in-Council 1901-551, March 11, 1901.

23  Amended commission of appointment issued to Lord Minto by King Edward VII, May 7, 1901.

24  *Canada Gazette*, June 14, 1902.

25  *Letters Patent Constituting the Office of the Governor General, 1905.*

26  Section 15 of the *Constitution Act, 1867* vests "the Command-in-Chief of the Land and Naval Militia, and of all the Naval and Military Forces, of and in Canada" in the Queen, although the authority has, since 1905, been vested in the governor general.

27  *Letters Patent Constituting of Office of the Governor General of Australia*, October 29, 1900.

28  *Journals of the Senate of Canada*, proclamation proroguing Parliament, November 23, 1904.

29  *Letters Patent* of 1935, amending the *Letters Patent* of 1931.

30  The provision-1935 amendments to the *Letters Patent 1931* were first exercised when Lord Tweedsmuir officially visited Washington, D.C., in March

1937. The timing of their implementation was fortuitous, as the Second World War brought about more frequent viceregal visits to the United States. Lord Athlone would make two significant official visits to meet with Franklin Roosevelt, the first in October 1940 and the second in March 1945.

31  McCreery, "Myth and Misunderstanding," 33.

32  LAC R5047-0-4-E, Esmond Butler Fonds, Léger Stroke File.

33  Percy Scott Flippin, *Royal Government in Virginia, 1624–1775* (New York: Longmans, Green & Co, 1919), 80.

34  Colonial Office Despatch 88, Lord Carnarvon to Lord Dufferin, April 8, 1875.

35  Order-in-Council 1875-123, April 28, 1875.

36  Minto to Senator Richard Scott, November 25, 1899. in *Lord Minto's Canadian Papers*, ed. John T. Saywell and Paul Stevens (Toronto: Champlain Society, 1983), 199.

37  Ibid.

38  Sir Alan Lascelles, *Government House Ottawa Confidential*, "The Green Book" (Ottawa: King's Printer, 1934).

39  Lascelles, 37.

40  Maurice A. Pope, ed., *Public Servant: The Memoirs of Sir Joseph Pope* (Toronto: Oxford University Press, 1960), 158–59.

41  Minto to Herbert, January 3, 1902, *Lord Minto's Canadian Papers*, 241.

42  Pope, 158.

43  David Ricardo Williams, *Duff: A Life in the Law* (Toronto: Osgoode Society, 1984), 141.

44  Twomey, 847.

45  Ibid., 846.

46  Christopher McCreery, "Confidant and Chief of Staff: The Governor's Secretary," in *The Evolving Canadian Crown*, 211.

47  *Kassongo Tunda v. The Minister of Citizenship and Immigration*, [2001] FCA 151.

48  Ibid. This occurred in Fiji in 1971, when a writ was issued challenging the appointment of the chief justice as acting governor general. Twomey, 847.

49  Quentin-Baxter and McLean, 140.

50  McCreery, "Confidant and Chief of Staff," 197.

51  Twomey, 847.

52  Pope, 158.

53  Farewell message from His Excellency Richard Wagner, Administrator of the Government of Canada, July 20, 2021, gg.ca/en/media/news/2021/message-canadians-administrator.

54  The administrators listed on the website of the Office of the Secretary to the Governor General are not accurate, gg.ca/en/resource-centre/administrator-government-canada (accessed February 26, 2022).

## Chapter 10
## A Right Honourable Journey: The Queen and Her Canadian Prime Ministers

1    Visiting the United Kingdom while prime minister in 1921, Meighen voiced his belief in the importance of the Crown in Canada and on the wider stage. "It falls to me to propose the toast the members of the Royal Family," he said during a speech before the Royal Colonial Institute in London (now the Royal Commonwealth Society). "This is a duty which is peculiarly pleasurable to one who comes to London on behalf of the Dominion of Canada. No tie which binds together our far-flung Empire is more valued or respected than the universal attachment of British subjects throughout the world to the House of Windsor ... These feelings of human attachment which we are accustomed, in our somewhat inexpressive way, to sum up in the phrase, loyalty to the Crown, are a part, a large part, of that common sentiment that binds the British Empire together. Long may it live and flourish." See Arthur Meighen, *Overseas Addresses, June-July 1921* (Toronto: Musson, 1921), 29.

2    Roger Graham, *Arthur Meighen: A Biography*, vol. 3, *No Surrender* (Toronto: Clarke, Irwin, 1965), 186.

3    Readers may be interested to learn that another historical figure, like Meighen, far removed from past glories, was also invited aboard the *Britannia*. Grand Duchess Olga, the sister of the last Tsar of Russia, Nicolas II, who herself lived quietly in exile in Toronto and area, was also received by Her Majesty in June of 1959 in Toronto. For many Canadians this was the first time they had learned of Olga's presence in their country.

4    It is also likely the future Queen met R.B. Bennett, particularly as he served in the House of Lords in London from 1941 until his death in 1947. To date the author has found no direct reference to Princess Elizabeth meeting Viscount Bennett.

5    Interview by the author with Justin Trudeau, December 3, 2021.

6    Ibid.

7    Former prime minister Joe Clark recalls a story involving his daughter that confirms Prime Minister Justin Trudeau's memories of Her Majesty's abilities and skill in interacting with children. "Our daughter Catherine (then turning eleven) came with us to the Vancouver Commonwealth Heads of Government Meeting in 1987 and attended the reception in the Hotel Vancouver for Her Majesty," Clark said. "As the Queen made her way in, Catherine curtsied appropriately, and the Queen was, as usual, gracious. Catherine then scurried around the reception for an hour or so, then got tired, so sat herself down on a chesterfield near the exit door. A little later, the Queen was on her way to the door, noticed Catherine and said 'Are you still here?' Catherine replied: 'Yes, my parents told me I can't leave before you do.' The Queen said: 'Well then, let's go out together,' and off

they walked through the door, then said good-bye, and Catherine waited for her parents to catch up." Email correspondence, Joe Clark to Arthur Milnes, November 3, 2021. Brian Mulroney, in a private journal entry he wrote after his first meeting with the Queen, offers a possible explanation for Her Majesty's special efforts to take time for the children she meets. "Her Majesty offered a private, intimate meal in honour of the new prime minister and his wife," the eighteenth prime minister wrote. "I think about twenty attended, all told. At dinner, the Queen told me of her affection for John F. Kennedy's mother, Rose, because when she and Margaret were young, a relative died, and the two girls were banished to a small room when important guests called. Only Rose Kennedy came into the room and chatted with them. They were ignored by the other guests — and she remembered it, some forty years later! One shouldn't really cross the Queen I concluded." Brian Mulroney, Memoirs (Toronto: McClelland and Stewart, 2007), 326.

8   "Justin Trudeau's Toast to the Queen Elicits Cheeky Royal Response," *CBC News*, November 27, 2015, cbc.ca/news/politics/full-text-trudeau-toast-queen-1.3340584.

9   LAC MG 26 J5, Mackenzie King Diary, Library and Archives Canada, December 8, 1936.

10   Mackenzie King Diary, August 31, 1941.

11   Mackenzie King Diary, October 23, 1945.

12   Mackenzie King Diary, May 24, 1946.

13   Christopher McCreery, "The Politics of St-Laurent on the Crown, Rituals, and Symbols," in *The Unexpected Louis St-Laurent*, ed. Patrice Dutil (Vancouver: University of British Columbia Press, 2020), 315–16.

14   John Diefenbaker, *One Canada*, vol. 2, *The Years of Achievement, 1957–1962* (Toronto: Macmillan of Canada, 1976), 83.

15   Ibid., 62.

16   Lester B. Pearson, *Mike: The Memoirs of the Rt. Hon. Lester B. Pearson*, vol. 3 (Toronto: University of Toronto Press, 1975), 291.

17   Brian Mulroney, *Memoirs* (Toronto: McClelland and Stewart, 2007), 61–62.

18   The author served as Mr. Mulroney's memoirs assistant between 2003 and 2008.

19   Ibid., 62.

20   Pearson, *Memoirs*, vol. 3, 299.

21   Ibid., 300.

22   Ibid., 300–01.

23   Ibid., 301–2.

24   LAC MG 26 02, vol. 23, file 2, Pierre Trudeau Papers. Interview between Ron Graham and Pierre Trudeau, May 12, 1992. The author would like to thank Thomas Axworthy and LAC's Michael Macdonald for facilitating access to the interview transcript. Former prime minister Joe Clark also recalled interacting with the Queen at the Commonwealth Heads of Government Meeting

(CHOGM) he attended in Africa as prime minister in 1979. "I also remember, at the Lusaka CHOGM how impressed (we were) by the sincerity and skill of her engagement with small luncheon groups of her prime ministers — she joked with us, asked pointed questions, was always both well-informed and respectful." Email from Joe Clark to the author, November 2, 2021.

25  Interview by the author with Justin Trudeau, December 3, 2021.

26  Interview by the author with Thomas Axworthy, September 17, 2021.

27  Pierre Trudeau, *Memoirs* (Toronto: McClelland and Stewart, 1993), 313.

28  Interview by the author with Brian Mulroney, November 16, 2021.

29  Ibid.

30  Ibid.

31  Mulroney, *Memoirs*, 326.

32  Jean Chrétien, *My Stories, My Times* (Toronto: Random House Canada, 2018), 32.

33  "Nunavut Gives Queen a Warm Welcome," *The Globe and Mail*, October 5, 2002, theglobeandmail.com/news/national/nunavut-gives-queen-a-warm -welcome/article25423087/.

34  Interview by the author with Paul Martin, December 3, 2021.

35  Interview by the author with Stephen J. Harper, November 1, 2021.

36  Ibid.

37  Ibid.

38  Ibid.


## Chapter 11
### The Rise and Fall of French Canadian Loyalism

1  Pierre Vallières helped popularize this notion in his best-selling *Nègres blancs d'Amérique*, though it was perhaps novelist and literary scholar Adrien Thério who developed it most fully in an anthology published in 1999. [Pierre Vallières, *Nègres blancs d'Amérique* (Paris: Maspero, 1969), 30; Adrien Thério, *Un siècle de collusion entre le clergé et le gouvernement britannique. Anthologie des mandements des évêques* (Montreal: XYZ Éditeur, 1999).]

2  Yvan Lamonde, *Histoire sociale des idées au Québec*, vol. 1: *1760–1896* (Montreal: Fides, 2000), 47.

3  Donal Lowry, "The Crown, Empire Loyalism and the Assimilation of Non-British White Subjects in the British World: An Argument against 'Ethnic Determinism,'" *Journal of Imperial and Commonwealth History* 31 (2003): 99.

4  Jean-Olivier Briand, "Mandement pour faire chanter un *Te Deum* en action de grâce du mariage du roi George III (14 février 1762),"in *Mandements, lettres pastorales et circulaires des évêques de Québec*, ed. Henri Têtu and Charles-Octave Gagnon, vol. 2 (Quebec City: A. Côté, 1888), 160–61. No doubt anticipating resistance to this change from some parish priests,

Briand appended a revealing note to his *mandement*: "Monsieur … Peut-être blâmerez-vous quelques-uns des articles de mon mandement; s'il m'avait été possible, j'eusse demandé sur une matière aussi difficile, le sentiment de messieurs les curés; je m'en suis rapporté à celui du clergé de la ville, qui pense presque unanimement qu'il n'est point défendu dans les prières publiques de nommer un hérétique non dénoncé. Au reste, je vous prie d'expliquer à vos paroissiens dans quel sens nous pouvons prier pour ceux qui sont hors de l'Église." (Jean-Olivier Briand to the clergy of the Diocese of Quebec, in ibid., 162). In a subsequent letter to the vicar general of Montreal, Étienne Montgolfier, Briand acknowledged that he had hesitated before ordering the change and that it had been met with skepticism by various clerics. However, he wrote, "Je n'ai pas souffert qu'on m'apportât pour raison qu'il est bien dur de prier pour ses ennemis, etc., etc. Ils sont nos maîtres, et nous leur devons ce que nous devions aux Français lorsqu'ils l'étaient. Maintenant l'Église dé-fend-elle à ses sujets de prier pour leur prince? Les catholiques du royaume de la Grande-Bretagne ne prient-ils point pour leur roy? C'est ce que je ne puis croire." (Jean-Olivier Briand to Étienne Montgolfier, Quebec City, February 1762, *Rapport de l'archiviste de la province de Québec* (1929): 50).

5   Marcel Hamelin, "Chartier de Lotbinière, Michel-Eustache-Gaspard-Alain," in *Dictionnaire Biographique du Canada*, ed. F.G. Halfpenny and Jean Hamelin, vol. 6 (Quebec City: Presses de l'Université Laval, 1987), 144.

6   Jerry Bannister, "Canada as Counter-Revolution: The Loyalist Order Framework in Canadian History, 1750–1840," in *Liberalism and Hegemony: Debating the Canadian Liberal Revolution*, ed. Jean-François Constant and Michel Ducharme (Toronto: University of Toronto Press, 2009), 126.

7   Joseph-Octave Plessis, "Mandement pour des prières publiques (29 octobre 1812)," in Têtu and Gagnon, *Mandements*, 3, 95. Joseph-Octave Plessis to George Prévost, Quebec City, October 24, 1812, *Rapport de l'archiviste de la province de Québec* (1927): 291. Already, in a 1799 sermon, Msgr. Plessis had underscored Britain's newfound role as a global barrier to revolution: "Au reste, messieurs, si d'un côté l'Angleterre tend une main secourable aux vic-times de la révolution, et les comble de bienfaits et de largesses; elle arrête, de l'autre, une partie des désordres dont ses monstrueux instruments menacent l'univers entier." (Plessis, *Discours à l'occasion de la victoire remportée par les forces navales de sa majesté britannique dans la Méditérrannée le 1 et 2 août 1798, sur la flotte française, prononcé dans l'église cathédrale de Québec le 10 janvier 1799* (Quebec City, 1799), 14).

8   Papineau, quoted in Yvan Lamonde, "Britannisme et américanité de Louis-Joseph Papineau à l'époque du deuxième projet d'Union (1822–1823)," *Cahiers des Dix* 66 (2012): 63.

9   Lamonde, ibid., 83–94.

10  Charles Larocque, "Lettre pastorale concernant l'inauguration du gouverne-ment fédéral (18 juin 1867)," in *Mandements, lettres pastorales et circulaires*

*des évêques de St-Hyacinthe*, ed. Alexis-Xiste Bernard, vol. 2 (Montreal: Beauchemin, 1889), 430.

11  Wilfrid Laurier, *Le libéralisme politique* (Montreal: Beauchemin, 1925 [1877]), 12, 15, 22.

12  A.I. Silver, *The French Canadian Idea of Confederation, 1864–1900*, 2nd ed. (Toronto: University of Toronto Press, 1997), 224–25.

13  Paul Bruchési et al., "Lettre pastorale de NN. SS les archevêques et évêques des provinces ecclésiastiques de Québec, de Montréal et d'Ottawa sur les devoirs des catholiques dans la guerre actuelle," in *Mandements, lettres pastorales et circulaires des évêques de Québec*, vol. 11 (Quebec City: Chancellerie de l'archevêché, 1912–1919), 92.

14  Canada, *House of Commons Debates* (March 1, 1901), 747 (Mr. Henri Bourassa, MP).

15  C.A. Bayly, *Imperial Meridian: The British Empire and the World, 1780–1830* (London and New York: Longman, 1989), 75.

## Chapter 12
## Royal Tours of Canada in the Reign of Queen Elizabeth II

1  A complete list of royal tours of Canada since 1953 is available online at canada.ca/en/canadian-heritage/services/past-royal-tours.html.

2  See Carolyn Harris, "Royalty at Rideau Hall: Lord Lorne, Princess Louise and the Emergence of the Canadian Crown," in *Canada and the Crown: Essays on Constitutional Monarchy*, ed. D. Michael Jackson and Philippe Lagassé (Montreal and Kingston: McGill-Queen's University Press, 2013), 17–32.

3  Michael Valpy, "The Queen Drops a Perfect Puck," *Globe and Mail*, October 7, 2002.

4  For more about Prince Edward, Duke of Kent and Strathearn in Canada, see Nathan Tidridge, *Prince Edward, Duke of Kent: Father of the Canadian Crown* (Toronto: Dundurn Press, 2013).

5  R.H. Hubbard, *Rideau Hall: An Illustrated History of Government House, Ottawa from Victorian Times to Today* (Montreal and Kingston: McGill-Queen's University Press, 1977), 259.

6  See Carolyn Harris, "Canadian Women's Responses to Royal Tours from the Eighteenth Century to the Present Day," *Royal Studies Journal* 5, no. 1 (2018), 15–33.

7  C.W. Jeffries, *Recollections of the Royal Tour of 1901*, Unpublished Manuscript, cwjefferys.ca/recollections-of-the-royal-tour-of-1901.

8  Jonathan Parry, "Whig Monarchy, Whig Nation: Crown, Politics and Representativeness 1800 to 2000," in *The Monarchy and the British Nation 1780 to the Present*, ed. Andrezj Olechnowicz (Cambridge: Cambridge University Press, 2007), 70.

)    Arthur Bousfield and Garry Toffoli, *Fifty Years The Queen: A Tribute to Her Majesty Queen Elizabeth II on Her Golden Jubilee* (Toronto: Dundurn Press, 2002), 132.

10   See R.W. Sandwell, "Dreaming the Princess: Love, Subversion and the Rituals of Empire in British Columbia," in *Majesty in Canada: Essays on the Role of Royalty*, ed. Colin M. Coates (Toronto: Dundurn Press, 2006), 44–67.

11   Philip Buckner, "Casting Daylight Upon Magic: Deconstructing the Royal Tour of 1901 to Canada," in *The British World: Diaspora, Culture and Identity*, ed. Carl Bridge and Kent Feodorowich (London: Frank Cass, 2003), 176.

12   Bousfield and Toffoli, 185.

13   William Borders, "As the Queen Visits, Canadians Debate Monarchy," *New York Times*, June 30, 1973, 2, nytimes.com/1973/06/30/archives/as-queen -visits-canadians-debate-the-monarchy-what-about-the-others.html.

14   Jill Mahoney, "Make Commitment to Nation, Queen Tells Canadians: Diversity of People and Country Amazing, Monarch Tells Ottawa Crowds at 130th Birthday Celebration," *Globe and Mail*, 2 July 1997, A4.

15   Nathan Tidridge, *Canada's Constitutional Monarchy* (Toronto: Dundurn Press, 2011), 197.

16   Stephen Bates, "William and Kate Celebrate Canada Day with Its Newest Citizens," *The Guardian*, July 1, 2011, theguardian.com/world/2011/jul/01/ william-kate-celebrate-canada-day.

17   Ian Radforth, *Royal Spectacle: The 1860 Visit of The Prince of Wales to Canada and the United States* (Toronto: University of Toronto Press, 2006), 20.

18   The Royal Collection Trust, "Canada Made Us: Royal Tours," in *Canada: Canadian History, Art and the Royal Family's Relationship to the Country*, rct.uk/collection/themes/Trails/canada/canada-made-us-royal-visits.

19   Kenneth Rose, *King George V* (New York: Alfred A. Knopf, 1984), 43.

20   Philip Buckner, "The Last Great Royal Tour: Queen Elizabeth's 1959 Tour to Canada," in *Canada and the End of Empire*, ed. Philip Buckner (Vancouver: UBC Press, 2005), 67.

21   Robert Trumbull, "Queen, in Address to Canadians, Makes Appeal for National Unity," *New York Times*, October 17, 1977, 2, nytimes. com/1977/10/17/archives/queen-in-address-to-canadians-makes-appeal-for -national-unity.html.

22   Philip Murphy, *Monarchy and the End of Empire: The House of Windsor, the British Government, and the Postwar Commonwealth* (Oxford: Oxford University Press, 2013), 131.

23   Bruce Campion-Smith, "Nelson Mandela Thanked Brian Mulroney for Canada's Anti-Apartheid Pressure," *Toronto Star*, December 5, 2013, thestar.com/news/world/2013/12/05/nelson_mandela_thanked_brian_mulroney _for_canadas_antiapartheid_pressure.html.

24  For more about the history of royal tours, see Arthur Bousfield and Garry Toffoli, *Home to Canada: Royal Tours 1786–2010* (Toronto: Dundurn Press, 2010).

25  Buckner, "The Last Great Royal Tour," 81.

26  For the complete itinerary of the 1954 royal tour, see Department of the Secretary of State of Canada, *Visit to Canada of His Royal Highness the Duke of Edinburgh, July 29 to August 17, 1954, Arrangements* (1954).

27  Michael Valpy, "Nunavut Gives Queen a Warm Welcome," *Globe and Mail*, October 5, 2002, theglobeandmail.com/news/national/nunavut-gives -queen-a-warm-welcome/article25423087/.

28  Tom MacDonnell, *Daylight upon Magic: The Royal Tour of Canada, 1939* (Toronto: Macmillan of Canada, 1989), 50.

29  McKenzie Porter, "How the Queen Talks and What She Says," *Maclean's*, October 12, 1957, archive.macleans.ca/article/1957/10/12/how-the-queen-talks -and-what-she-says.

30  "Canada's Monarchy," *Globe and Mail*, May 23, 1994, A12.

31  Buckner, "The Last Great Royal Tour," 85.

32  Jamie Bradburn, "Two Days with the Queen: Were Canadians Feeling Indifferent Toward Queen Elizabeth II During her 1959 Royal Visit?" *Torontoist*, March 16, 2013, torontoist.com/2013/03/historicist-two-days -with-the-queen/.

33  Martin Stone, "Canadian Leader Commits Queen-Sized Gaffe," UPI News, October 8, 2002, upi.com/Top_News/2002/10/08/Canadian-leader-commits -queen-size-gaffe/41411034106168/.

34  Graham Fraser, "We Want to Keep Monarchy," *Toronto Star*, May 31, 2002, A16.

35  For recent polling date concerning Canada and the monarchy, see St. John Alexander, "Canadian Support for Monarchy Hits 'Lowest Level,' Poll Results Suggest," *CTV News*, March 2, 2022, Mbc.ctvnews.ca/canadian -support-for-monarchy-hits-lowest-level-poll-results-suggest-1.5802174.

36  Elizabeth Thompson, "Protecting Prince Harry Cost Canadians More Than $334,000," *CBC News*, December 8, 2021, .cbc.ca/news/politics/ prince-harry-rcmp-protection-1.6276872.

37  Peter Zimonjic, "Governor General-Designate Mary Simon Speaks with the Queen," *CBC News*, July 23, 2021, cbc.ca/news/politics/mary-simon -the-queen-audience-1.6114444.

# About the Contributors

## Damien-Claude Bélanger

D.C. Bélanger is a graduate of the Université de Montréal and McGill. He is an associate professor of Canadian history at the University of Ottawa and a co-founder of *Mens: revue d'histoire intellectuelle et culturelle*. His research interests include French Canadian intellectual history and Canadian-American relations. He is the author of two monographs, *Prejudice and Pride: Canadian Intellectuals Confront the United States, 1891–1945* (2011) and *Thomas Chapais, historien* (2018), and is currently working on a history of loyalism in French Canada.

## Keith Thor Carlson

Keith Thor Carlson holds the Canada Research Chair in Indigenous and community-engaged history at the University of the Fraser Valley, where he has additionally been appointed Director of the Peace and Reconciliation Centre. He has been working with Coast Salish Knowledge Keepers since 1992. Individually or with partners, Dr. Carlson has authored or edited eight books and over fifty articles. His scholarship has been translated into three languages, transformed into video documentaries and works of public art, and found expression in expert-witness legal reports. Keith Carlson was made an honorary member of the Stó:lō Nation in 2001 and was appointed a member of the Royal Society of Canada's College of New Scholars in 2017.

## John Fraser

Author and journalist John Fraser is executive chair of the National NewsMedia Council of Canada. He was Master of Massey College in the University of Toronto from 1995 to 2014. Previously, he was the award-winning editor of *Saturday Night*. He is the author of eleven books, including the internationally acclaimed *The Chinese: Portrait of a People* (1980), *Eminent Canadians* (2000), and *The Secret of the Crown: Canada's Affair with Royalty* (2012). A Member of the Order of Canada, he is founding president and a Fellow of the Institute for the Study of the Crown in Canada. In 2020 he received the Michener-Baxter Special Award from the Michener Awards Foundation for long-term achievement in public service journalism.

## Carolyn Harris

Author, historian, and royal commentator, Carolyn Harris received her doctorate in European history from Queen's University and teaches at the University of Toronto School of Continuing Studies. She is the author of *Magna Carta and Its Gifts to Canada* (2015), *Queenship and Revolution in Early Modern Europe* (2015), and *Raising Royalty: 1,000 Years of Royal Parenting* (2017). Dr. Harris is the proofreading editor of the *Royal Studies Journal* and co-editor of *English Consorts: Power, Influence, Dynasty*, a four-volume series about English royal consorts, to be published in 2022.

## Andrew Heard

Andrew Heard is a Fellow of the Institute for the Study of Crown in Canada, a professor in the Department of Political Science at Simon Fraser University, and a past president of the British Columbia Political Studies Association. He previously taught at Dalhousie University and in South Africa. His research interests cover Canadian constitutional and institutional issues: the Crown, constitutional conventions, Senate reform, parliamentary privilege, federalism, and the courts. His publications include a second edition of *Canadian Constitutional Conventions: The Marriage of Law and Politics* (2014).

## avid Johnston

The Right Honourable David Johnston was Canada's twenty-eighth governor general, serving from 2010 to 2017. During his mandate he established the Rideau Hall Foundation (RHF), a registered charity that supports and amplifies the Office of the Governor General in its work to connect, honour, and inspire Canadians. Today he is actively involved as chair of the RHF board of directors. Prior to his installation as governor general, Mr. Johnston was a professor of law for forty-five years. He served as president of the University of Waterloo for two terms and principal of McGill University for three terms. He is a Fellow of the Institute for the Study of the Crown in Canada.

## Serge Joyal

The Honourable Serge Joyal was a senator from 1997 to 2020. He had been a member of Parliament, a minister and secretary of state, and in 1980–81 co-chaired the joint committee that recommended the adoption of the Canadian Charter of Rights and Freedoms. A collector and patron of the arts, he is the author and publisher of articles and books related to parliamentary and constitutional law, as well as essays in social and political history. Serge Joyal is an Officer of the Order of Canada, *Officier de l'Ordre national du Québec*, and *Commandeur de la Légion d'honneur* (France). He is a Special Fellow of the Royal Society of Canada, Advocatus Emeritus of the Quebec Bar, and a Fellow of the Institute for the Study of the Crown in Canada.

## Carolyn King

Carolyn King is a nationally recognized advocate for Indigenous and First Nation Peoples in Canada. She was appointed a Member of the Order of Canada in 2021 for her advocacy of Indigenous-led initiatives and her efforts to improve Canadians' understanding of First Nations. She is also the creator/founder of the Moccasin Identifier Initiative. With over forty

years of work experience in the field of First Nations community econom
development and communications, she has served on many organizatio
from the local to the national level. Carolyn King is a member and residen
of the Mississaugas of the Credit First Nation, located in Southern Ontario,
and a former elected Chief of her First Nation community.

## Barbara J. Messamore

Barbara J. Messamore, professor of history at the University of the Fraser
Valley, is the author of *Canada's Governors General, 1847–1878: Biography
and Constitutional Evolution* (2006), co-author of *Narrating a Nation:
Canadian History Pre-Confederation* (2011) and of *Conflict and Compromise:
Pre-Confederation Canada* (2017), and was the co-founder and editor-in-
chief of the *Journal of Historical Biography*. With a PhD from the University
of Edinburgh, she is a Fellow of the Royal Historical Society (UK). She is
also a vice-president and Fellow of the Institute for the Study of the Crown
in Canada.

## Arthur Milnes

Arthur Milnes, an award-winning journalist, served as the research assistant
to the Right Honourable Brian Mulroney on the latter's best-selling memoirs
from 2003 until 2008. He later worked in the Prime Minister's Office as a
speechwriter to then prime minister Stephen Harper. His thirteen books include studies of prime ministers Sir John A. Macdonald, Sir Wilfrid Laurier,
Arthur Meighen, R.B. Bennett, John N. Turner, and Brian Mulroney.

## Warren J. Newman

Warren Newman is senior general counsel in the Constitutional, Administrative and International Law Section of the Government of Canada's
Department of Justice. He has been legal adviser to the Government of
Canada and a constitutional specialist for forty years. He acted as counsel
for the Attorney General of Canada in cases before the Supreme Court,

cluding the *Manitoba Language Rights Reference*, the *Quebec Secession Reference*, and the *Senate Reform Reference*, as well as before trial and appel-
te courts, including the *Motard* case on the validity of the *Succession to the Throne Act, 2013*. Dr. Newman has appeared frequently as an expert witness before parliamentary committees and is an adjunct professor at the Faculties of Law of the Universities of Ottawa, McGill, Queen's, and York. He is a Fellow of the Institute for the Study of the Crown in Canada.

## Jonathan Shanks

Jonathan Shanks is senior counsel with the Privy Council Office Legal Services Sector. He has a varied practice relating to democratic institutions, the machinery of government, the division of powers, the royal preroga-
tive, and various aspects of Crown law. He served in the Constitutional, Administrative and International Law Section of the Department of Justice from 2008 to 2020. In 2020, Jonathan Shanks joined the Privy Council Office. Between 2010 and 2020 he taught public and constitutional law at the University of Ottawa and Queen's University. He is the co-author (with David E. Smith and Christopher McCreery) of *Canada's Deep Crown: Beyond Elizabeth II, The Crown's Continuing Canadian Complexion* (2022).

## Nathan Tidridge

Nathan Tidridge teaches Canadian history, government, and Indigenous studies at Waterdown District High School, Ontario. He is author of *Canada's Constitutional Monarchy* (2011), *Prince Edward, Duke of Kent* (2013), and *The Queen at the Council Fire* (2015). He is a board member of the Ontario Heritage Trust, a member of the national advisory council for the Prince's Charities Canada, and a vice-president of the Institute for the Study of the Crown in Canada. He was awarded a Meritorious Service Medal in 2018 for his work in educating Canadians on the role of the Crown and its relationship with Indigenous communities. He received a Governor General's award for excellence in teaching history in 2020.

# Image Credits

# INDEX

# About the Editors

Chief of protocol of Saskatchewan from 1980 to 2005, D. Michael Jackson, CVO, SOM, CD, coordinated ten tours by members of the Royal Family and developed the province's honours program. A founding member of the Institute for the Study of the Crown in Canada, he is president and a Fellow of the Institute and has coordinated four national conferences on the Crown. Dr. Jackson is co-editor of *The Evolving Canadian Crown* and *Canada and the Crown: Essays on Constitutional Monarchy*; author of *The Crown and Canadian Federalism*; and editor of *The Canadian Kingdom: 150 Years of Constitutional Monarchy* and *Royal Progress: Canada's Monarchy in the Age of Disruption*. He was appointed a Commander of the Royal Victorian Order by the Queen in 2005 and a member of the Saskatchewan Order of Merit in 2007. He was awarded the Sovereign's Medal for Volunteers in 2021 for his services to the Institute.

Christopher McCreery, MVO, PhD, FRHistS, has served as private secretary to the Lieutenant Governor of Nova Scotia since 2009. He holds a doctorate in Canadian political history from Queen's University, Kingston. Dr. McCreery has served as an advisor to the federal government and a number of provincial and Commonwealth governments on matters related to honours and symbols. He has also regularly been consulted on the role of the Crown reserve powers, protocol, and the historical position of the monarchy in Canada. Prior to being appointed private secretary, he served with the Priv Council Office and as an advisor in the Senate of Canada. He has al: served as a member of the board of trustees of the Canadian Museum History from 2012 to 2018. Dr. McCreery's publications consist of mor. than a dozen books, including two Canadian non-fiction best sellers. In 2010 the Queen appointed him a member of the Royal Victorian Order.